POLAND'S DAUGHTER

Books by Daniel Ford

Poland's Daughter: How I Met Basia, Hitchhiked to Italy, and Learned About Love, War, and Exile

Remains: A Story of the Flying Tigers

A Vision So Noble: John Boyd, the OODA Loop, and America's War on Terror

Flying Tigers: Claire Chennault and His American Volunteers, 1941-1942

Michael's War: A Story of the Irish Republican Army

The Only War We've Got: Early Days in South Vietnam

The Country Northward: A Hiker's Journal

The High Country Illuminator: A Tale of Light and Darkness and the Ski Bums of Avalon

Incident at Muc Wa: A Story of the Vietnam War

Now Comes Theodora: A College Novel

As editor

Glen Edwards: The Diary of a Bomber Pilot

When I Am Going (with Anne Crowley Ford)

The Lady and the Tigers (with Olga Greenlaw)

POLAND'S DAUGHTER

HOW I MET BASIA, HITCHHIKED TO ITALY, AND LEARNED ABOUT LOVE, WAR, AND EXILE

Daniel Ford

Warbird Books 2014

Contents

On September 1, 1939, Hitler's forces stormed into Poland from the north, west, and south, followed on September 17 by Stalin's Red Army from the east. They divided the country between them, while 43,000 Poles escaped to Romania to continue their fight in French or British uniform.

CHAPTER ONE

We Meet in Caf
1955

TO BE HONEST, I'm not sure whether my love for Poland led me to Basia, or it happened the other way around. They came into my life a very long time ago. By now, I'm afraid, the unlucky nation and its fortunate daughter have more or less merged in my mind. When I think of Poland, it's Basia's dark blue eyes that I see – her impossibly blue eyes, like cornflowers in the summer fields. And when I think of her, I hear the tanks clanking toward the ancient city in which she was born, and where she was a five-year-old in September 1939. From Germany comes the gray Panzer IV, squat and gray, with a short-barreled 75-mm howitzer in its turret. And from Soviet Russia, the green BT-7 *Betuska*, smaller and faster and more lightly armed.

In sour salute to the despots who unleashed those machines upon Basia's birthplace, I think of the German tanker as Corporal Adolf, with a square mustache and a twitchy white face, while pockmarked Comrade Josef drives the smaller, faster cavalry tank from Soviet Russia. Bad cess to both of them, as my Irish mother would have said. They were the first killers of the Second World War, the worst thing that ever happened.

But then . . . but then! If Germany and Russia hadn't invaded Poland – if those tanks had turned back before they crossed the frontier – I would never have met Basia. It's a terrible thought, I know, but if 60 million people hadn't died in the Second World War, and if thrice that number hadn't been bereaved, wounded, raped, and exiled, I would never have kissed that pretty girl on the road to Italy. And not only did the War bring us together, but all the rest of her personal tragedy was likewise necessary to our meeting. What for Basia was a loss beyond imagining –

her father, her brother, the very cobblestones of Potocki Street – even the language she'd learned as a child – were stages on the journey that brought her to the University of Manchester in the dreary northwest of England, where I came to know her in the winter of 1955.

I think we met in Caf, the vast room where undergraduates gathered at ten o'clock for cigarettes and coffee. That would have been early in the Lenten term, the months between Christmas and Easter. I was one of two Fulbright Fellows at what the English called a redbrick university, though in truth the buildings weren't brick but stone, and not red but black from the coal fires of Manchester. This was a considerable disappointment. I had expected smooth lawns, spacious Georgian halls, and white shutters against the brick, much like the University of New Hampshire from which I'd come.

I was also distressed to find that, as the English understood the matter, my field of study – Modern European History – had come to an end with the Victorian era, which to me seemed ancient history. And it wasn't just the history department: the entire city seemed dedicated to the Widow at Windsor. When I arrived at Victoria Station and carried my suitcase to the red double-decker bus, I found myself under the protection of a grand gray statue of the seated Queen, holding the world in her palm like an anarchist's bomb. Nearby were Victoria Square, Victoria Street, and the Victoria and Albert Hotel. Indeed, I now find that the formal name of my institution of higher learning was the *Victoria* University of Manchester, though I didn't know that at the time. I doubt that any of us did.

And the classrooms weren't heated. I was always cold in Manchester, but never colder than in class. In my 1848 seminar, the more rebellious students (an Irishman named Callahan, a lesbian Marxist named Joan, and me) abandoned the table and perched on the ribbed iron radiator. Up against that tall, drafty window, streaked on the outside

2

with sooty raindrops – like coal-miners' tears! – we might catch a bit of the warmth that gurgled through it from time to time. As for the lecture rooms, I don't believe they had any radiators at all.

Then too, I felt adrift in the English system of self-tutoring. In our first meeting of "1848: Year of Revolution," Professor Lewis handed out mimeographed packets of books we might like to read, about the Second Republic, the Frankfurt Assembly, and so on. I scarcely knew what to do with these bibliographies, accustomed as I was to reading chapters from a common textbook, a chapter per class. However, I gritted my teeth and decided to concentrate on Giuseppe Mazzini and Young Italy, because they seemed so similar to my father's service in the Irish Republican Army. But when I went to the University library, I found that its catalog consisted of bound books with many handwritten additions, utterly baffling to one accustomed to card catalogs in alphabetical order.

What with one thing and another, by the time the Lenten term began, I'd stopped going to class. Instead I wrote and rewrote a novel whose central character was Stephen Faust, in joint tribute to Joyce's young hero and to Goethe's elderly alchemist, who had pledged his soul to the devil in return for unbridled experience. I sat fully clothed at my typewriter, with a bathrobe over all, and a pair of fingerless wool gloves from Burtons, the chain haberdasher on Oxford Road near the University.

I read *Faust* and *Portrait of the Artist* that winter, and much else besides: *The Magic Mountain*, *Nineteen Eighty-Four*, *Brideshead Revisted*, *Tender is the Night*, and Hemingway's *Fiesta*, which turned out to be *The Sun Also Rises* in disguise. These were orange Penguin paperbacks at two shillings sixpence the volume. I also bought and read a six-volume set of Winston Churchill's *The Second World War*. It wasn't Senator Fulbright's intention, I'm sure, but my year at Manchester enabled me to catch up on the books

I'd been too busy to read as an undergraduate. (To my shame, I also read a quantity of post-apocalypse Pan paperbacks with garish covers, nuclear war being an English preoccupation of the time.)

And I wrote for the *Mancunian*, the student newspaper, where Frank the editor assured me that it would be quite all right, indeed rather amusing, if I retained American spelling and usage in my reporting. The English were much intrigued by the way I handled their language. I was asked: "Do all Yanks talk like you?" And: "When one stages Shakespeare in your country, do the characters speak with American accents?" I hadn't, up to my arrival in England, realized that I actually had an accent. Southerners did, and even Midwesterners had an accent, as I'd discovered coming over on the *SS United States*. But New Englanders spoke the language just as it was meant to be spoken, or so I believed before I became part of the Victoria University of Manchester.

The newspaper staff became my particular friends. We drank great quantities of room-temperature beer, called bitter though it really wasn't. We saw foreign-language movies at the Piccadilly Cinema uptown – *Wages of Fear*, *Sawdust and Tinsel* – another way of keeping warm. We joined the Union debates on one side or another; it didn't matter which side; the debate was the thing. I loved the debates, for which we donned academic gowns, and where I was addressed as the Gentleman from the Colonies.

And we went to Caf every morning. Coffee was twopence for a tall white cup, straight-sided, with a saucer, identical to those served at Victoria Station or at the Lyons Teashop on Oxford Road. The coffee was dreary, like most things in 1950s England, slippery stuff, probably adulterated with chicory.

I keep saying "England." That's correct for the era. My friends thought of themselves as English, or Welsh or Irish. (I didn't know any Scots.) "Britain" was a geographical notion, referring to the island that contained the glorious English nation and its subsidiaries. As for today's favored term, "United Kingdom," that was a theoretical construct, so that London could continue to rule the six Irish counties that made up its last colony, as my father reminded me in his letters.

Poor Dad! As a boy he'd gone to war against the "bloody damned English," using one of their own rifles for the purpose. He must have been puzzled that his younger son wanted to study in their company. I'd applied for every fellowship on offer, variously named for Cecil Rhodes, George Marshall, and William Fulbright. The last of these came through for me, and in September 1954 I took the train to Grand Central Station and walked across town to Pier 86 on the Hudson river, just the third time in my life I'd ventured more than a hundred miles from home.

SOMEWHERE IN CAF – a cavernous room, with tables covered with oilcloth – was a table of students who fancied themselves literary, mostly drawn from the *Mancunian* staff. The group invariably included my best friend in Manchester, a tall Liverpudlian named Malcolm Hopson, with a mop of black hair and a quiet, bespectacled girlfriend named Sheila. She was generally the only girl at our table, whether in Caf or in the pub to which we adjourned in the afternoon, and she seldom spoke. She loved Malcolm and tolerated the rest of us because we were his friends. He'd done his National Service in the Royal Air Force, which he called the "Raff." That brought his age close to mine although he was a fresher, a first-year student.

Less often, Frank the editor would be there, stroking his beard. I was much in awe of Frank, who'd served with the British Army in Korea while I enjoyed myself as an under-graduate. Oh, and Antony Bolcover, a portly, heavy-faced lad with smooth, shining cheeks, well dressed and well spoken. I have a photo of our gang in Caf, taken before

Basia entered my life: serious Antony, bushy-haired Malcolm, placid Sheila, and a bright lad named Ian Fellowes who lived in the same digs as I, on Mauldeth Road in the suburb of Withington.

Did my wandering eye spot Basia even then? She tells me that she and her best friend, an English girl named Margaret, weren't far away, at a table made up mostly of medical students. Evidently they regarded us as deep thinkers, rather than the brilliant writers we fancied ourselves to be. In an email, Basia recalls those long-ago mornings in Caf:

One day someone mentioned a table of intellectuals. I did look across at your table occasionally but didn't find it of great interest. Maybe because at the time I had more interest in Paul, an Irish medical student. We were getting on fine but it finished badly. He was meeting his parents in London and invited me for dinner with them at the Ritz. I then spoilt it all by writing to Margaret and to Paul and putting the letters in the wrong envelopes. Those were not the days of easy telephone access, so I only learned about the mistake when I met him back in Manchester and he said "Thank you for letting me know what you think of me." I can't imagine what I could have written. I liked him and his parents, and the dinner was enjoyable, especially when the waiter suddenly materialized in front of me and produced a lighter for my cigarette.

For a while I moped, was too embarrassed to go on meeting him at the medics' table, and didn't go to Caf very often. Finally Margaret and her boyfriend established their own table so I would join them. I think that was the time I started to notice your group. You seemed quieter than the others and had a good smile.

All these years later, I am pleased to learn that in 1955 I had a good smile!

WITHINGTON WAS A TWO-PENNY ride on the upper

deck of the Number 42 bus. There was a pole by the entryway, to hold onto, and a broad step, as if designed for the express purpose of letting students swing on and off. It was a point of honor for us to do this, while the Indian conductor watched us impassively. The entry was at the back of the bus, and there was no door to hinder us.

Number 42 ran past the Gothic university buildings on Oxford Road – a scaled-down Houses of Parliament, as they seemed to me, though without the gold leaf, and with towers that were oddly flat-topped – and down Wilmslow Road to Withington, where I lived, and where I dined too often on fish and chips served in a cone of yesterday's *Manchester Evening News.* "Fish and four!" we would say.

"Food for the body and food for the mind!" the vendor agreed, handing me sixpence worth of codfish – white, flaky, and steaming inside the brown crust – and a fourpenny portion of potato. The chips, as the English called them, were heavily salted and flavored with vinegar that the vendor dispensed from a round-bellied bottle, like a barber shaking hair tonic on a newly shorn head. Thus an evening at leisure in Withington cost tenpence for dinner, plus sixpence for a seat in the front stalls of the Scala Cinema, a total of nineteen U.S. cents at the exchange rate then prevailing. Cheaper, indeed, to go out for dinner and a movie than to stay home and feed coins into the gas meter.

The Scala was said to be one of England's oldest cinemas. It was situated on a corner, its second story half-timbered behind the marquee. The film was generally from Janus, Rank, or Ealing Studios, and it generally starred Dirk Bogarde or Jack Hawkins as a war hero, or perhaps Alec Guinness dressed as a woman, transvestism being a traditional vein of English humor. Ah, the glow of the projector's beam through the shifting veil of cigarette smoke! At the Scala, or indeed any English cinema, each seat was equipped with a tiny ashtray, on the armrest or attached to the back of the next seat forward.

Cigarette smoke was the least of our pollutants. Most Mancunians relied on coal-fueled fireplaces for their heat, and their electricity likewise came from coal-burning plants. The soot was everywhere – begriming the university buildings, streaking the windows, and mixing with winter fog to produce what were known as "pea soupers." On one occasion, walking from Mauldeth Road to Withington, the fog was so thick that I couldn't see the sidewalk beneath me: I missed the curb and fell into the street. Probably on the same evening, Basia's bus was led on its route by a man on a bicycle, with a lantern slung behind him.

Each morning I bought the *Manchester Guardian* and wrote the previous day's statistics in my diary. *Temperature: 55 high, 40 low. Rain: trace. Sunshine: nil.* In my recollection, the sun never shone in Manchester that year.

EXCUSE ME; I meant to introduce you to Number Two, Mauldeth Road West. I lived at the back of the house, on the third story, and Ian Fellowes had a room on the second story front. Like Malcolm Hopson, he was a fresher, but he hadn't done his National Service so was only eighteen. He was "reading" – that is, majoring in – biochemistry, and he was my boon companion on those evenings on the prowl in Withington. We got on remarkably well together, considering our differences in age and aspiration.

Ian came from Hull, and he was the first to alert me to the fact that the War I had enjoyed as a youngster was regarded somewhat differently by Europeans. It seems that he lived near the docks, and that the docks were often bombed. "That must have been exciting," I said.

"No, it was terrifying," Ian said.

He also spiced my vocabulary with Yorkshire sayings such as "Ne'er shed a clout till May is out" and "If once naught's naught, twice naught must be sommat." We'd met at the Mayfield Hotel nearby, where we'd lodged during Michaelmas term – three pounds sixpence a week for bed, breakfast, and dinner, which generally consisted of brussels sprouts, mashed potatoes, and pot roast, followed by pie or cake smothered in a sweet white sauce called custard. The clientele was entirely male. Like Ian, all the lads were younger than I, and all were virgins except for me. I felt quite the international playboy at the Mayfield Hotel. This wasn't just vanity: not long after my sojourn there, the sociologist Ferdynand Zweig (born in Poland, as it happens) interviewed Manchester students on a variety of topics, including their sex lives. Scarcely a third of the lads claimed to be sexually experienced. Considering that this is a subject upon which young men are notorious fabulists, I am tempted to put an exclamation mark after that sentence. And get this: *Mr. Zweig didn't interview the girls.* The 1950s were indeed a different age, closer to Queen Victoria than to Lady Gaga.

But back to Caf! Unlike most spaces in Manchester, it was warm, thanks to the body heat of a hundred or so undergraduates. Sometimes, indeed, we actually felt overheated in our jackets, ties, and long university scarves, which were our primary protection against fog, rain, and even snow. I did own a plaid winter coat from Sears, Roebuck that was much envied by Ian Fellowes, who had no overcoat.

One morning at Caf, Ian joked that he was so warm that he might take off his jacket. This met with no protest. So, glancing uneasily around the table, Ian actually did shed the jacket, and sat there rather proud of himself with his shirtsleeves tucked up. (English shirts were sold by neck size only, with sleeves long enough for any contingency; if there was sleeve left over, and there usually was, you took it up with a garter worn above the elbow.) One or two others followed this daring example, but not Antony Bolcover, in whom gentility ran strong. Antony was also, I think, one of the few students at Manchester not receiving a government grant, which for most of them was forty pounds a month.

My own stipend was fifty quid, so for the first time in my life I was just about the wealthiest person in my immediate circle. Fifty pounds, about $140, bought more beer than a twenty-two-year old could drink, if he knew what was good for him . . . but who does know what's good for him, at twenty-two?

At some point in the Lenten term, Basia joined the journalists' table. Basia, I learned, is the Polish diminutive for Barbara, and I now know that one of the reasons she liked me was that I pronounced it more or less correctly. The English made three crisp syllables of her nickname: *bass-ee-ah*. My lazy American tongue rendered it as two: *bash-ah*. That is almost correct, it seems.

She'd turned twenty-one during the Christmas holidays, so like Frank and Malcolm was closer to my age than most of the students. There was just the slightest difference in her speech – not what could be called a Polish accent, which is quite impressive given that she didn't really learn English until she entered secondary school. The Poles, it seems, have very agile tongues. And Basia had been exposed to *so many* languages. Almost every week, it seemed, I discovered yet another language she'd had to cope with on the way to her final linguistic home: Polish, of course, then Russian, Farsi, Italian, and French. All this before the age of fourteen, when she had to master English along with high school Latin.

As a rule, students in English universities didn't stray far from their chosen subject. Ian Fellowes, for example, was taking his sole elective in German, because most scientific research at the time was written in that language. Basia was much more adventurous: in addition to honours Italian, which required her to study English and French as well, she was studying philosophy:

I did logic that year, and I will never forget the lecturer. He would talk for the whole hour, and every fortnight or so he would set us some exercises. When he came into the lecture room with a batch of papers in his hand, we knew we had it coming. He would start by waving the whole packet, making derogatory remarks. Then, taking each paper separately, he would wave it even more forcefully, read out a name, and say what he thought of the – usually "poor, very poor" – effort. When he came to mine, it was always the same. He would say quietly, with pity in his voice, "Miss Deszberg," then shout "Miss Deszberg!" Then he'd go through an exercise or two, picking out all the faults and finishing off with, "You may have the right conclusion." A pause. "Sometimes." Another pause. "But no premises." Another pause. "Where are your premises?" By that time he was thundering, and I would give a sigh of relief. It was over. But I liked him, and I did enjoy his lectures.

SHE WAS A SMALL GIRL, standing five foot four and weighing eight stone on the English scale – 112 pounds. Her hair was light brown and worn fairly short, curling over her forehead and under her ears. She had high, arched eyebrows, high cheekbones, an elegant nose, and lips that begged to be kissed.

What I saw first, though, were her eyes. They were not merely *blue*. Everyone in my family had blue eyes, of a shade that one might find in a box of marbles from Woolworth's: a medium blue, an inexpensive blue. Basia's eyes were very dark, as if purple had been added. When I asked her about this, she only said: "Oh, it's my sister who has the exceptional eyes! They're dark brown. In Poland, *brown* is the color that turns men's heads. Lalka, my sister – Lalka was always the pretty one, and I was the ugly duckling."

Duckling?

Ugly?

Sheila and most of the girls in Caf had no jewelry, but Basia wore four gold bangles on her right wrist. She told me that her mother had given them to her when they lived in Tehran, "for luck," when she was ten years old.

But really, what does any of this matter? I found her enchanting, and no doubt I fell in love at my first sight of her. One does that sort of thing at twenty-two. All the sadder, then, that I really don't remember meeting her, though I'm sure it was at Caf.

FOR HER PART, BASIA thinks we met at Rag Ball, the culminating event of Rag Week, an English university carouse to raise money for charity. I find that it still exists: Manchester has a Rag organization and a Rag Week, though no longer a Ball. Oxford does, but it entails black tie for men and party dress for women. God help us! I never saw a tuxedo at the University of Manchester. Antony Bolcover might have inherited one, but if so he never wore it. I don't even know if one could *rent* a tux in Manchester. We wore the same invariable jacket to Rag Ball as to Caf, the pub, or the cinema, and the same striped tie and university scarf, wound once around the neck and hanging down rakishly in back and front. It was the same with the girls: Sheila in her pleated dress, with a brown cardigan over it; Basia in her gray suit and demure white blouse. She only had the one costume; all of us only had the one costume. As she emails now:

I am glad we didn't meet in my first year at Manchester. I was still wearing my school blazer with the coat of arms on the pocket, my school shoes and blouse, and a skirt I borrowed from my sister. (At convent school we wore a tunic or long wide shorts that looked like a skirt, and a blouse and tie. I didn't take the shorts to Manchester, and I cut off my plaits.) Later Uncle Jan gave me the two-piece suit, and much later I bought a beautiful pair of high-heeled bright green shoes.

Basia underestimates the effect she had on me. Never mind the blazer, the borrowed skirt, and the clunky brown shoes! If she'd worn a burqa, I would have concluded that full body concealment was the very height of female fashion.

Rag Ball was held in the Men's Union, an ancient building that contained a club-like lounge, offices for student organizations – including the *Mancunian* – and an upper-story auditorium where we otherwise gathered for those Thursday afternoon debates. I remember wandering with Malcolm and Sheila from floor to floor and from room to room, some with dance bands and some with open bars. By midnight I was rather drunk, and I kept getting into scrapes that almost but not quite ended in fistfights. At some point I linked up with Basia, who'd come to the ball with her friend Margaret. Perhaps it was Margaret and the boyfriend who pushed her into my orbit, or perhaps Basia made it happen.

In any event, I stayed close to her for the rest of the evening. In one of those many rooms with many bars, I realized that another lad had draped his arm across her shoulders. I was hugely offended, so I grabbed his thumb and peeled it back, neatly removing his arm from the shoulders that I regarded as my own acquisition. With some justification, he set out to punch me. He was a sturdy lad, and big across the shoulders, so he probably would have made a good job of thrashing me, if Malcolm hadn't stepped in. He drew the outraged young man away and smothered him with eloquence. I heard him speak of "hands across the sea and all that," no doubt arguing that he would be leaving a blot on England's honor if he punched out a guest from the colonies.

Late at night, we wound up in an actual ballroom, almost empty as I recall. We sat along one wall in folding chairs – Malcolm, Sheila, Basia, and I – while a dance band played forlornly on the stage. Perhaps, come to think of it, this was the same auditorium in which the Union debates took place, with the chairs removed to supply a dance floor.

Nobody was dancing, however. Instead we sat with our heads hanging, with the exception of Basia, whose dark blue eyes lighted upon the artwork decorating the stage behind the band. This depicted a square-rigged ship, all sails set, and above it in fancy letters the legend, *Frigging in the Rigging*.

"What does 'frigging' mean?" she asked.

If this seems impossibly naive, take note that I was the product of a rather coarse background, yet at the age of twenty-two I'd only once heard the ultimate obscenity spoken in what was known as "mixed company." On that memorable occasion, I'm sorry to say, I was the speaker. I was driving a 1934 Chevrolet sedan over a hump-backed bridge, en route to Boston, and on the downslope the accelerator stuck wide open. The Chevy kept increasing speed, causing me to shout: *"What the fuck?"* The slip was met with strangled laughter, was never again mentioned, and I'm sure was never forgotten. So I was not about to interpret for the language student from Poland. But again Malcolm came to the rescue. He raised his fine head and its great burden of black hair, shook it once, and said: "Why, it means *fucking*, my dear."

All these years later, I find that I remember some parts of our friendship very clearly, while Basia remembers different moments altogether, and sometimes to opposite effect. This conversation is among the events she challenges, though it is word-for-word graven upon my memory. I couldn't be mistaken, as I tell her in an email. She answers:

Okay, if you are sure. But Malcolm's explanation would not have enlightened me as I didn't know that word either.

WHAT A THING IS MEMORY! That late-night ballroom, with the forlorn dance band playing for the four of us, is as vivid to me as if Rag Week were yesterday. Yet I don't remember if I took Basia home, whether I kissed her in parting, if I even arranged to meet her again.

Indeed, I don't really know how much of an item we were that winter. We lived on opposite sides of the city, I in Withington to the south, Basia in a northern suburb with her Uncle Jan, Aunt Jadzia, and two baby cousins. Nor could I have courted her by telephone, because phones were still a rarity in England. (I remember a *Manchester Guardian* advertisement for a tailor who boasted, "Telephone," without troubling to include the number.) Still, we had some sort of relationship, because Basia tells me:

I went to great length to save for my green shoes, and you gave me a perfectly matching pair of gloves. Real colour sense! You managed to get the same colour without me, and without looking at the shoes.

I did? It seems very unlike me, but even more unlikely that Basia would be mistaken, given that she had so little money that generally she ran through her stipend before the end of the month. For the final week or so Uncle Jan would send her off to school with two shillings to buy a ham sandwich for lunch. As feckless as us lads, she often spent the florin on a ten-pack of Player's. Her grant was twenty pounds a month, half of what Malcolm, Ian, and the others were getting, whether because "boys were privileged over girls," in the words of a scholar of the times, or because the money came from Polish funds rather than English.

And always there were our mornings in Caf. Every morning at ten o'clock, Basia joined us at the *Mancunian* table, and the early arrivals shifted places so that she and I could sit together. A courtship based on coffee and cigarettes!

We devoted hours to this pursuit. (Never again, after Ian's daring breakout, did any of the lads remove his jacket at table.) If I brought out my packet of Player's Navy Cut, it was mandatory to send it around the table, often enough returning empty. At three shillings sixpence the pack of twenty, this was a considerable offering. Never mind! Next time, Malcolm would hand his pack around, or Ian would, or Frank or Antony. The girls were not expected to participate in this ritual.

Basia also went to the pub with us from time to time, and to the Piccadilly Cinema uptown. I particularly remember *La Strada*. Malcolm and Sheila were there, and we picked up Ian Fellowes en route. I spotted him, Malcolm called to him, and he swung about the bus in the best student fashion as it swayed along Oxford Street.

I sat next to Basia, casting covetous glances at her profile in the reflected light from the screen – the soft lips, the elegant nose, the tousled hair still damp from rain. I considered the merits of leaning across and kissing those lips, which were pouting disapproval of Anthony Quinn's cruelty to Giulietta Masina, the circus strongman and his simple-minded protégé. (A year earlier, in the Franklin Theater at home, I'd have canoodled with my girlfriend without a second thought. What a mystery! Faced with a different woman, how does one get from here to *there*?) I ventured a whisper: "Do you read the subtitles?" Basia shook her head and lightly spanked my knuckles on the armrest. Well, she knew where my hand *was*, at any rate!

Apart from that tap on the hand, I got little of value from Signor Fellini's fable, though I did enjoy the Fool's wonderment at the heroine's appearance: "What a funny face! Are you a woman, really? Or an artichoke?"

The pubs were opening when we emerged from the movie at half-past six, in the rainy night, but Basia pleaded that she was overdue at home. She fled in the direction of Piccadilly Gardens.

I didn't see her home? No, I watched her duffle coat – white, it seemed in the night – vanish amongst the double-decker buses, bound for all points of the compass. The wet asphalt reflected their headlamps and the red of brake lights, along with the gleam of the cinema marquee and the pub window toward which the rest of us were bound.

It wasn't much of a date, to be sure, but I could console myself that my love at least was no artichoke.

THEN EVERYTHING CHANGED. The Fulbright office sent out a list of ships sailing for North America in the summer of 1955: which one did I prefer? I settled on *RMS Ivernia*, her maiden voyage scheduled for June 30 from Liverpool to Montreal. Flush with the prospect of this new adventure, I met Basia for our morning excursion to Caf . . . which, come to think of it, means that by this time we had a regular rendezvous. Probably I'd developed the habit of lurking in the corridor of her classroom building at ten o'clock, or on the steps outside, so as to share a private moment while we walked to the Union. It's a pity, really, that I don't remember more about our friendship in Manchester – when and where I bought those green gloves, for example.

It was Sheila who reacted to my news. "You'll be going home?" she said, and reached across the table to pat my hand. "We will miss you!" I have always admired women for their ability to say things like that, which men keep to themselves. I would miss this gang when *Ivernia* steamed out of Liverpool, but I would never have said so.

Then Basia delivered her own news: she'd been accepted at Perugia's *Università per Stranieri*, School for Foreigners, to spend the Easter term perfecting her spoken Italian.

"How wonderful!" Sheila said, while my heart slid into my shoes. No more coffee and cigarettes at Caf? No more movies at the Piccadilly Cinema uptown?

The University of Manchester still followed the pleasant tradition of dividing the year into three terms – Michaelmas, Lent, and Easter – with a four-week break between them. We were expected to use the time for independent study or to write a "long essay" or research paper, but for most of us it was an excuse to travel. In Basia's case, because the school calendars weren't the same, she'd have

17

two weeks between her last class at Manchester and her first at Perugia. "I will visit Paris on the way," she said, "and Florence of course. I would love to have company! Won't one of you go with me?"

"Yes," I said, before anyone else could speak. "I will."

On September 22, 1939, German troops withdrew from Lwow and were replaced by their Russian allies. Red Army cavalry tanks paraded down the cobblestone streets of Basia's home town, while the NKVD arrested the Polish defenders and sent them into the Gulag.

CHAPTER TWO

War Comes to Potocki Street
1939

IN SEPTEMBER 1939, when German and Russian armies crashed into Poland – two hammers beating the anvil! – I was a barefoot boy on Chestnut Cove Road in East Alton, New Hampshire.

The Fords were a smaller family than the Deszbergs, and not nearly so affluent. We lived in what was called the Caretaker's Cottage, provided as a bonus to my father's wage of $80 a month. We had no relatives within three thousand miles, though in time I would discover quantities of them in Ireland, Australia, and South Africa – the Irish diaspora. But as a boy I knew only the four of us: Mom, Dad, my brother Joe, and myself. I was the second-born and often in trouble.

I've always suspected that Joe didn't entirely approve of me. In one of my earliest memories, he is leading me along the top of a stone wall after a considerable snowstorm. (All snowstorms are considerable when you are forty inches tall.) We are walking on stones we cannot see, between our house and the barn where we play, where there is a horse named Alfred, and where there is a room set aside as a privy. Probably that is where we are bound – the privy. But inevitably, at some point along the stone wall, I take a false step and sink deep into the snow on one side or the other.

Joe goes back to the house, takes off his coat and over-shoes, and settles down to read the comic strips in front of the fire. Some little time elapses before Mom notices I am missing, and sends Dad to retrace our footprints and pull me out of the snowbank.

Well – Poland! We didn't learn about its agony on the radio, for the very good reason that we didn't own a radio. Nor did the Caretaker's Cottage have any of the other amenities that were common even in 1939, such as electricity, running water, refrigeration, or a source of heat apart from a fireplace in the living room and the Glenwood range in the kitchen. Because they were wood-fueled, neither held a fire overnight, so the family ritual called for Dad to rise at six o'clock and build a fire in the kitchen. On top of the Glenwood range was a kettle filled with water, which in the winter froze solid in the early hours of morning. It had thawed by the time Mom got up, so she could pour a cup into the throat of the hand pump at the sink, to prime it, since the handle had been raised to let the water run back into the well. (Otherwise the pipe would have "caught a little," as New Hampshiremen say.) Then Joe and I raced from the bedroom with our clothes in our arms, to dress by the radiant heat of the Glenwood range.

So at best I learned about the onset of the Second World War, as we called it from its very first week, in the Sunday edition of the Boston *Post*. The Sunday paper was the only one Dad felt we could afford; he bought it at McGrath's General Store in Alton Bay, as we drove home from Mass. Dad liked to patronize McGrath's because the name seemed Irish. The news might therefore have reached us as early as September 3, two days after German tanks crossed the Polish border. As it happened, this was the same day that Britain and France declared war on Germany, with high-blown sentiments – "Our hearts are with you, and, with our hearts, all our power, until the angel of peace returns to our midst" – but little practical effect.

I absorbed the War's beginning through photographs in *Life* magazine, the oversized weekly that cost five cents and covered the wide world in its fashion. (Dad didn't actually spend the nickel. The magazines were passed along to him by Mrs. Damon, whose lakefront home Dad cared for. Alfred the horse belonged to Mrs. Damon, as did our house.) *Life* tutored me about the Spanish Civil War, the Japanese invasion of China, and Adolf Hitler orating from a balcony in some dark German city.

Thus with the invasion of Poland. I especially remember a photo of women and boys digging trenches in a park, where people could shelter from aerial bombardment. How I envied those Polish boys in short pants, soon to be heroes in war! *Life* also brought us full-page drawings of German bombers attacking hypothetical cities, and of hypothetical fighter planes intercepting the bombers, along with photos of actual tanks, motorcycles, and horse cavalry.

The invasion, and the War's first terror bombing, got much more attention in *Life* than the Russian invasion that followed. The onslaught was a gigantic affair, and it would seem even more astonishing now: with a million and a half men under arms, Germany fielded an army nearly three times the size of the American army of today. At least ten thousand died in the struggle to subdue Poland, even with help from Soviet Russia.

LIFE INTRODUCED a new word to my vocabulary: *blitzkrieg*, or lightning war. Since the Industrial Revolution, armies had gone to war across a broad front, guarding their flanks and protecting their supply lines as they advanced. If the advance stalled, they dug trenches and defended them in depth. Such combat involved stupendous numbers of men, of whom stupendous numbers died. The American Civil War was the first industrial-scale conflict, though it paled against the "universal feast of death" that was the First World War.

To break the bloody stalemates of conventional warfare, the Germans developed blitzkrieg. Speed, flexibility, and violence would be the strategy: they would smash through Poland's defensive line at its weakest points, taking huge chances in the hope of confusing and demoralizing the defenders. To be sure, this wasn't an entirely new concept. Genghis Khan, when he led his horsemen on the gallop across four thousand miles of Asia and Eastern Europe, was a blitzer. There have been blitzers in every conflict, including the First World War, when T. E. Lawrence led his Arab Legion against the Turks, and German storm troopers broke through the lines in France.

What Germany added in September 1939 were tanks, dive bombers, radios, and the principle of "leading from the front" – putting the commander in the lead tank, or letting Corporal Adolf make the decisions as he clattered along. The wide plains of western Poland were ideal for fast-moving armored columns. Where they could, German troops bypassed Polish strongpoints and attacked their supply lines, without which the Poles could not fight. The chaos was compounded by fleeing refugees: "All along the road, the farmers stared in amazement at this winding river of people, without beginning or end, this river of anguish." In addition to contending with multiple German thrusts from the west, the defenders had to deal with invasions from north and south, from the German enclave of East Prussia and across Poland's almost undefended border with Czechoslovakia.

This southern attack was spearheaded by the 1st Mountain Division, a "light" force of 12,000 Bavarians and Austrians, who in the last week of August had passed through German-occupied Czechoslovakia in order to hook into Poland, far behind the front line. In the lead was the 98th Regiment under Colonel Ferdinand Schörner from Munich. His men traveled on foot and on horseback, by motorcycle, truck, bicycle, and city bus. They covered up to thirty-five miles a day, with the rest of the German 14th Army trailing on behind. Their target was the city of Lwow – Basia's home town – and their task was to seal the country's southern border. This would prevent the Polish army from escaping into Romania and Hungary.

Lwow was Poland's second city. It was a regional capital, university town, commercial center, and home to a wonderful medley of people: "golden-skinned Poles with steel-blue eyes, Armenians with velvety eye-balls, Jews whose long pale faces are framed by the ritual cork-screw curls" – and Ukrainians, a fraction of the urban population but a majority in the countryside. "Lwow," writes the Anglo-Polish historian Halik Kochanski, "was a Polish intellectual and social island in an ocean of Ukrainian peasants."

And it was a beautiful city, which the Austrians had called Little Vienna for its resemblance to their own imperial capital. The novelist and poet Joseph Wittlin adopted Lwow as an adult. He loved its cafe society, its manifold hills and "fantastic wooded gorges," and the glass-roofed railroad station that greeted him whenever he returned from abroad. "I have reached many stations in this tortuous journey called life," he wrote, "but none, except perhaps Gard du Nord in Paris, raised in me such excitement." In his novel of the First World War, *Salt of the Earth*, Wittlin limned his city as "the capital of the largest crownland in the Austro-Hungarian Monarchy, the pearl of the Hapsburg crown, the great garrison town . . . and the dream of all officers buried in tiny Galician stations – Little Vienna."

LWOW! BASIA TAUGHT ME to pronounce the first letter as a syllable unto itself – a shortened *leh* – and to follow it with a soft "voof." So: *L'voof!* It was one of the few Polish words I could voice with absolute certainty. (Being certain, of course, is not the same as being accurate. Polish is a hard nut to crack.)

The first Deszberg seems to have been a Hungarian named Jan Deshegyi. After serving in the Austrian army, he settled in southern Poland, then a province of the Austro-Hungarian Empire. German was therefore the dominant language, so when he married, Jan changed his surname to Deszberg. *Hegi* means "mountain" in Hungarian, like *berg* in German.

Jan and Eufrozyna Deszberg reared two daughters and three sons. The eldest was Kazimierz, Basia's father, born in 1875. He attended the Polish-language gymnasium in Lwow – not an obvious choice, since to get ahead in Little Vienna one had to speak the language of the Emperor Franz Josef. He then studied veterinary medicine, and for six years after graduating he remained at the college as a clinician and researcher. In 1905, at the age of thirty, he moved to Busk, a fair-sized town to the east of Lwow, as its municipal veterinarian. The move was probably prompted by a young woman named Stanislawa Korostenska, whom he married about this time, and who presented him with two sons before she died at a young age – in childbirth, probably. Soon after the younger boy, called Jurek, was born in 1909, *Pan Doktor* (Mister Doctor) Deszberg moved yet farther east, almost to the Russian frontier.

Then came 1914 and the First World War, when Poles found themselves serving in four armies and sometimes fighting against one another. Their country had been occupied and partitioned toward the end of the 18th Century. Russia conscripted the eastern Poles, Germany the western Poles, and Austria-Hungary those living in the southern province of which Lwow was the capital. Meanwhile, tens of thousands of Polish-Americans and other exiles volunteered to fight under French command on the Western Front, in what was called Haller's Army.

The thirty-nine-year-old Doctor Deszberg was called to duty in the Austrian army, serving in the 1st Brigade of the Polish Legion under Colonel Jozef Pilsudski. Though little noticed by the history books, the Eastern Front was one of the bloodiest theaters of the First World War, and the most extensive, nearly a thousand miles from north to south. It was much more fluid than the trench warfare on the Western Front. Cavalry and infantry charges regularly broke the line, though to no great result other than the eventual ruin of the empires that had once partitioned

Poland – first the Russian, then the Austrian, and finally the German.

Captain Deszberg was twice decorated for his services to Emperor Franz Josef, winning the Gold Cross with crown and combat ribbon, *für treue und bewährte Ergebenheit gegenüber dem Herrscher und den Vaterland*, for true and lasting devotion to Emperor and Fatherland. It was a handsome trinket, the cross with splayed arms in the Teutonic tradition, decorated with gilt and red enamel. Since gold was in short supply, it was actually made of bronze, with the promise of an upgrade when victory came, as of course it never did. In 1919, in the great reshuffling of European frontiers that was the Treaty of Versailles, the Austro-Hungarian Empire of 1914 shrank to a tiny and fractious republic, one-tenth its former size. One of its disgruntled citizens was a sour, scrawny war veteran named Adolf Hitler.

Among Austria's losses was Lwow, which became part of the newly independent Republic of Poland – free and united after more than a hundred years of occupation. War promptly broke out again to the east. Poland's new chief of state, Jozef Pilsudski, wanted to take back the eastern lands that had once been Polish. In Russia, meanwhile, the Bolshevik government under Vladimir Lenin wanted to export Communism to the west. "Over the corpse of Poland leads the road to global revolution," cried Mikhail Tukhachevsky, the Red Army's brilliant young commander. "On to Vilnius, Minsk, and Warsaw – march!" And march the Red Army did. Most of eastern Poland (though not Lwow, which held out as a fortress city) found itself under the rule of a stocky and ruthless commissar who had adopted the name of *Stalin*, Man of Steel.

Captain Deszberg joined the newborn Polish army along with nearly a million others, including thousands of Polish-Americans who had served in France. He was commissioned a colonel in the 14th Infantry Division, based at the gingerbread town of Torun in western Poland. The Red Army almost got that far, reaching the outskirts of Warsaw before the Poles rallied at what they still celebrate as "the miracle at the Vistula." The Russians lost all the land they'd conquered, and more besides, enabling Pilsudski to achieve his dream of pushing Poland's frontier deep into Russian territory. *Pan Pulkownik* – Mister Colonel – Deszberg was twice decorated in the conflict, winning a Silver Cross and the Russo-Polish War Service Medal.

This vicious little war had immense consequences. For the Russians, it marked the end of Lenin's dream of exporting Communism. Henceforth, he would concentrate on "revolution in one country," a policy affirmed by Joseph Stalin when he took control of what was now called the Soviet Union. But he never forgot the humiliation that had been inflicted upon him and the Red Army in the Russo-Polish War. Until the day he died, Stalin went out of his way to punish the Polish nation and the Polish people, wherever he could find them, even in petty ways. A favorite opera was Glinka's *Ivan Susanin*, though he stayed only long enough to see the Poles lured into a forest where they would freeze to death. His enmity satisfied, he would leave the theater without waiting for the final curtain.

For Western Europe, the Russo-Polish War seemed a lucky turn of events, preventing Lenin's dictatorship of the proletariat from reaching France or even the English Channel. In defeat, General Tukhachevsky lamented: "There can be no doubt that if we had been victorious on the Vistula, the revolutionary fires would have reached the entire continent," and British historians tend to agree. The Polish victory "largely determined the course of European history for the next twenty years or more."

Military observers took note of the mobile warfare practiced by the Poles, in contrast to the earlier, trench-bound stalemates in France and Belgium. They included Major Charles de Gaulle, an advisor to the Polish army who became France's leading advocate of tank warfare. And there was General Tukhachevsky himself, who not only introduced tank warfare to the Red Army but also experimented with airborne infantry as a "deep battle" (*glubokaya operatsiya*) tactic. These experiments were shared with the German officers who – forbidden by the Treaty of Versailles from developing an army of their own – trained secretly in Soviet Russia. So it is not entirely fanciful to note that the Poles themselves helped create the blitzkrieg strategy that would stagger them in September 1939.

THE "MIRACLE AT THE VISTULA" convinced Poles that they were a great power in Europe. Jozef Pilsudski became a national hero on the scale of George Washington, though one who did not retire when his day was done: he led a coup against the civilian government that succeeded him, and for all practical purposes ruled as a dictator until his death in 1935. As with Pilsudski, so it was with the military he'd led to victory. "Army officers," wrote Norman Davies of interwar Poland, "occupied the pinnacle of social respectability and in due course the seat of political power."

Alas, the proud new country had two fatal weaknesses, both partly attributable to its victory in the Russo-Polish War. For one thing, its eastern border was arbitrary, largely undefined by mountains, rivers, or other obstacles that would slow an invader. For another, those eastern lands were heavily populated with Ukrainians, Belarusians, and Jews, to the extent that ethnic Poles were merely the largest minority in a region made up entirely of minorities. Indeed, Poland itself was not so much a nation as a confederacy. Of 32 million people, nearly a third did not think of themselves as Polish. Perhaps six million regarded Ukrainian, Belarusian, or a local dialect as their mother tongue; three million spoke Hebrew or Yiddish; and nearly a million thought of themselves as *Volksdeutsch*, ethnic Germans.

Such divisions were common to the nations midwifed by

the Treaty of Versailles. "It's a Europe of hatred," says an American historian of the interwar years; "it's a Europe of fears." Beyond these tensions, the Continent suffered from an agricultural depression during much of the time that the Polish Republic existed – and seventy percent of its people were farmers. The new country also had to pay reparations to France and Britain, since its west and south had been part of the defeated German and Austrian empires.

BUT LIFE GOES ON. About 1928, the widowed Colonel Deszberg married a young woman named Zuzanna Brachaniec, born the same year as his son Zdzislaw. This was the lady whom I would come to know as Mama. In a photograph taken when she was twenty or so, Zuzu is remarkably pretty, with plump cheeks and dark hair, though the hair color is evidently a photographic quirk. "Mama was always blonde," Basia assures me, and in later photos she is indeed lighthaired. Moreover, her round cheeks have become more angular – less *pretty*, more beautiful. For his part, the colonel was in his fifties and wearily handsome, his hair cut short in the tradition of Continental army officers. His nose might have been borrowed from the eagle that appears as Poland's national symbol.

Their first child was Maria Magdalena, born in Torun and named for the sinner whom Jesus cleansed of demons. She was nicknamed Lalka, Doll, because she was so pretty. Soon after her birth, the colonel moved his young family to Lwow, where Zuzu's brother and two sisters were living. About the same time, at the age of fifty-seven, he apparently went onto reserve status with the Polish army, for his military record shows no duty assignment after 1933.

In Lwow that December, Zuzu was delivered of a second daughter. She wanted to call the newborn Ewa, or Eve, the cause of mankind's fall from grace, but the colonel demurred. "One sinner in the family is enough!" he decreed. So the little girl became Barbara. Her pet name was *Chabrus*, derived from the Polish word for cornflower. This was a tribute to the startling blue of her eyes . . . and indeed, there is a painting by Igor Grabar that shows baskets of cornflowers of precisely the shade of Basia's eyes. I got quite a pang when I first saw a reproduction of that painting.

LIKE MOST YOUNGER CHILDREN, Basia thought of herself as the runner-up, second always to her more perfect sister. "Lalka was a socialite," Basia says, with a sibling's combination of love and exasperation. Perhaps she is remembering herself in a family grouping in 1936. Polish mothers believed that if they cut a child's hair short, it would grow out strong and thick, so Basia in the photo is cropped as close as her officer-father, giving no hint of the handsome young woman she will become. Lalka by contrast is poised and perfect, with a ribbon in her hair. She is adorable, and she knows it.

They lived at 99 Potocki Street in Lwow's southwestern quadrant. At its upper end, near the city center, Potocki is the very model of an Old World avenue, paved with cobblestones, a tram line running down the middle and three-story stone houses crowding the sidewalks. There is even a "palace" at Number 50, an ornate corner building that once belonged to a Polish nobleman, or so I am told by a current resident.

Halfway down the street, a redbrick Catholic church stands on a grassy lot, after which the tram jogs off to a parallel street to serve the southern railroad station. (Lwow was encircled by railroad tracks, with a large and handsome central station and three suburban ones.) Potocki Street at this point becomes quite leafy, with widely separated houses. Number 99 today is a small, rather elegant stone house, standing by itself in a forested park. In the 1930s it had close neighbors, later destroyed by the War – and in fact, Basia's home was probably also a casualty of Lwow's recurrent bombardments, with the present building added more recently.

Zdzislaw Deszberg, the colonel's older son, was a banker and a man of many gifts and graces. He too married about this time, so that his bride – Waleria by name – found herself with a mother-in-law only a year or two older than herself. This led to a certain coolness between the two young women. Or perhaps, as Basia recalls, it was only that *Pani* Waleria couldn't bear the chaos of the two young children running about the Potocki Street flat:

Years later, Waleria told me that their visits to us were usually short. She would tell Zdzislaw that half an hour of "those brats" was more than enough. She thought we were terribly spoilt, especially by our father. I was very happy to hear that. After all, it was for only a short time.

Mama's family was closer. She had two older sisters, one of them married with a son, and a younger brother who had settled into a career as perpetual student and ladies' man. This branch of the family – Aunt Krysia, her husband and son, Aunt Nuna, and Uncle Jan – shared a house on Karpenski Street in the city center, not far from Potocki Street. Every summer, they went on a holiday with Mama, Lalka, and Basia:

We used to spend August in the mountains, covered with pine trees. The smell was gorgeous. One day when we were waiting for Aunt Krysia, she appeared with what looked like blood on her face. She gave everyone a fright, but it turned out that she had only rubbed her face in wild strawberries – very good for the complexion, she said.

Aunt Krysia had many such beauty tricks. Indeed, in a photograph taken in August 1936, at Kosmacz in the Carpathian Mountains south of Lwow, she astonishes with her youthfulness. She looks like a college student, though she is the oldest of the siblings, and her son Zbyszek is a leggy ten-year-old.

Colonel Deszberg does not appear in these souvenirs of

summers in the country. No doubt August was the occasion of the annual call-up expected of an officer in the army reserve.

THEN THERE WAS THE COLONEL'S younger son, Jurek Deszberg, who followed his father and grandfather into the army. Jurek graduated from Lwow's military high school in 1927, and after three years' further education – in Torun, I think – was commissioned a lieutenant in the Polish army. After serving with the 27th Field Artillery Regiment, he became a staff officer, probably at the divisional level. He was Basia's favorite relative. She especially remembers that he once gave her a ride on his motorcycle – just the sort of thing an older brother ought to do, though I suspect it distressed Mama at the time.

Basia also remembers the Sisters of Charity at the convent on Potocki Street, with their great winged cornettes, as if swans had alighted on their heads. Lalka went to school with the sisters, and Basia was supposed to follow, but made such a fuss that her kindergarten education lasted only a single day. In Lwow as in East Alton, the second-born tend to rebel against those who have the charge of them.

And she remembers going to the cinema and seeing Shirley Temple eat spaghetti. That would have been *Poor Little Rich Girl*, in which a child goes missing in New York City and is taken up by two Italian entertainers. For Basia, the film was so life-changing that she acquired a doll in the likeness of the American film star, though with blonde hair and blue eyes. She also saw *Snow White and the Seven Dwarfs*, which as it happens was my first movie. Lwow had a proper cinema – several of them, indeed – whereas in Alton we went to the town hall, where a portable screen was erected in front of the stage, and we sat in wooden folding chairs. The Wicked Queen gave me nightmares for a week.

31

Basia's mother at twenty or so, about the time she met Colonel Deszberg, who was thirty years her senior.

Basia's father when he retired from active duty, wearing two decorations from the 1919-1921 war and a medal honoring his years of service.

A family outing in the Carpathian Mountains south of Lwow in August 1936. Left to right: Aunt Nuna, two-year-old Basia with her hair closely cropped, Mama, Uncle Jan, Aunt Krysia, Jan's most recent sweetheart, Lalka, and Krysia's son Zbyszek. Three years later, those same pine-shrouded mountains would become the escape route for tens of thousands of soldiers heading for Romania and eventual service in 1st Polish Corps of the British Army.

IT WAS A PLEASANT LIFE on Potocki Street, with servants to help Mama with housework, cooking, and caring for the little girls:

I remember the snow in Lwow and going sledding with a nanny. She got distracted by a young soldier and let the sled go. It went down the hill and I landed in a brook. The ice must have been thin because I was wet through and my white fur coat ruined. Then I see myself in the kitchen with Mama, another woman, and the nanny bustling about and making a lot of noise.

When I told Lalka about it, ages later, she said it was her coat that was ruined, and that the whole thing happened to her. Maybe she was right. She was a good storyteller, so maybe I just took it over.

Number 99 Potocki Street had a lawn and garden, a dog named Nana, a swing, and other children for the Deszberg girls to play with. Basia even had an admirer among the neighborhood children, a boy named Stanislaw:

Tas was thirteen years old. He looked after me when we played in the garden. One of our favorite games was to leap off the swing when someone with closed eyes would cry, "Jump!" When the other children got fed up with that game, they would start another, and I was left trailing behind them. Tas saw to it that I got my turn and that the swing was not too high when I had to leap. He was my guardian.

While we were on holiday in the country, he wrote me a letter to say that Nana's puppies had opened their eyes, were doing well, and not to worry about them. He addressed the letter to "Chabrus," signed it as "your fiance" with a big red heart and a small red heart, and said he would love me to the end of his days.

I wonder what happened to him?

Mama tucked the letter into her treasure box, and it would accompany her into exile, as a memory of happier days. As for Stanislaw, his fate was probably dire. With

Poland occupied by Nazi Germany and Soviet Russia, turn and turn about, Tas was almost certainly conscripted as a soldier or slave laborer for one side or the other, and perhaps for both.

BASIA REMEMBERS HER FATHER as an army officer with knee-high polished boots. An enlisted soldier – what the English call a batman – came to the house from time to time to care for the colonel's kit, and especially those boots. They were "a prestige and status symbol" in the Polish officer corps, "made from the softest leather brought to perfect luster by hours of tedious polishing."

The colonel was called up at some point in 1939, though at sixty-four probably not with a front-line unit. Jurek too would have been on active duty that awful summer, while the German dictator blustered and threatened. Adolf Hitler regarded Eastern Europe as Germany's proper sphere of influence, and in short order he had erased Czechoslovakia from the map, annexed part of Lithuania, renounced Germany's treaties with Britain and Poland, and replaced them with new pacts with Italy and Soviet Russia. The Hitler-Stalin agreement was signed in the late hours of August 23.

Basia recalls those last weeks of peace, when the family went on its customary holiday in the country, leaving the Potocki Street flat in the care of an acquaintance:

My father would usually stay with us only for a fortnight or so, on leave from the army. In August 1939 on his return home, he found the flat empty. Our carpets, Mama's fur coats, Lalka's coat, my coat, and most of the movable furniture were gone. The lady who was supposed to look after the flat had also disappeared. Mama often spoke about the shock, about how she had to look for material to have new coats made for us, with bombs falling on the city and shops emptied of goods and of Dad's worrying about how on earth she was going to cope in the War.

Our garden now had a shelter where we all ran when there was an air raid. Except for Nana the dog, who was left tied to a tree and who howled desperately.

THE BOMBERS WERE SUPPORTING Colonel Schörner's 98th Mountain Regiment as it neared Lwow. On September 11, a Monday, his two leading companies – three hundred men – reached the outskirts but were thrown back in a bloody encounter with Lwow's defenders and their two 75 mm (three-inch) cannon. Next day, the Germans reinforced and broke through to the city center, but were again driven out. Settling in for a longer fight, four companies of the 98th fought a two-day battle at the hilly suburb of Zboiska, north of the city. By sundown on Thursday, September 14, the Germans held Zboiska and the high ground west of it, which they called Hill 374 after its elevation in meters.

Hill 374 was a steep, forested upland, its sides cut with gullies, standing three hundred feet above the rooftops of Lwow. Here the Germans placed their heavy weapons, including infantry mortars and 75 mm pack cannon. As his trailing elements caught up, Colonel Schörner threw a cordon around the city except for a gap on the northeast side. He maintained his headquarters in a streamlined bus, perhaps army issue, perhaps seized along the way. The Germans pressed especially close on the southwest, where the Polish defenses were actually inside the railroad line, cutting across Potocki Street a few blocks south of Basia's home.

The resistance was led in the early days by General Franciszek Sikorski, brother of Poland's once and future prime minister. Sikorski commanded a hodgepodge of regular army units, stragglers from the west, and the *Straz Obywatelska*, an ad hoc Citizen's Guard of retired officers and civilian volunteers. Sikorski had no fighter planes to stop the German Heinkels and Stukas – Lwow's airport was bombed from the first day, then occupied by Schörner's troops – and no way to reinforce against two more regiments of 1st Mountain Division coming up.

Then the Red Army stormed across Poland's eastern border. That was Sunday, September 17. Russian propaganda presented the invasion as a rescue mission, "to render immediate assistance to our brother Belarusians and Ukrainians" – that is, to the ethnic minorities in the borderlands. History is full of curious twists. Here's one involving the recurrent sieges of Lwow: when the Red Army invaded Poland in 1919, the commissar in the eastern part of the country had been Joseph Stalin himself. Now he was Nikita Khrushchev, the plump bully who in 1953 would replace Stalin as the overlord of Soviet Russia and its vassal states.

The Polish military staff, or what remained of it, had moved east to organize a last stand in the marshy borderlands, hoping that the French would come to the rescue by attacking Germany from the west. The Russian invasion gave the staff no option but to escape into Romania. (The civilian government had already crossed the border and been interned.) By radio they ordered the troops not to resist the Red Army, in the forlorn hope that it might actually have come to help, or anyhow would be less destructive than Hitler's fast-moving legions.

The first Russian tanks reached Lwow on Tuesday, September 19. Ignoring their orders to cooperate, the defenders pounded the Red Army with shells from their two small cannon, whereupon the Russians pulled back and contented themselves with completing the encirclement of the city. Now it was Germans on the west, Russians on the east, much like the fate of Poland itself.

About this time, the 1st Mountain Division commander, General Ludwig Kübler, flew into the Lwow airport in a Fieseler Storch lightplane. Under his direction, a German lieutenant walked down a dusty city street under a white flag of truce, to meet a Polish officer carrying a similar flag.

The surrender was signed on Thursday, September 21, by which time Kübler's forces had lost 250 men killed and 400 wounded. (Some of the casualties may actually have been inflicted in skirmishes with the Russians.) The Polish dead, including civilians, were probably in the thousands. Among them was the young man whom Basia's Aunt Nuna was engaged to marry. He had been killed in a bombing raid in the first week of the War.

The Germans withdrew to the line that had been agreed upon in the Hitler-Stalin pact of August 23. Poland was now almost exactly divided between its two traditional enemies, who were also traditional enemies of one another. Fighting continued in the German sector, with Warsaw holding out until September 28, and Lublin until October 6.

And the Polish army didn't cease to exist! Forty-three thousand sailors, airmen, and soldiers managed to escape across Poland's southern frontier. With them fled civilian officials to replace the government that had been interned in Romania. Through tortuous routes (some literally went around the world, through Soviet Russia, across the Pacific, through the United States, and back across the Atlantic) they reformed in France and then in England. In time the country's gold reserves caught up with them, to finance the Polish government in exile.

I Kiss Your Hand
1955

WHICH OF US HAD THE IDEA of hitchhiking to Italy? For fifty-odd years I thought the plan was Basia's, to save the money she'd otherwise spend on train fare. She thinks it was my idea, for the sake of adventure, and no doubt she's right. Thumbing rides had been my invariable mode of travel at home, whereas English students seldom hitch-hiked. English cars were small and the roads were awful, while the trains were cheap, frequent, and on time – much better than the diesel-powered Budd Liner cars that ran between Boston and the University of New Hampshire. Anyhow, hitchhiking to Italy had a particular attraction for me. It promised me a week as Basia's sole companion.

However it happened, we agreed to take the boat and train to Paris, spend three nights in the City of Light, then hitchhike in stages to Lyon, Turin, Florence, and Perugia. Or so we charted our route on a BP map of Europe that I bought at a bookstore on Oxford Road. (English oil companies *sold* their road maps, instead of giving them away at service stations.) As matters turned out, we didn't take sufficient notice of the mountains that stood athwart the road to Italy, repeating an error that Hannibal had made in 218 BC.

I'd joined the Youth Hostel Association for my travels around England, and I'd bought a guidebook to European hostels, an orange sleeping bag, and a steel-frame rucksack of a design that proved miserably uncomfortable for carrying more than twenty pounds for any length of time. It was as if a small boy were hanging from my shoulders.

"We will stay the night with Mama in London," Basia said. "You will meet her, and she will know that I will be safe with you."

We would set out on April 4, a Monday, so we could cash our monthly checks. It also enabled me finesse the question of whether I would accompany the Deszberg ladies to Sunday Mass. I was not a churchgoer, and they almost certainly were.

My check arrived on Friday, so I could go to the bank before it closed. I returned with a stack of fifty one-pound notes, green and crisp, with the young Queen's portrait on the front. I folded this small fortune into a parcel and tied it at the bottom of my sleeping bag. The War had bankrupted England, so its people were allowed to take just £25 out of the country. Though the Fulbright was an American fellowship, my monthly stipend actually came from Her Majesty's Treasury, as part payment on the Marshall Plan aid that had kept the country afloat during the hungry years after the War. It would be a brave customs officer who unrolled my dank orange bag to look for the surplus banknotes. This was dishonest of me, no doubt, and it was certainly illegal. At the time, the question didn't trouble me at all, as such niceties seldom trouble a lad of twenty-two.

For clothing I had the tweed jacket, wool trousers, and leather shoes that I wore every day to class, Caf, the pub, and the cinema. (Did I hope to impress Mama with my schoolboy attire?) I had a nylon shirt from Burtons that was supposed to dry overnight, and two polo shirts for sunny weather. What else? Well, my passport, in the leather billfold that Dad had brought from Ireland in 1927. My Speed Graphic press camera – a monstrous thing, but I was a journalist! A toilet kit with the usual stuff, including a hairbrush and a Gillette razor. (I didn't need the razor, because since Christmas I'd grown a rather dashing beard, but I took it anyhow.) Oh, and a towel. And a fat white tube of Macleans toothpaste.

What surprises me now is the things I didn't take. No aspirin, Band-Aids, or Imodium – no condoms! Youth is the time before we know enough to take precautions.

SUNDAY EVENING AT SIX-THIRTY, Basia met me at Piccadilly Gardens for a celebratory drink. This was her idea, and I now realize that she was thrilled to be escaping dreary Manchester and the oversight of Uncle Jan. I regarded her as a sophisticated young woman, much more sophisticated than I. She spoke all those languages! She'd been to all those cities – she'd seen the *Pyramids*, for crying out loud! To be sure, she'd accomplished this as a child, guarded by Mama or Aunt Krysia, but that didn't occur to me at the time. Despite my American bravado and my comparative affluence, I felt a bit of a hillbilly in the presence of Basia Deszberg, late of Lwow, Tehran, Beirut, and London.

We went to the pub near the Piccadilly Cinema and ordered gin and Rose's Lime Juice. This was the lounge bar, where drinks were a penny dearer and the atmosphere quieter than in the "public" room. With the second drink, Basia said: "When you meet Mama, you must kiss her hand. She will like that."

"Oh, I don't think so!" For an American of the 1950s, everything European and decadent – old world and sinister – the mindset behind those recurrent wars – was symbolized by a monocled and mustachioed army officer, clicking his heels, bending at the waist, and kissing a lady's hand.

"It's important," Basia said. She extended her right hand across the table, palm down. "You may practice on me."

Well, that was different! We were the only people in the lounge bar, and the publican had his back to us, drawing pints of bitter for the men standing at the counter in the other room. I took Basia's downturned fingers between my thumb and fingertips; then I dipped my head, raised her knuckles to the level of my chin, and kissed the back of her hand. For the honor of my country, I then turned it over and kissed the palm, for which I got my own hand spanked. "Enough!" Basia said. "The nuns would grade you *c'est suffisant*." This, I gathered, was the convent's equivalent of a

Gentleman's C, undistinguished but enough to keep one advancing from grade to grade. I desisted, but I resolved to practice further at my next opportunity. It wasn't far, after all, from Basia's hand to the sweet bow of her lips.

MONDAY AFTERNOON, WE MET AGAIN at Piccadilly Gardens and walked over to the glass-roofed railroad station for the train that would take us to London and my meeting with Mama. Basia had a rucksack like mine, and she wore sensible black trousers and the light duffle coat that made my heart jump whenever I spotted it in Caf or on the street.

Now I must explain what at the time I didn't know. There'd been a family blowup over Basia's plan to perfect her Italian in Perugia. Uncle Jan in particular was outraged, threatening to write the University to protest its careless ways with the virtue of its young women. As I have said, Jan had been a bit of a rake in Lwow, where he had dallied through ten years as an undergraduate. It took the Second World War to straighten him out:

He learned English, finished his degree within a year, married, became an exemplary husband and father, and sat on a high moral horse. He was a pain in the neck during my years at Manchester, though I was glad of his supervision at times, like the time in the pea-soup fog when he met me at the bus stop.

After all, who knows better than a reformed ladies' man the dangers that face young women? Basia was twenty-one years old that spring, but Uncle Jan waited for her at the bus stop whenever she stayed late at the University. She'd never brought an admirer home to meet her aunt and uncle – not Paul the medical student, not me.

Oddly, the sticking point for Uncle Jan wasn't the idea that his niece planned to live and study in Italy. Rather, he couldn't accept the notion that she'd have to *travel* there. She would take the ferry and boat train to Paris – sinful

Paris! – followed by a night and a day in a second-class carriage to Florence, hip to hip and knee to knee with seven French and Italian strangers, some or all of them certain to be male. Basia mustn't travel by herself! Thus her ever-so-casual invitation at Caf, thrown out to the table but actually, it seems, directed at me:

I was offered the chance to go to Perugia. We were talking about it on the way to Caf, you and I, when I realized that you had a grant only for the year and would go back to the United States before I returned from Italy.

To my surprise, I didn't like the idea of your going away, so I thought it would be nice if you came to Perugia with me. I have now worked out the reasons, a little late. There were the obvious ones: you looked good, you were intelligent. But also I was brought up with stories of my highly idealized father and the heroes of Polish literature. And in my Italian course we were going through courtly poetry. I must have attributed some of those qualities to you. . . . As Mama would have said, you were a perfect gentleman.

So I asked if someone wanted to go to Perugia with me. I was hoping that you would volunteer. I could have ignored the answer if it came from someone else.

The family was much relieved when Basia announced that she'd found a traveling companion. Then, honorably but unwisely, she revealed that not only was I male, but – an American! After the Deszbergs had escaped from Russia, Mama worked for a time at the U.S. Army officers' club in Tehran, where louche young lieutenants had presumed to call her "Susie" and perhaps to give her a pat or a pinch as she cleared the table.

After much discussion, the family reached a compromise: Basia would produce me for inspection, and Mama would decide whether it was safe for her to proceed to Italy in my company. Once Mama made her decision, the rest of the family – Uncle Jan, the aunts, Lalka, and various in-laws – would fall into line. Like the launch of the Space Shuttle, therefore, our Easter vacation was subject to cancellation at the last moment, and this without Mama's knowing that we meant to hitchhike.

FROM EUSTON STATION WE TOOK the Victoria and the Piccadilly line to North Ealing, then walked a few blocks to Basia's home. I ought to have been terrified, but I don't think I was, and to my eternal regret I don't remember meeting Mama or kissing her hand, though Basia assures me that I did. (I certainly didn't click my heels!)

The house was a pretty one, "semi-detached" as the English say, joined to its neighbor with a common wall. A low brick fence guarded it from the sidewalk, with an iron gate and a curving flagstone path to the door. It was two stories high, and I remember the rooms as very large, with high ceilings. We ate in a breakfast room off the kitchen, with Basia to my right and Mama across from me. She was an older, taller, plumper, and blonder version of her daughter, with the same pretty lips, all of which made her a very comforting presence.

To my shame, I asked Mama not one question about Poland, about the prison camp in Siberia (as I understood her exile at the time), or about how she'd managed to reach England. There is no underestimating the incuriosity of the young. At least until we are into our thirties, we assume that the world we experience is the world as it has always existed, and as it should exist. We have no idea that it was forged by people who grew old in the process.

Luckily for me, there had been one individual whom Mama excepted from her disdain for Americans. His name as I now know was Tom, and evidently I more closely resembled him (quiet? a nice smile?) than the young lieutenants at the officers' mess in Tehran. In any event, I managed to pass my exam without ever knowing I had sat for it.

44

And perhaps I wasn't quite as gauche as I remember, as Basia points out:

You wouldn't have had much of a conversation, anyhow. Mama's English was very rudimentary. "How much is that? Five shillings? Too much!"

WE SET OUT AFTER BREAKFAST, to Victoria Station and the nine o'clock train to Dover. Basia left her gold bangles with Mama, so that her only jewelry was a small school ring on her right hand. I am pretty sure that I kissed Mama's hand in parting, and I know that I drew myself up and said: "I will see Basia safe to Perugia." I had sense enough for that, anyhow. I'd rehearsed it all through breakfast.

The train was the usual English coal burner, though our carriage was labeled second class instead of third as was the practice elsewhere in England. From Victoria Station onward, we were for all practical purposes on the Continent.

The ferry was a splendid turbine steamer called *Invicta*. Even as the boarding ramp was being wheeled away, an American girl in the second-class cabin corralled everyone of student age, demanded to know where we were from, and announced that we would play Twenty Questions to ward off seasickness. She had the right idea, at that, for the Channel was rough, and about halfway across I began to feel distinctly green. Basia and I went on deck, as far forward as we could get, to stand in the salt breeze and watch the White Cliffs of Dover shrink behind us and the more modest cliffs of France grow large before us. The sun was brilliant. I had not seen an afternoon so clear since the *SS United States* steamed past the Lizard Lighthouse, seven months before.

Then the most astonishing thing happened. As *Invicta* steamed into the harbor of Calais, four or five schoolboys scrambled along the seawall at just our level, keeping pace with the ferry and shouting at us – in French! I'd studied Latin and Spanish in high school, and there were several

French Canadian families in Wolfeboro, where I lived at the time, and where the parish priest was required to be a French speaker, so he could hear the confessions of the older women. Yet somehow it had never occurred to me that children might speak a foreign language. I was awed, humbled, entranced, and also a bit dismayed to realize how much I would now depend on Basia as my interpreter.

At the Calais ferry hall we queued for customs, queued again to have our passports stamped, again to change pounds to francs, and a fourth time to board a bus to the railroad station. Like the boat train to Dover Marine, this one had American-style open carriages, with seats that faced one another and a table between. It was electrified, however, and it was brighter and faster than the English version, never mind the Budd Liners of the Boston & Maine Railroad. This seemed all wrong to me. Hadn't England won the war, while France was invaded once in 1940 and again in 1944?

Much the same proved to be true of Paris when we clattered through the suburbs: they were much brighter than London's, and I saw no vacant blocks where bombs had fallen. In modern combat, it seemed, a country might be better off losing than winning. Better to be ravished Marianne than embattled John Bull.

We'd been traveling for eight hours, Victoria Station to Gare du Nord, so we plunged into the Metropolitaine at five o'clock, along with everyone else in Paris. A ticket cost thirty francs, which struck us as ominous. (We were accustomed to paying twopence for a bus ride, and a halfpenny more on the Underground.) We found an illuminated map, and I checked the YHA guidebook for the address of the hostel. Then all we had to do was press the button for Place d'Italie and – *voila!* – our route was displayed for us by little yellow bulbs.

We had to stand with our rucksacks, swaying in the smelly second-class carriage as we hurtled beneath the

Seine to the Left Bank, steel wheels clattering and screeching on steel rails.

When we emerged again into daylight, Basia smiled at the first pedestrian we encountered on the Avenue d'Italie: "*Excusez-moi, m'sieur, où est l'auberge de jeunesse, s'il vous plaît?*" – a phrase I silently memorized. The hostel was just a few blocks farther along, but we were desperate to be footloose in Paris, and we needed groceries. So we dallied up side streets until we spotted a boulangerie where we could buy a two-foot-long loaf of bread. Then to a tobacconist's for a stubby pack of *Gauloises Bleues*. And a vintner's for red wine, which involved three distinct purchases: the bottle, the cork, and the wine, decanted from a vat behind the counter. Lastly we found a fromagerie for half a kilo of hard cheese. Basia bargained; I did the conversions. "How much is 100 francs?" she would ask.

"Two shillings." She returned to the negotiation with renewed zest. I was as impressed with her bargaining as with the fact that she could do it in French.

"When we lived in Tehran," she explained, "I learned Farsi at school, and I used to go to the bazaars with Aunt Kyrsia. They were full of color and excitement, and we haggled like mad. Aunt Krysia liked the haggling so much that when we got to London she tried it in Harrod's, with me still interpreting. I wished the floor would swallow me!"

My role was to do the math and to parcel out 20-franc coins and 100-franc banknotes. (The notes were lavender, depicting a young farmer with his ox and a digging fork.) We spent 600 francs all told, a dollar and a half, one-third of that for the blue pack of thick, heady Gaulois cigarettes. Basia was much relieved to find that she and I were twins for frugality. "I was afraid," she admitted, "that an American would want to buy the best of everything."

All of which now strikes me as a risky way to pursue a romance. We'd never before spent more than a couple hours in each other's company, but here we were in a strange city, on the first day of a week-long journey, and one of us was head over heels in love with the other. I think we did very well to reach the youth hostel as happy as when we'd set out from Mama's house, ten hours before.

The hostel was a rectangle of concrete blocks, like a police station in a bad neighborhood, with a trampled yard behind it where a few tents were pitched. We paid Madame 600 francs, three nights' lodging for the two of us, and in return got an impressive stamp on our YHA membership cards. Then we each went off to our assigned dormitory, where double-decker bunks were ranged in rows, with mattresses so thin they were rolled at the head of the bed. I claimed an upper bunk by unrolling the mattress and spreading out my sleeping bag, which had a sort of hood into which it was tucked for traveling. I stuffed this hood with spare clothing for a pillow, then went out to the common room to await Basia. I didn't think to secure my bankroll in any way, nor would I ever do so while hitchhiking in Europe. The hostels were locked during the day, and again at ten or eleven at night, but anyone could have pilfered the dormitories during the evening hours. It didn't happen to me, nor to anyone else that I knew of.

AFTER A SUPPER OF BREAD, cheese, and wine, we went out to explore. The first thing Basia wanted to see was the basilica of the Sacré Coeur, so we set off on the Metro, clanging and screeching. We got out at Anvers station on the south side of Montmartre, where artists had their paintings on display. Most depicted the Sacré Coeur with its splendid domes, one large and one small, and drawn out at the top like a Hershey's Kiss, except bone white instead of chocolate.

It was a stiff climb to the basilica. There were others on the steps, a dozen or so, but most were either Parisians or young travelers like ourselves – *vagabondi*, as we'd been called at the youth hostel. I almost never met a tourist as I knocked about Europe that year, even in high summer. Tourism really didn't exist in the decade between the War and the Boeing 707. Just about the only people traveling from country to country were American soldiers, students of whatever nationality, and young carpenters with their tool boxes and *wanderjahre* costumes.

The moon was nearly full, and the great basilica shone white above us, a moon reflecting the moon. And Paris – even in 1955 a city of light! – sparkled like a galaxy below us. I'd never seen anything so beautiful as Paris at night. No wonder so many of my heroes had chosen to live here when they were young: Ernest Hemingway, James Joyce, Scott Fitzgerald, Ezra Pound, and John dos Passos. (Nobody reads *Manhattan Transfer* today, and few read the *Cantos*, more's the pity. Even Hemingway and Fitzgerald have lost their cachet, the one scorned for his chauvinism, the other for sentimentality.)

On the plaza in front of the basilica, a young Frenchman fastened upon us. The basilica, he lectured us in fast and very passable English, was the work of two businessmen who during the Franco-Prussian War pledged that if Paris were delivered from the Germans, they'd build a monument to the Sacred Heart of Jesus. "This was a limestone quarry," he said, "so she was made from limestone. She is always white because in the rain, the lime comes out like new." How long had he waited here, to impart this information, and was he was hoping to improve his English or to impress a pretty girl? The knowledge was welcome in any case. Neither Basia nor I were believers in guidebooks; it was as if we thought that knowing about a place in advance might spoil our enjoyment of it.

Then the great bell began to ring, pealing as though it would never stop. The sound seemed to move inside my head, and as the vibrations built up, my cheekbones seemed to ring as well. The notes sometimes softened, then rose again, to a volume so overwhelming that ranking it on some sort of scale was just impossible. "She is *La Savoyarde!*" our guide shouted during one of the quieter moments. "She weighs seventeen thousand kilograms! The how do you say – the hammer? – the hammer is eight hundred kilograms!"

A one-ton clapper, falling endlessly upon a nineteen-ton bell – or upon my skull, as it seemed.

What does a young man do when overwhelmed by the pealing of the Savoyarde? Why, he turns to the young woman beside him, puts his arms around her, and kisses her on the lips. . . . Or tries to! Alas, Basia was quicker than I. She fended me off with her right hand extended, slightly inclined from the wrist. It was like a dance step, as if she'd practiced before a mirror in Uncle Jan's flat in Manchester. "You may kiss my hand," she told me.

All sorts of questions ran through my mind, so recently filled with that magnificent bell. Should I try my luck again? Would Gary Cooper have kissed Grace Kelly's hand, before or after that shootout at high noon? It seemed unlikely, and I was positive that Humphrey Bogart would never have kissed Lauren Bacall's hand. But it was too late to fall back on my national honor: I'd already compromised it, over gin and Rose's Lime Juice in the lounge bar off Piccadilly Gardens. . . . Never mind! I took her fingers in mine, raised her hand to my lips, and kissed it just above the knuckles.

Basia seemed pleased, and to tell the truth so was I. Indeed, I was rather proud of myself, especially when I turned the hand over and pressed my lips to her palm, and got away with it this time. Ah, me. There are more things in heaven and earth, Yank, than are dreamt of in your philosophy.

WE SPENT THREE NIGHTS at the hostel off Place d'Italie. We visited the Eiffel Tower and climbed the 600 steps to the second level. We went to Mass at Notre Dame, in the company of a dozen large women in black, kneeling on the cold stones and fingering their rosaries. They ignored the priest, far distant at the altar, and he ignored us, the tourists. The experience made me rather weepy, and on the way out I bought a postcard of the cathedral to send home to Wolfeboro, to let Mom know that I hadn't entirely sold my soul to the devil.

We browsed the bookstalls along the Seine, in honor of my literary heroes of the 1920s. We drank *cafe au lait* at an outdoor cafe on the Champs-Élysées while we read the Paris edition of the *New York Herald Tribune*. (The newspaper office, I learned from the masthead, wasn't far off. Sitting there on the Champs, reading the expatriate newspaper, seemed so natural that I decided that I would work there some day.)

Indeed, we did all the things young lovers do in Paris, except make love. This was a disappointment to me, but only a minor one. I felt very close to Basia. We'd become friends, whereas in Manchester we'd been acquaintances. I could take her hand without feeling awkward, and she trusted me enough to doze on my shoulder on the Metro. I knew that some day soon I would kiss her on the lips, that before long I would share her bed – indeed, that someday I would marry her, though to be sure I hadn't worked this out in any great detail.

The hostel had a common room with a gas range and two trestle tables where we vagabonds cooked, ate, and socialized. One evening I fell into conversation with an American who lived in one of those tents in the back yard. "I lost my passport," he explained, "so I'm stuck here until the new one comes. Madame lets me camp out back." When I admitted that I too was an American, he asked the inevitable question: "Yeah? Where from?"

This caused Basia to smile – an effect I enjoyed, because when the corners of her mouth turned up, so did the tops of her cheeks, causing her eyes to crinkle prettily. Our team leader on *Invicta* had asked everyone the same question –

"Where you from?" – so Basia considered it an American ritual, like dogs circling one another when they meet. If you live in a small country, I suppose, your geographical location is of much less significance.

"New Hampshire," I said.

"Well, did you ever live in Massachusetts?"

"Yes."

"In Concord?"

"Yes, as a matter of fact."

"Well," he said. "I'm Gordon Olson."

Yes! He'd been my best buddy in sixth grade, toward the end of the War, when Dad worked on Mr. Laughlin's estate on Old River Road in Concord. After graduating from the University of Massachusetts last June, Gordon worked on a road gang to pay his passage to Norway, to meet his cousins and aunts and uncles, much as I had done in Ireland over the Christmas holiday. He'd spent the winter skiing in Austria. Then he shipped his skis home and set out to visit Paris and London. Alas, a pickpocket had lifted his wallet and passport in the Metro. His father sent him $100, but as a personal check that the American Express office wouldn't cash, so he was living on the cheap while he waited for his replacement passport. I gave him my address in Manchester. "I'll be back there at the end of April," I told him. "I'll cash that check for you."

Gordon knew all the bargains in Paris. On Friday afternoon, we followed his directions to the municipal baths on the Isle St. Louis, where we luxuriated under hot showers, and afterward to the market on Boulevard St. Germain. We lunched on fresh *pâté*, heavy with herbs and spread on just-baked bread, with olives and cheese on the side. When we were done, we bought a block of cheese and a loaf of bread to provision us on the road to Italy.

"It's a pity you can't stay another day," Gordon said that evening, after we recounted our adventures. "The Louvre is free on Saturday."

CHAPTER FOUR

A Death in the Forest
1939-1940

THOUGH LWOW HAD SURRENDERED to the besieging German army, its defenders were required to make their peace with the Russians as well. This they did the following morning: September 22, 1939. After posing for a propaganda photograph – a German officer, a Russian officer, and a Polish officer, smiling for the camera in an open touring car – General Kübler and his 1st Mountain Division withdrew from the wrecked city in deference to Hitler's new best friend. That it was the Germans who had conquered Lwow was an inconvenient fact that was promptly expunged from the history of the Second World War.

For the Red Army, the surrender was signed by General Semyon Timoshenko. He generously granted every favor asked by the defenders: enlisted soldiers must register with the Soviet authorities but could then return to their homes; officers could keep their personal kit and, if they wanted, could leave for any country willing to take them. This last concession was especially important to the Poles, most of them hoping to continue their country's fight in French or British uniform.

The Red Army entered Lwow at noon, accompanied as always by the *Narodnyy komissariat vnutrennikh del* – Communism's enforcers, the NKVD, the paramilitary police who were virtually a second army in Soviet Russia. The Bluecaps (as they were called, for the color of the identifying band around the officers' headgear) promptly broke all of General Timoshenko's promises. Officer or enlisted man, Lwow's defenders were arrested and marched at gunpoint to the Market Square, where they were herded into groups of fifty or so and trucked to the main railroad station. There a boxcar awaited them – the blood-red freight wagon that the survivors of such treks always describe as a "cattle car." In filth and hunger they were transported 750 miles east to a prison camp at Starobilsk, in the Soviet republic of Ukraine.

The mostly Catholic Poles found themselves sleeping on the stone floor of a church and convent, formerly the property of the Eastern Orthodox church. The quarters were impossibly crowded, though they improved somewhat when the enlisted men were moved to another camp, leaving the officers at Starobilsk.

OF THE ADULT MEN in Basia's family, only her father and her half-brother Zdzislaw were still at liberty. Jurek, the younger brother, had been sent to a prisoner of war camp at Kozelsk, near Moscow, where like the Starobilsk captives he was lodged in a former monastery. ("At that time," as Aleksandr Solzhenitsyn tells us in his chronicle of *The Gulag Archipelago*, "the authorities used to love to set up their concentration camps in former monasteries: they were enclosed by strong walls, had good solid buildings, and they were empty.") Uncle Jan had set out for Romania, hoping to join the Polish army abroad; he was caught and jailed for the peculiarly Russian crime of border crossing. Aunt Krysia's husband was a prisoner of war in Germany. And Aunt Nuna's sweetheart was dead, a victim of the bombs that had fallen on Lwow.

AT 77,710 SQUARE MILES – about the size of Nebraska – the Russian half of Poland was actually larger than the German west, and in addition to rich farmland it contained oilfields and mines that were coveted by both invaders. Its population of 12 million, however, made it much the smaller half, even including the hundreds of thousands of refugees who'd fled the German advance only to find themselves under Russian occupation.

Germany and Russia now set out to extinguish the

conquered nation. "Poland never will rise again," boasted Hitler in the city he called Danzig but the Poles knew as Gdansk. This pledge was echoed by Stalin's foreign minister, Vyacheslav Molotov. "One swift blow to Poland," he told the Supreme Soviet on October 31, "first by the German Army and then by the Red Army, and nothing was left of this bastard offspring of the Versailles treaty."

In dismembering Poland, the Russians were infinitely more clever (and in the long run more successful) than their partners. "German methods," wrote the commander of the Polish underground, "unified and strengthened the nation, those of the Soviet weakened and split it." A resistance fighter in Lwow made a similar caution: "The men of the Russian secret police are more clever and better trained [than the German Gestapo]. . . . They are less crude, more scientific and systematic. Many of the ruses and practices that work in Warsaw will not do at all in Lwow."

The Hitler-Stalin agreement of August 23 had split Poland more or less along a line conveniently drawn in 1919 by the British Foreign Office and named for the then-foreign secretary, George Curzon. As Dad was fond of saying, wherever in the world you found a mess of bloody feathers, an English fox was certain to be at the bottom of it. (The line had been intended to separate the two sides in the Russo-Polish War, but was made irrelevant by Pilsudski's victorious drive to the east.)

West of the "Curzon Line," German death squads began to line up Poles (and especially Polish Jews) in front of open pits that the victims themselves were forced to dig. They were shot at its edge, so that the dying fell upon the dead – or upon the still living, for it sometimes happened that a victim tumbled into the pit lightly wounded, to crawl out of the mass grave in the night.

We like to think that this work was done by depraved Nazis, particularly the SS. (The paramilitary *Schutzstaffel*, Protection Squad, was Germany's equivalent of the NKVD.)

Not at all! Most of the killers were, in Daniel Goldhagen's memorable phrase, "ordinary Germans." Soldiers did this work. So did policemen, and not only German police, but men from allied countries and even from the conquered nations. "During the first try," an Austrian policeman wrote to his wife, "my hand trembled a bit as I shot, but one gets used to it. By the tenth try I aimed calmly and shot surely at the many women, children, and infants. I kept in mind that I have two infants at home, whom these hordes would treat just the same, if not ten times worse. The death that we gave them was a beautiful quick death. . . . Infants flew in great arcs through the air, and we shot them to pieces in flight, before their bodies fell into the pit and into the water."

One gets used to it! In this fashion, good men become monsters. On the road to Lwow, the 98th Mountain Regiment had conscripted the Jews of Przemysl to rebuild a bridge destroyed by the retreating Polish army; following along behind, the Germans rounded up 500 of the town's Jews for a more fatal encounter. "I saw a ragged line of people running down the street," as a witness recalled the roundup. "Along the line, revolvers in hand, German soldiers were running, young boys about eighteen years old, dressed in dark uniforms with swastikas on the sleeves, with light blond hair and rosy faces." The Jews were taken to a nearby village and slaughtered by machine guns. "The corpses were lying on their backs and sides . . . some on top of others, with their arms outstretched, their heads shattered by the bullets."

Though German anti-Semitism ensured especially cruel treatment for Jews, they were by no means the only target. In Krakow, the SS arrested 183 university professors and sent most of them to the concentration camp at Sachsenhausen, there to be brutalized and worked to death. "For the non-German population of [Poland]," declared Heinrich Himmler, the SS commander, "there must be no higher school than the fourth grade. . . . The sole goal of this schooling is to teach them simple arithmetic, nothing above the number 500, writing one's name, and the doctrine that it is divine law to obey the Germans." Universities and high schools were closed, works of art were confiscated, and the daily ration for a Pole was set at 609 calories – 503 if he were Jewish.

East of the Curzon Line, the Russians were less bloody-minded and more methodical. They organized elections, selected the candidates (mostly Soviet citizens, including Red Army officers), saw to it that they were elected over-whelmingly – Communist governments are very good at getting out the vote – and let the new assemblies petition to be joined to the Soviet Union. The Lwow assembly was chaired by the pudgy Nikita Khruschev, who had exchanged his army uniform for an ill-fitting suit.

So Basia's homeland ceased to exist. Lwow became Lviv, and with the rest of southeastern Poland was annexed to the Soviet republic of Ukraine. The northeast was similarly joined to Belarus. Any Pole who chose not to accept Soviet citizenship thus became a foreigner in his own home. In time, this maneuver would have immense consequences for the 12 million residents of eastern Poland.

Meanwhile, the Russians stole everything that could be prised loose. They took whole factories, along with the workers; they took hospitals, with doctors and nurses but not the patients; they took crops from the fields, trees from the forests, goods from the shops, and furniture from the houses. Zoe Zajdlerowa, an Irishwoman married to a Pole, recalled how she saw "whole convoys of common cabbages, used household brooms, three-legged stools and floor-boards torn out of private houses, barracks, and school-rooms," leaving for Soviet Russia in the fall of 1939.

They also took the young men, conscripting 210,000 to serve in the Red Army. Many were former prisoners of war, allowed to go home and promptly rounded up again.

Polish wealth was confiscated by the simple act of decreeing that the Polish zloty and the Russian ruble would trade at par, wiping out four-fifths of everyone's savings. This of course was followed by inflation on a ruinous scale. Before the War, a Polish blacksmith or carpenter might have earned 150 zloty a month, in purchasing power the rough equivalent of $150, or nearly double what my father earned as Mrs. Damon's caretaker. The ruble's value was about twenty cents, so the once-prosperous craftsman found himself earning the equivalent of $30 a month. From this sum he had to pay a dollar for a kilogram of potatoes – $6 for the same weight of meat – $10 for sugar – $140 for a kilo of tea! "A pair of second-hand shoes," recalled Zoe Zajdlerowa, "could easily be sold for five hundred rubles" – the equivalent of $100 in 1939, and something like $2,000 in today's much-depreciated greenbacks.

The inflation was fed by a spending spree on the part of the *Krasnoarmiejcy*, Red Army Men, as they were called by the Poles. In some accounts, each soldier was given 300 rubles to distribute to the local population; in other versions, an advance of three months' pay. Whatever the case, he spent the money wildly. "The soldiers ran in town from shop to shop, bought up whatever they could, mostly watches, rolls, sausages, dress fabrics, and bicycles." The Krasnoarmiejcy found themselves in one of Europe's poorest regions, yet to them eastern Poland seemed a land of undreamed-of riches. "Torn uniforms," a boy from Lwow said of the Russians, "dirty coats, hands, and faces, they washed their boots in puddles, they picked papers off the streets and rolled cigarettes, they were pitiful."

In December, the zloty was abolished. A family could exchange no more than 300 for rubles, thus completing the confiscation of Polish wealth. "As a result," wrote another Pole, "farmers stopped selling food to the town entirely, and people returned to the archaic barter system. The whole town turned into one enormous marketplace, with people carrying all manner of goods in their arms or on their backs offering to trade them for what they needed. There were few takers, for most people had nothing at all, and the number of the poor increased daily."

When the Russians were finished with eastern Poland, as Zoe Zajdlerowa concluded, "The whole infinitely costly storehouse of generations had been burst open and destroyed . . . [with] profound contempt for the care and toil of the individual and for the mystery of man's long husbandry of the soil. Even the village hearths had grown cold." But it would be a mistake to conclude, as she did, that this was the accidental result of poor men and thieves exploiting a society they didn't understand. Rather, as the American scholar Jan Gross has argued, spoliation was the essential nature of Soviet Russia, and indeed of any totalitarian society: "But it is precisely arbitrariness, lawlessness that epitomises the common destiny, rendering everyone vulnerable, indistinguishable." The destruction, the contempt, the upending of everything – this was how the brave new world was created – this *was* the brave new world. It was the same in Russia, and it would be the same wherever the Red Army established Joseph Stalin's dominion.

THE WINTER OF 1939-1940 was described by the survivors as the coldest in memory. A cavalry officer – wounded and captured as he tried to slip across the border with his men – was brought into Lwow as a prisoner of war toward the end of September. He was driven through "a sad city with empty shops and long queues of ragged, dispirited people," to be locked in the cellar of a looted villa. He was later moved to a cell at NKVD headquarters and finally to Brygidki Jail, on Kazimierzowska Street near the city center. "Though the winter was a severe one," he wrote, "the temperature being 30° C below freezing-point [-21° F], I was not given my uniform but was put into a thin drill overall. A warden brought in a bucket of water, which immediately froze, and another bucket for excrement. . . . Occasionally a piece of bread was thrown in to me and I was given a plate of a horrid liquid pompously called soup."

This was General Wladyslaw Anders, commander of a cavalry brigade that had spent most of the war trying to find the front that kept slipping out of its reach. Evidently the Bluecaps thought he might be helpful in the Russification of Poland. As a decorated veteran of Tsar Nikolas's army in the First World War, Anders spoke the language and understood the Russian military culture. So the NKVD kept him alive, after a fashion, and in time he would bend the trajectory of Basia's life in my direction. *Na zdrowie*, General Anders – here's to you, and to the little girl you inadvertently rescued!

ALONG WITH THOUSANDS of other Polish soldiers, Basia's father escaped this dragnet for a time. Colonel Deszberg returned to the family home at 99 Potocki Street soon after the surrender, passing himself off as a civilian. He was, after all, sixty-four years old. Probably the Bluecaps knew perfectly well who he was, and were only waiting for an opportune moment to sweep up the leftover officers from prewar Poland. That sweep was ordered on Sunday, December 3, with the work to be accomplished a week later. Meanwhile, on December 6, the Deszbergs celebrated Basia's sixth birthday along with the feast of St. Nikolas, when Poles exchange Christmas presents. There was very little in the way of gifts, anywhere in occupied Poland that year, while the Bluecaps prepared to spring their trap.

The dragnet was cast on December 9, as Saturday edged into Sunday morning. A nocturnal visit was more likely to find the wanted man at home and unprepared, and his neighbors less attentive. Basia remembers the intruders as Red Army soldiers, and perhaps they were, but more likely they were uniformed troops of the NKVD. At 99 Potocki Street, Basia was awakened by the clamorous arrival of the

Bluecaps:

I have a very few snapshot memories from childhood, and the most vivid is of the soldiers crowding into the room and taking my father away. The soldiers said he could take his gold watch with him, but he gave it to Lalka, as the older one. I somehow think that he knew he wasn't coming home. . . . I don't panic. If something really bad happens, I simply go blank. And I suspect I went blank when they took my father away. I remember standing there and watching, and I have the scene before my eyes, every time I think of it.

We waited for him to come home, and for months Mama went to the prison every night hoping to see him, or to hand in a food parcel for him.

A few years later, as a boy soldier in the "Anders Army" of Polish exiles, Basia's cousin Zbyszek – Aunt Krysia's son – wrote about that December roundup. He too recalled that the intruders were Red Army Men: "Lorries with a dozen or more Krasnoarmiejcy would stop in front of the houses which had been previously marked," he wrote in the firm, right-sloping script of Europeans of that era. (My mother's handwriting was very like Zbyszek's.) "And despite the late hour – one or two o'clock in the night – the Krasnoarmiejcy would burst in [and] conduct searches, throwing everything they could upside down, and taking with them the officers, for what they said was an interrogation." Though Zbyszek's father was already in a German prison camp, the house indeed proved to be the hideout of an officer – a friend of the family – who was duly arrested.

Zbyszek was thirteen that winter, and an occasional minder for his cousins, as Basia recalls:

When my mother spent her nights queuing up in front of the prison gate, hoping to see my father, Zbyszek would sometimes come to look after Lalka and me. We had a great time. Once we had a pillow fight; a pillow burst and the room was covered with feathers. Only when I had

61

children of my own and realized how exasperating they can be, I thought with admiration of Mama, who didn't scream at us or start crying.

AS ALWAYS WITH THE NKVD, there was a precise accounting of the men taken to Brygidki Prison: "The arrested include 5 generals, 23 colonels, 42 majors, 28 lieutenant colonels, 61 captains, 22 lieutenants, and 46 2nd lieutenants."

Brygidki was a vast, U-shaped building, a city block in length and three stories high. Originally a convent, where the nuns of St. Bridget had schooled the children of noble families, it was turned into a jail by the Austrians toward the end of the 18th Century. It now became an NKVD hell-hole where *bytoviki*, common criminals, were jammed together with military officers, priests, peasants, black marketeers, and schoolboys, so tightly that in some cells the men had to take turns standing and sleeping. A typical cell measured thirty square meters – say sixteen feet by twenty feet. Under Polish governance, it might have housed seventeen men – bad enough, God knows. The NKVD tripled the number on the average, and one cell held no fewer than sixty inmates, so that each could claim less than six square feet of floor space. In the end, Brygidki held thirteen thousand men, and it was only the largest of several formal and informal jails in Lwow. The historian Jan Gross estimates that, between September 1939 and June 1941, the NKVD arrested half a million people. Almost all were men, meaning that one out of twelve males in eastern Poland was jailed by the Bluecaps.

A prisoner couldn't shave; he seldom got water to wash, and never enough to wash thoroughly; he ate badly; he had an overflowing slop bucket for a toilet; and he was ridden with lice and bedbugs. "At first," as Aleksandr Solzhenitsyn described the inmate's battle with the bedbugs, "he waged war with them strenuously, crushing them on his body and on the walls, suffocated by their stink. But after several hours he weakened and let them drink his blood without a murmur." At intervals each man was taken out for interrogation, which meant a beating at best, perhaps torture, sometimes death.

His sixty-four years would have spared Colonel Deszberg none of these torments. Indeed, everything that had earned him honor and respect in the Polish Republic – his education, his profession, his affluence, his smooth hands, his good manners, and above all his military service and medals – these were liabilities in the topsy-turvy world of Brygidki. Here, the doctor or banker discovered that his success was precisely the crime for which he'd been arrested, and the army officer learned that his honorable service was his worst offense. This was especially true of men like Colonel Deszberg who had served in the Russo-Polish War of 1919-1921. If he protested that he had only served his country, like any man of honor, he was told that his duty in fact was desertion: he should have come over to the Russian side.

THE WORLD REMEMBERS so much about Hitler's conquests, and so little about Stalin's! "People talk of Prussian militarism but not of Russian militarism," writes Norman Davies, "of the 'German jackboot' but not of the Russian or Soviet jackboot. Russian imperialism and expansionism, though far more extensive than anything in the German record, are somehow taken to be normal."

In their August 1939 agreement, Hitler and Stalin did more than divide Poland: they essentially split all of Europe between them, with the western half subject to invasion by the Germans, the eastern half by the Russians. After the two dictators digested Poland, it was Stalin who first took advantage of his designated sphere, sending the Red Army into Finland on November 30, 1939. As was his custom, he had first signed a non-aggression pact with his victim, meanwhile organizing a puppet government to rule the country after the conquest. For every defending Finn, there were three Russian soldiers; for every Finnish warplane, thirty Russian aircraft; for every Finnish tank, one hundred clanking monsters from the Soviet Union. For all that, the "Winter War" was a debacle for the invaders.

Five thousand miles to the west, in the Caretaker's Cottage in East Alton, Joe and I studied the photographs in *Life*. Here were Finnish soldiers in white camouflage uniforms, on white skis; here they emerged from a sauna bath, whipping their backs with birch branches and rolling naked in the snow; and here was my favorite, a brave lad wearing six fur hats piled one atop the other, taken from the Russian soldiers he had killed.

Dad grew husky of voice and moist of eye when he spoke of "little Finland" and how, of all the people of Europe, the Finns were the only ones to repay their First World War debt to the United States. Religion also had an influence on Dad's political loyalties. He'd backed General Franco in the Spanish Civil War, then Catholic Poland against Lutheran Germany and godless Russia, and now he backed the Finns. They weren't Catholics, but they were fighting the Communists, and that was almost as good. Very likely the parish priest encouraged these sentiments. But it wasn't just us Catholics! All but the most leftist of Americans were delighted when the Russians stumbled and froze in the snows of Finland.

The Winter War had great consequences for the tens of thousands of Polish soldiers in Russian prison camps. Even a country as vast as the Soviet Union, with a security force as huge as the NKVD, had a finite capacity to absorb prisoners of war. The war with Finland yielded new masses of captives, and they had to be put somewhere. Weirdly, not all of them were Finns. When the peace treaty was signed in March 1940, the Finns released 6,000 Red Army prisoners. As would become Stalin's policy during the wider war to follow, the returnees were viewed as traitors, and straight into holding camps they must go. To prepare for this influx, the Poles had to be cleared out.

By the NKVD's count, its prison camps – notably Starobilsk in Ukraine, and Kozelsk and Ostashkov in Russia itself – held 14,300 Polish "officers, officials, landowners, police, gendarmes, prison guards, settlers, and intelligence agents." (The "settlers" were veterans of the Russo-Polish War who had been granted farmsteads along the eastern frontier.) Another 10,700 were jailed in eastern Poland, including Basia's father in Brygidki Prison.

Their ultimate jailer was Lavrentiy Beria, head of the security police. He was a fearsome man, with cold eyes behind rimless, pince-nez spectacles, a gourmand and a rapist, whom his colleagues feared as much as his victims did – "an ugly, shapeless toad," in the words of one woman who suffered his attentions. He was gifted at guessing Stalin's intentions and pandering to him. Thus, though the initiative for murdering the Poles came from Beria, it's safe to assume that he was voicing Stalin's wishes. As Beria explained the situation in a memo to the dictator, these 25,000 captives were "all hardened, irremediable enemies of Soviet power." He recommended that the NKVD hold "special tribunals" to weigh the merits of each case – without the prisoner being present, of course – and afterward to apply "the supreme penalty, shooting." Stalin had been responsible for the deaths of some 10 million of his own citizens in the famine and the Great Terror of the 1930s. Why would he blink at shooting 25,000 prisoners of war? He countersigned the execution order that same day.

BASIA'S FATHER WAS AMONG those "enemies of Soviet power" in local jails. Evidently it did not seem politic to carry out a massacre on what had so recently been Polish soil, so it was decided to send them east, into Soviet Russia. On March 5, Beria gave orders to this effect. Those jailed in the northeast – now considered "western Belarus" – went to Minsk, where they met their death in circumstances still unknown. A larger number – nearly 1,000 in Lwow alone – were jailed in "western Ukraine." They were dispatched to Kiev, a 300-mile journey by train that today takes ten hours but in 1940 probably lasted several days. Again, not a great deal is known about the circumstances of their deaths, though locals recall that they were murdered in the cellar of the NKVD building in the capital, then transported in "canvas-covered" trucks about eight miles to Bykivnia, a village on the east bank of the Dneiper River.

Today Bykivnia is a compact suburb on the north side of Brovarsky Avenue, the main road to the east. South of the highway is a pine forest – a forbidden zone during the Communist years. After the 1991 collapse of the Soviet Union, 240 mass graves were found here, covering a four-acre tract just half a mile from the well-traveled highway. Most of them hold the bodies of Ukrainian peasants who in the 1930s resisted the government takeover of their farms, and who in consequence were shot by the NKVD. One burial would be laid upon an earlier one, mingling the bones. In 1942 during the German occupation, some of the graves were excavated, then reburied by the NKVD when the Red Army retook Kiev. The confusion was compounded in the wild years after the Soviet Union collapsed, when grave robbers dug up the charnel pits in search of jewelry and souvenirs. In consequence, no one can know who was buried where, or when, or even how many bodies there are, with estimates ranging from 30,000 to 300,000.

Mixed with the bones are Polish army insignia, remnants of uniforms and knee boots, Polish coins minted as late as 1939, and more evocative *mementi mori*. Among them is a tiny comb made of a plastic soft enough that its owner could scratch the names of the towns through which he traveled, from January 21 to May 24, 1940, along with twenty-one names of his comrades on the journey through the Gulag to the dank cellar room in which he was killed.

In the period of openness that followed the collapse of the Soviet Union, the Russians released what came to be known as "the Ukraine list," containing the names of 3,390 men and 45 women transported to Kiev in the spring of 1940 to be shot. About one-fourth of the way through the list I find this entry: *862 Deszberg, Kazimierz s. Jana ur. 1875 55/5-25.*

So at some point in his journey, Basia's father became Number 862 to the Bluecaps, who to further distinguish him noted that he was born in 1875 and that his father's name was Jan. The concluding notation is less clear, but Mark Turkowicz, a Canadian of Polish descent, believes that it can be deciphered as follows: Colonel Deszberg was in the fifty-fifth group of condemned men, and he was the twenty-fifth member of that group to be shot, by an executioner identified as "Five." If this is correct, his killer was likely a high-ranking Bluecap, for there are five numbered shooters, and of the 3,435 known victims of the Kiev massacre, only 38 names are laid to his account. Perhaps he was a major, called upon to shoot the higher-ranking Polish officers. Or perhaps he was the commander of the NKVD in Kiev, who lent a hand only when the schedule was crowded.

However that may be, Bykivnia is Colonel Deszberg's almost certain resting place. Others in the March "clearing out" may have been sent farther east to a mass execution site at Kharkov, a Ukrainian city near the Russian border. Kharkov was also the destination of the Polish prisoners of war at Starobilsk, including General Franciszek Sikorski and the other defenders of Lwow, arrested on September 22 the previous year.

WE KNOW MORE ABOUT the manner in which the prisoners of war – those captured by the Red Army during the hostilities of September 1939 – met their deaths. Beria set up a system of *troika* boards, whose three members briskly reviewed each case of the 14,300 prisoners of war. Ninety-seven times out of a hundred, they sentenced the prisoner to death. (The exceptions were mostly *nasedka*, NKVD informants who'd been planted among the prisoners to gauge their mood and look for signs of rebellion. A few others were protected by a German, Latvian, or Russian connection. Thus a Polish lieutenant was saved by a telephone call from his uncle, who happened to be a film director in the Soviet Union.)

The condemned men were marched onto buses or trains, often with an honor guard of fellow prisoners, sometimes with a marching band laid on by the NKVD. The Bluecap in charge at Starobilsk, where the defenders of Lwow had been sent, made this heartbreaking observation about the clearing-out of the camp population: "The overwhelming majority of officer POWs are certain they are going home. . . . [A] mood has been noticed to get going as quickly as possible, and they are turning to the camp administration [with requests] to be included in the next transport for departure."

At Kharkov, one man survived to tell the story, and we have the recollections of some of the Bluecaps who took part, from which to reconstruct how the men from Starobilsk met their final hour: "Though they could not have known this," writes Timothy Snyder of Yale, "they had been brought to one of the main killing centers of Poles in the Soviet Union. . . . [T]hey went to their deaths ignorant of the past, ignorant of what would happen to them. After a day or so in prison they were taken to a room where their details were checked. Then they were led to another room, this one dark and without windows. A guard would ask 'May I?' and then lead in the prisoner. As one of the NKVD men remembered, 'there was a clack, and that was the end.' The bodies were piled onto trucks. Jackets were pulled over the heads of the corpses so that the truck platform would not be stained by the blood. The bodies were loaded head first, then feet first, so they would stack."

The trucks drove to a park near the village of Piatik-hatski, where an NKVD sanatorium was located. Open pits awaited the Poles. They were thrown in, sprinkled with lime, and covered with earth by bulldozer tractors. Of the Starobilsk prisoners, 3,739 are known to have been buried at this spot.

THEN THERE WAS BASIA'S HALF BROTHER, the lieutenant of artillery. Jurek Deszberg's name appears in the NKVD list of prisoners at the Kozelsk monastery near Moscow. These men were sent to Smolensk, a walled city on the Dnieper River, still in Russia but near its border with Belarus. Like the Starobilsk victims, the Kozelsk prisoners thought they were going home, and in some instances their comrades formed an honor guard for them as they marched to the waiting trains. Their journey – in purpose-built prison cars, evidently – took them 200 miles west to Gniazdovo, a station just west of Smolensk. Here they got down, stiff from the journey, and walked through a corridor of NKVD troops armed with rifles and fixed bayonets. In groups of thirty or so, they were loaded into a bus whose windows had been whitewashed. There seems to have been just the one bus, which returned half an hour later for another group of thirty. (This from the testimony of a university professor saved by a Bluecap colonel who wanted to question him.) In this fashion, 4,410 Polish prisoners disembarked at Gniazdovo in April 1940 and were taken away by that bus with the whitewashed windows or by *chorny voron*, "black raven" prison vans. The latter were built on a Ford Model A chassis, with the back divided into cells intended for one man but routinely jammed with half a dozen.

One Polish major kept a detailed diary of his final journey. His entry for April 4 suggests that he at least knew that he would not be going home: "A few minutes before five in the morning – wake-up call in the prison railway cars and preparations to leave. We are to go somewhere by car. And what then?" A few hours later he continued: "Departure in a prison car in cells (awful!). We were driven to some place in a wood; something like a summer resort. Here, a detailed search took place. They took my watch, showing 6:30. They asked about my wedding ring. . . . They took rubles, main belt, penknife." They didn't take his diary, which was later found on his body.

The "place in the wood" was three miles west of Smolensk, between the east-west road and a horseshoe bend in the Dneiper River. Here the NKVD maintained a rest and recreation area called *Koze Gory*, Goat Hills, on the edge of the Katyn Forest.

Katyn, pronounced more or less as "*Kah*-tin," has since become the common name of an atrocity spread among five or six killing fields in Russia, Belarus, and Ukraine. Likely the executions followed the usual procedure, with each Pole taken at night to a windowless room, as if for further interrogation. As he stepped inside, his arms were pinned by two NKVD soldiers, one on either side of him. The executioner, wearing high boots, elbow-length gloves, and a leather butcher's apron, stepped up from behind and shot him in the back of his head. Usually only one bullet was necessary. The dead man was then carried out the opposite door and stacked in a waiting truck.

The NKVD favored the German-built Walther PPK semi-automatic pistol for this work. It had less recoil than a Red Army revolver. An executioner might have to shoot 250 men a night; the service revolver would have bruised his hand so badly that he couldn't have worked the following day. The PPK was also a bit lighter and had a nicer balance. The Bluecaps used German-made 7.65 mm Geco cartridges that, like the pistols, had been bought during the 1930s, a detail that would later help the Russians blame the atrocity on the Germans.

Altogether, over the course of two months in the spring of 1940, the NKVD murdered 21,892 Poles, including Basia's father and half-brother. (And also including several dozen women. Among them was Lieutenant Janina Dowbor, a pilot in the Polish air force, who as the story is told was shot down by the Germans but parachuted into the false safety of the Russian zone.) "It was their social status that landed them in front of NKVD execution squads," wrote an analyst for the U.S. Central Intelligence Agency. "Most of the victims were reservists who had been mobilized when Germany invaded. In all, the NKVD eliminated almost half the Polish officer corps – part of Stalin's long-range effort to prevent the resurgence of an independent Poland."

Their bodies ended in a pit, much like those murdered by the Germans, with the difference that these Poles usually didn't have to dig their own graves. That work was done more efficiently by the backhoe and bulldozer blade on a Caterpillar tractor.

I think of the Deszberg men – Kazimierz and Jurek, father and son – as the two victims at the end of that curiously precise number: 21,892. History happens to one person at a time. Of the 60 million who died in the course of the Second World War, each had a name, a past, work to finish, and hopes for the future. He may even have had a young daughter or sister who would remember him, the father with his gleaming boots, the adored brother who gave her a ride down Potocki Street on his motorbike.

We were in Yonne before noon, having covered 180 kilometers since breakfast. It was not long after this that we caught a ride in an American land yacht with two students at the University of Burgundy, who took us to Dijon.

CHAPTER FIVE

The Road to Italy
1955

ON SATURDAY MORNING, April 9, we shouldered our rucksacks, shook hands with Gordon Olson, and walked to the Porte d'Italie. It was a fine day, cool and sunny. Basia wore her duffle coat, while I closed and buttoned the lapels of my jacket. The great thing about that Harris tweed was that it so readily became an outdoor coat. It could even withstand a light rain, of the sort that went along with urban life in England. (We had no rain gear with us, as if we knew that foul weather couldn't possibly trouble us – and it didn't.)

A few hundred meters down the Avenue d'Italie, we found a spot with good sight lines and room for a car to pull over without blocking traffic. "This will work," I promised, putting down my rucksack and holding up my open palm, as Gordon had instructed us. The American thumb-jerk, he said, might offend Europeans.

Sure enough, in a very few minutes we caught our first ride in a gray Citroën *Deux Chevaux* with a canvas top that could be rolled back, the way you'd open a can of sardines. Basia sat in front and charmed the driver in what seemed to be flawless French. I sat mute in back with the rucksacks, knees against my chest. I was entranced to see that the gear shifter was located on the dashboard, a curved handle that seemed to have a limitless number of positions. (Only four, as I now know. The impression of multiple gears probably came from the driver's constant shifting of what amounted to a nine-horsepower motorcycle engine.) The Deux Chevaux carried us just far enough to put us in the countryside. The driver left us on a long, straight, tree-lined stretch of highway while he turned off on a gravel road. "What were you talking about?" I asked.

"All about his wonderful automobile," Basia said. "The queue is five years, but he could jump ahead because he is a farmer."

"What else?" I planned to master the language by first getting the gist of things, then sorting out the words.

"The next town is Fontainbleau." I loved the way she said it, the "u" soaring to the sky, or so it seemed to me. I had her repeat the name until I could more or less pronounce it the same way. Then a delivery van picked us up and took us not only to Fontainbleau but a kilometer or two beyond.

South of the city, we put down our rucksacks and faced the traffic. The day was warming up, and we were comfortable in the shade of a tree. Rather than the spreading elms of New Hampshire, these were tall, tailored Lombardy poplars, all the same height, same shape, and spaced at an identical distance, on both sides of the road. We were now on National Route 6, the road signs alternating between *Rue de Paris* and the more thrilling *Route d'Italie.* I could have whooped for joy. I was hitchhiking through France with the girl I loved! We were on our way to Italy!

The rides came quickly, in miniature cars and luxurious ones, and once or twice in an intercity truck with a potbellied driver, dribbling ashes onto his sleeveless undershirt from a Gaulois stuck to the corner of his mouth. In the afternoon we were picked up by a handsome Chevrolet convertible, a land yacht that could have stowed a Deux Chevaux in its trunk. It belonged to an American couple, students at the University of Burgundy in Dijon. Basia and I spread ourselves and our packs along the back seat, of sumptuous red leather and wide enough to furnish a country-house parlor. "Dan's an American too!" Basia volunteered, to encourage the ritual exchange of home states. And when they left us off, she said: "Before I met you, I thought all Americans were like that automobile, big and rich and noisy." Which I took as a great compliment.

74

What a happy day that was, from Paris to Fontainbleau, Yonne, and the wonderfully named Châlon-sur-Saône! Basia too was thrilled by the progress we were making, the ease of it, and the excitement of wondering what our next ride would be like:

I'd had no experience in that sort of travel. I'd seen some beautiful things – the Cedars of Lebanon, the mosque in Damascus, the beach in Beirut, the bazaar in Tehran – and met charming people. But mostly it was poverty and the heavy iron-studded gates of the convent schools. I hadn't even seen much of London at that time.

During those few weeks we lived in an unknown territory. Every crossing of the border was an exciting experience. We enjoyed the truck drivers and the insouciant way they drove. For me, any car which took us was a luxury, and the proud drivers were endearing.

You noticed Europe's poverty and the scars of the War. For me, it was rich beyond belief. And both of us were enthralled by its glory. At that time also there were many more open spaces in Europe, and many more differences between countries.

Yes. Everything was different. In the 1950s, every country boasted its own automobiles, currency, clothing, and food. As for open space, I find that most of the towns we visited have since tripled in population; they have sprawled into the countryside and been bisected and bracketed with superhighways.

Seriously, Dan, traveling with you to Italy is one of my happiest memories. I was exhilarated. I was free, I had good company, there were so many things to see. On Sundays, the bells were ringing but with great satisfaction and a little guilt, I didn't go to church. A manifestation of rebellion, I suppose.

I also had a feeling of doing something not "done," and you were my collaborator. That added to my excitement.

IT WAS DUSK WHEN WE were left off in downtown Lyon, having covered 500 kilometers since breakfast. This time it was I who accosted the nearest pedestrian: "*Excusez-moi, m'sieur, où est l'auberge de jeunesse, s'il vous plaît?*" He instructed us (instructed Basia, actually, since I could parrot the question but, like the parrot, couldn't understand the reply) to cross the river and follow the east bank north. We would pass the university in a few kilometers, he said, and the hostel was just beyond.

This we did, strolling beneath the trees on a riverside promenade. A trolley rattled past with *Université* on its signboard, but neither of us made a move to hail it. Night had fallen, and the street lamps on the far bank were doubled by their reflection in the water. On our side of the river, the lamps were bright enough to light our way, yet not so bright that they dimmed the stars. The Saône seemed to radiate warmth to us, but I suspect that what we felt was actually a breeze from the Mediterranean. Whatever caused it, the evening was *balmy,* as if we were sailing through a tropical night. Coming off six months in the soot, fog, and chill of Manchester, I felt as though my body were thawing and the once-sluggish blood was surging through my veins.

I was happier that evening, walking along the Saône, than ever before in my life. The young woman beside me was of course a very large part of that. I knew, as surely as I'd known anything in my young life, that I would kiss Basia on the mouth before the night was much older. I stole side-glances at her lips, as at *La Strada* a few weeks earlier: I could almost taste them!

I HAVE BEEN AT SUCH PAINS to describe my pretty companion that perhaps it's time to turn my gaze inward. Normally this is a difficult chore, especially for a writer looking at his much younger self, but I once took a walk-on role in one of my novels, so I have something to quote. The character was called What's-his-face, showing that by this time I was more influenced by *Catch 22* than by *Portrait of the Artist*. (The hero was still called Stephen, though his family name had morphed into something more Irish.) This is how Major Barker saw What's-his-face: "The new clerk-typist was a tall, thin private first class with a triangular face and a gigantic pair of spectacles, the kind with brown-black frames and little silver doohickeys beside the hinges. Fruit glasses, the Major called them."

Though this deals with my later involuntary service in the U.S. Army, it's a fair description of the young man who accompanied Basia to Italy in April 1955. I was wearing the identical glasses, in fact.

And serious? Oh my goodness. "In his heart," Major Barker mused of the new clerk-typist, "that bespectacled fruit thinks he's Secretary of Defense." Which is indeed the impression I get when I look at photos of my youthful self. As an old man, I often catch myself capering with happiness when I would be better off borrowing some of that youthful gravitas. In exchange, I'd give the solemn lad of 1955 a heartier sense of humor. Things might have turned out better at the hostel in Lyon, that balmy night on the east bank of the Saône.

I don't remember the details, and if Basia does, she won't share them with me. But from a letter I afterward wrote to friends and family at home, I find that we walked for an hour along the river, that the distance was six kilometers, and that the hostel when we reached it was empty except for a Scotsman and five German journeymen with their toolboxes, black hats, bell-bottom trousers, and fancy waistcoats. The letter, alas, is purged of romance: I mention Basia only as a linguist and maker of sandwiches.

Curiously, I don't remember the sandwiches! I thought we simply tore off bits of bread and cheese, and ate them in alternation. I do know that after supper we went out to look at the stars, that I pressed my luck too hard, and that I was firmly put down. Oh yes, and I clearly remember Basia's final declaration: "And I don't like it when you put your hand on my *pupka!*"

Which is how I learned my first word of Polish, the fond term that mothers use when referring to a baby's bottom.

TO MAKE MATTERS WORSE, next day was Easter Sunday, a fact that (like the Alps) had escaped our attention when plotting our route on that BP map of Western Europe. The French of 1955 were as Catholic as the Poles, or the Irish, when it came to lining up for the Communion wafer – "making your Easter duty," as my mother called it. As a result, there were precious few motorists leaving Lyon that morning.

We'd expected to hitchhike over the Col du Mont Cenis on Monday, crossing into Italy and sleeping in Turin, where the YHA guidebook promised that we would find a youth hostel. But for a wearisome hour, on the Avenue Franklin Roosevelt, nobody stopped for us. When we finally did get a ride, it was only for a few kilometers.

It went that way all morning, and the afternoon was worse. Family cars were all we got, often enough with the entire family inside, so we had to jam ourselves in back with the children. At three o'clock we still hadn't reached Chambery, and it was clear we wouldn't cross over the Col du Mont Cenis before nightfall, let alone reach that youth hostel in Turin.

Basia kept irritating me by suggesting that we walk for a bit, to change our luck. In vain I explained that the driver had to slow down at a crossroads, giving him a chance to see how harmless we were, and how deserving of his charity. If we walked, however, we'd be turning our backs to the Good Samaritan. He might have a poor view of the road ahead, so he'd be concentrating on the driving and not on the handsome young couple whom he might favor with a ride, the lass in her duffle coat and the lad in his tweed jacket.

Arguing with one's sweetheart is never a wise thing to do, and especially when it came to Miss Deszberg, who after all had studied logic for a term. Her premises might sometimes be missing, but her arguments were impressive.

I offered a compromise: let me choose the best place to face the oncoming traffic. For her part, Basia could decide when we'd stood in one place too long and ought therefore to move along. That worked for half an hour. Then we were stopping and starting at ever-shorter intervals, so that we might as well have set out to *walk* to Turin.

Did we really let such a squabble spoil our afternoon? I'm afraid so. I have a photograph of Basia taken that day, perched on her rucksack by the side of the road during one of those interminable waits. We are in a town, probably La Tour-du-Pin, halfway between Lyon and Chambery. She is wearing the duffle coat, and she is as beautiful as my memory assures me she was, her nose as elegant, her lips as full. However, she is looking sideways at me with her brows slightly arched, the perfect image of skepticism. Clearly we've had a falling out.

This quarrel, our bad luck on the road, and (above all, I suspect) last night's rebuke outside the Lyon youth hostel – taken together, they decided me to give up my quest. What was the point of a sweetheart one couldn't kiss, and who refused to defer to my superior knowledge of hitchhiking?

"This isn't going to work," I said.

"I suppose not," Basia said.

This wasn't the answer I'd expected – she was supposed to protest! So naturally I raised the stakes: "When we get to Turin," I said in a reasonable voice, one good friend to another, "I'll put you on a train to Florence, and I'll go to straight to Venice." It's true that my heart was set on roaming the alleys and squares of Venice, but I'd have let St. Mark's Basilica sink beneath the Adriatic, in exchange for a kiss from Basia's soft lips.

"You promised Mama," she pointed out. "You said you'd see me safe to Perugia."

I squirmed at this reminder. Dear Mama, with her trusting face, probably not understanding a word of my little speech!

"You'll be perfectly all right on the train," I said. "If you leave in the morning from Turin, you'll reach Perugia the same day. That's a lot faster than hitchhiking, at the rate we're going. Safer, too."

"All right," Basia said. "I will take the train, and you will go to Venice." Then the student of logic emerged: "But first we must reach Turin."

Perhaps it was after this exchange that the photograph was taken.

THE DAY GREW CHILL and dark as we tacked our slow path toward Chambery, gaining altitude in the process. No more warm breezes from the Mediterranean! On the high ground we could see the impossibly big-shouldered Alpine ridge that stood between us and our destination. I had never seen anything so huge or so white, and for the first time it occurred to me that it would be a considerable feat to hitchhike across it. I didn't share this thought with Basia. The day was discouraging enough already.

And our rides became fewer and farther between. Obviously we weren't going to cross into Italy today, nor even reach Modane at the foot of the mountains. Indeed, by six o'clock it was clear that we weren't even going to reach Chambery. Evening overtook us on the outskirts of Les Abrets, seventy-four kilometers from that youth hostel in Lyon. (It's not quite true that we could have walked that distance between breakfast and dinner, but at six kilometers an hour we could have come close.) Route 6 was shrouded in dusk, though the sun still sparkled on the Alpine snowfields beyond.

We walked the last kilometer, and a woman in a shawl, coming toward us with a basket hooked over her arm, confirmed what we had already guessed: there was no hostel in Les Abrets. She recommended an *auberge* that, she said, lay just a hundred meters farther along the Rue de la Republique, as Route 6 was locally known.

"The length of a football field," I said to Basia.

"Then why can't we see it?"

"Perhaps football fields are longer in France."

Basia sighed. "It will be less expensive," she said, "if we share the same room."

"Yes." Oh my, what was this?

She was silent for ten or twelve paces. Then she said: "But you should have been the one to suggest it, not leave it to me."

"Yes," I said. I didn't think she would have agreed to the arrangement as readily as I had done, but I wasn't going to risk the moment by pointing this out.

The auberge proved to be a HOTEL, as announced on a neatly painted sign above the front door. It was a two-story building of gray stucco, with lace curtains in the windows and the street number on a square blue tile beside the door. We went inside, careful not to swing our rucksacks into anything breakable, and were confronted by Madame at a concierge window, with her private parlor visible beyond it. Basia and she fell into deep conversation, and I saw that what seemed a window was actually the upper half of a Dutch door, with a shelf on the lower half to serve as a desk. As for Madame, she reminded me irresistibly of one of our rucksacks, skinny at the top but spreading out generously below.

"A thousand francs," Basia told me, a sum that would have paid for five nights at a youth hostel.

"See if she'll take six hundred," I said, delighted to bargain since I didn't have to do it myself. "Say we're poor students, that –"

Basia smiled for the first time in hours. She was ten years old again, haggling in the bazaar on Aunt Krysia's behalf. After several volleys, she announced the compromise: "Eight hundred francs."

"Well done," I said. Then, to show that I too had a part in this negotiation, I looked Madame in the eye and said: "*Avec petit dejeneur.*"

"*Comment?*" she said. Basia repeated it – in the same words and with the very same inflection, or so it seemed to me – and Madame beamed at her. "*Mais certainment!*" Yes, breakfast was included. Then: "*Passports!*"

This was my first encounter with the Continental custom of commandeering the passport of an overnight guest, but Basia assured me that it was perfectly in order. *La police* would come by in the evening to ensure that no desperate criminals were spending the night in their district. Besides, the passports were security that we wouldn't skip out without paying. "Wouldn't it be easier if we paid in advance?" I asked.

"That's not how it's done."

With great reluctance, I handed my precious green passport through the little window to Madame. She opened it to the photo page and a smooth-chinned lad with spectacles and narrow jaw. As deliberately as the immigration officer at the Calais ferry hall, she turned to the amendments page and nodded her head at the same lad in a photo taken after Christmas. "*Avec et sans barbe!*" she said approvingly.

Then she took Basia's book and thumbed through it. Strictly speaking, this was not a passport but a travel document, of the sort issued by European governments to resident aliens without passports of their own – displaced persons, they were called. It had a gray cover, some black diagonals, and the words *Titre de Voyage / Travel Document*. Though more substantial than mine, it nevertheless had a thrifty air, as if it might be revoked with the next change of government.

It satisfied Madame, in any event. She tucked the documents into a cubbyhole at her right hand, at the same time retrieving a key with a heavy brass disk. Then she swung open the half-door and led us up the stairs, wheezing as she went. She showed us into room number five, containing two narrow beds with a small nightstand between, an oak dresser, a washbasin with the customary warning – *eau non potable* – and a window overlooking the Route d'Italie. My heart fluttered nicely. I was in a hotel room with the love of my life! To be sure, I'd have preferred a double bed, but no doubt Basia had closed out that possibility.

Madame left us, wheezing and coughing down the carpeted stairs. I was hugely impressed by her sophistication. Once in a while I'd rented a hotel room or Kozy Kabin with my college girlfriend, a process that involved a great deal of sneaking about, separate arrivals, assumed names, make-believe wedding rings, and so on. And that was in the United States! In England, with a narrow-nosed landlady guarding the stairs, and reinforced by a phalanx of elderly permanent residents, I wouldn't have attempted it. But on the Continent, it seemed, our morals were our own affair. The only thing Madame wanted from us was our passports.

A hot bath would have cost another 100 francs, so we took turns at the washbasin and its somewhat spotted mirror. Basia went for a walk while I washed up, then I dressed again and went down to the front step to let her know the coast was clear. Madame watched me pass without comment, but when I returned, she'd shut the upper half of her Dutch door. Either she had seen it all before, or she had dismissed us as crazy foreigners. I saw no sign of the police, or of our passports.

Basia, like me, had no nightclothes, so she was dressed again in her black trousers and white blouse when I returned. Her hair was damp – she'd washed it! – and tousled from the towel, an effect that made me weak in the knees. She had folded back the nubbly spread on her bed, the one near the door. Since there were no chairs, we each sat on our own bed, knee to knee thanks to the close quarters. I pulled the cork on the wine bottle with my teeth and gave her the first drink, and she passed it back to me. It was a red wine, homely and smooth, decanted that afternoon from a vat behind the zinc counter of a *bar-tabac* in La Tour-du-Pin. I particularly liked drinking from the same glass lip that had just been kissed by Basia.

What did we talk about? Her family, I suppose. I learned a great deal about Basia's history in the course of our travels. I knew that her father had been killed in the Katyn Forest massacre, though I don't recall that she mentioned Jurek. I knew that Mama and the girls had been sent into exile and that in her sweet confusion Mama brought along a chamber pot as her only utensil. Basia told me this story, or anyhow I understood her to be telling it, as a little joke upon Mama, and I'm sure I laughed along with her. But if you are bound for Siberia in a boxcar with two little girls, forty or fifty strangers, and a hole in the floor for a toilet, could you bring any more serviceable bit of furniture than a chamber pot?

I knew about shopping with Aunt Krysia at the bazaar, and that Mama had worked in the officers' club in Tehran. I knew that in her travels Basia had acquired a working knowledge of Russian – she taught me to say *dosvedanya*, farewell – though somehow it never occurred to me to ask where she'd perfected her nearly flawless English. Since it was my native language, English was transparent. I took it for granted, as the natural order of things, the way a young person looks upon most aspects of the world around him.

But now that I open the tap – it was *dosvedanya* that did it! – more things come to mind. I knew that when she dreamed of home, about Mama and the aunts, she dreamed in Polish, but if about her classes at the University, the dream was in English. That when she sent a telegram to Ealing – Manchester students didn't use the telephone –

she addressed it to "Mama" followed by a few words in Polish instead of the family name, so as to keep the word count down. And she told me how she went with friends to the Hallé concerts at the Free Trade Hall, a glorious ark on Peter Street uptown, where she and some friends would eat fish and chips while they waited for the rush seats to open; then they sprinted into the auditorium, sitting on the floor if they couldn't find seats.

As for my half of the conversation, Basia thinks that I talked about books and my ambition to write them. Yes, no doubt I lectured her about my literary heroes, and perhaps something about Stephen Faust.

Anyhow we chatted, sitting on our separate beds, trouser knee to trouser knee, and passing the wine bottle back and forth. The disagreement of the afternoon was long behind us, and I suppose this new state of affairs – that I had accepted the fact that we were friends, but nothing more than friends – was a relief to me as well. And no doubt the wine helped put everything into a more comfortable perspective.

But after a bit, a strange and magical thing happened. Basia slid off the bedspread and sat on the floor, her back against the bed frame, and gave me the most bewitching smile I have ever seen on another person's face. It was as if she'd hooked me with a gaff and pulled me down to sit with her, my legs under her bed and my back against my own. My arms were around her waist. This was much more comfortable than an embrace among the trees behind the youth hostel in Lyon.

And that is how I came to feast upon the soft and perfect cupid's bow of Basia's lips.

I wasn't in the least bit tipsy, but neither was I thinking clearly. I once saw a cartoon – in *The New Yorker*, I think – purporting to show a cross-section of the brain of a middle-aged American male. Fully half of it was given over to the lyrics of a pop song:

Volare, oh oh,
E contare, oh oh oh oh.
How my glad heart sings;
Your love gives me wings.
This dream won't come again!

In the spring of 1955, my brain was similarly stuffed, with Basia's soft lips, firm breasts, and neat pupka substituting for the lyrics of *Volare*. All the rest – the Year of Revolution, the Young Italy movement, the masterpieces of James Joyce and Johann Wolfgang von Goethe – had to contend for the small remainder of my intelligence.

Ah, how we rolled about on the floor of that little hotel in Les Abrets! Eventually, though, we got off the floor and onto Basia's bed, a bit disheveled but fully clothed. And in time I kissed her goodnight and returned to my own bed.

DOES THIS SEEM impossibly innocent? It was 1955 – a different time. In the movies, Doris Day and Rock Hudson went to separate beds in ironed pajamas, and the beds were farther apart than ours in Les Abrets. Unmarried lovers did not go to bed at all. At most their coupling might be suggested by a fireworks display, as Alfred Hitchcock provided for Grace Kelly and Cary Grant in *To Catch a Thief*.

And Basia had been schooled almost entirely by the nuns, from childhood until she enrolled at Manchester, where Uncle Jan met her at the bus stop if she were expected home after the evening rush hour. She had experienced none of the furtive gropings that were a part of growing up in America:

I was eighteen years old when I started at Manchester, but my only experience of men was an altar boy at Kidderminster, when I was at school. He used to look at me when going from the side bench to the altar during Sunday Mass. But I am not sure even of that conquest. My friend sitting next to me told me he made eyes at her.

Anyway, at Manchester my studies were my main

concern. I did have a few not especially memorable dates during holidays, which I spent with my family in London. I went to dances with Lalka at the Polish Hearth Club. That was plenty enough.

There was Paul, the Irish medical student who took her to dinner with his family at the Ritz, but evidently he never pressed his luck as far as I had done. Indeed, I probably was the first to kiss Basia on the lips, or anyhow the first she kissed in return.

However that may be, I was wonderfully content, and next morning I felt as pleased with myself as any bridegroom. We were alone in the breakfast room – it was Easter Monday. Not many people were traveling, and those few were sleeping in. Madame led us to a corner table with hoop-backed chairs, somewhat creaky when we settled into them, and a tablecloth held in place by metal clips. There were cloth napkins, too, along with white cups and saucers, metal spoons, and a triangular Cinzano ashtray in white, red, and blue. Madame went off to the kitchen, wheezing and sighing, and returned with a tray containing two metal pitchers, one containing very strong coffee and the other a pint of hot, frothy milk, along with a basket of four croissants. Oh my goodness, the buttery taste of those croissants, flaking into my mouth, there to be washed down with *cafe au lait*, and finally the Gaulois that we passed back and forth across the table, fat and pungent. Was there ever a more satisfying meal?

Luckily I wasn't Doktor Faust and hadn't wagered with Mephisto, all experience to be mine, but my soul to the devil if I asked for the moment to linger:

> If I should say to the fleeting hour,
>   "Stop a while, you are so fair!"
> Then bind me with your iron chain;
>   I'll go down with you to Hell!

I'd surely have lost the bet that morning. If ever I wanted to stop the clock of my life, it was then and there, with the fresh croissants and the sweet cafe au lait, sharing a Gaulois with Basia Deszberg.

"Today," I said, with all the thoughtfulness I could muster, "we will reach Turin. Then Florence on Tuesday, Perugia the day after." Basia raised her left eyebrow, a perfect arch. "Or Perugia on Thursday," I added, thinking of yesterday's slog, and anyhow not eager for the adventure to end.

No more was said on the subject.

CHAPTER SIX

The Sky Was Green
1940

AND NOW IT WAS THE TURN of the wives and children. In the paranoid logic of Stalin and his enablers, if Colonel Deszberg was to be shot, something must be done about his wife, his children, his sisters-in-law, and *their* families. They too must be enemies of the regime – "counter-revolutionaries," in the jargon of Soviet Russia. Thus came the second knock on the door of Basia's childhood.

There had been an earlier roundup of Polish civilians, in February 1940, when the Bluecaps arrested tens of thousands of farmers, foresters, policemen, civil servants, and government officials, many of them young or middle-aged men. They were valued for their labor potential, so they were sent into the *Glavnoe Upravlenie Ispravitel no trudovykh Lagerei,* the Main Directorate for Corrective Labor Camps, known to Russians and eventually the world by its ugly acronym: *Gulag.*

The Gulag was a many-layered Inferno. The first circle was a labyrinth of conventional prisons, beginning with the infamous Lubyanka in Moscow. From there, most prisoners were sent deeper into the Gulag. They might go to a distant prison camp, surrounded by barbed wire and watchtowers, where men and women lived in segregated barracks while they were worked to death in mines and forests. Or, with a better chance of survival, they might find themselves in a loosely guarded labor colony where a family could stay together in a hut containing several such families, and where hunger, rather than the lash, was the principal motivation for work beyond the comprehension of westerners.

Such a colony was the destination for most of the February deportees: "During the night of the 9th of February," as Anna Poplewska described her arrest, "several

NKVD police troopers . . . broke into our home. Awakened from deep sleep, we were paralyzed with fear. They ordered us to dress quickly. . . . I did not know what to do, what to grab. I dressed the children. . . . [The Bluecaps] did not allow me to move around the house, and they hurried us as if the place were on fire. . . . The temperature outside was far below freezing; it was that memorable dreadfully severe winter. On instructions from the NKVD troopers, our [hired hand] got the sleigh ready and drove us to the railway station. . . . The train, that had been readied for us, was enormously long, stretching from Ozenina to Zdolbunow, a distance of five to six kilometers."

The midnight visit, the rush, the confusion – this was standard practice for the Bluecaps, calculated to terrify victims and shake their confidence from the first moment. A bewildered prisoner is easier to manage.

As befits a bureaucracy, the NKVD kept seemingly precise records of the Polish "echelons" as they went east. Each train was categorized by date, departure station, destination, the number of people it carried, and something about the Bluecaps who guarded them, including the commander's last name. Thus we know, or think we know, that ninety-eight trains left Poland in the great migration that had swept up the Poplewska family. When I add them up, the February deportations come to 141,134 souls, an average of 1,440 per train, though one carried 2,127 – the population of a small town, rattling deep into Soviet Russia on a journey that lasted two, three, or even four weeks. Most were destined for slave labor in Archangelsk or elsewhere in Russia's frozen north.

The deportees considered themselves *Siberyaki*, though they hadn't actually reached the dreaded place of exile. European Russia above the Arctic Circle, and the Asian steppes of Kazakhstan, served as well as the literal Siberia when it came to isolating undesirables and extracting the utmost in labor before they died.

The NKVD numbers for the exiles are routinely trebled by the Polish emigre community. In an early assessment of the four great waves of deportations, Janusz Zawodny concluded: "A sober and cautious estimate of the total number of deportees can be established at approximately 1,200,000" – that is, one out of ten residents of eastern Poland. Like the length of Anna Poplewska's train, this was always implausible, and, following the 1991 collapse of the Soviet Union, revisionists used newly released documents to drop the figure to 320,000. More recently, the consensus figure has been rising. In her 2012 history, Halik Kochanski concludes that "it now seems likely that there were at least 500,000 Polish citizens deported in 1940-41." Which may be as close to the truth as we will ever get.

A ROUND TRIP TO THE GULAG, in a boxcar or goods wagon behind a steam locomotive, traveling at ten or twelve miles an hour with frequent and prolonged halts, would tie up a train and its guards for two months – one month out, another month back. As a result, it was April before boxcars were available for a second mass deportation. The responsibility for scheduling them belonged to Stalin's henchman "Iron Lazar" Kaganovich. (His signature was on the Katyn Order that had condemned Basia's father and brother, and his name would brush across her life yet again in 1942.)

Planning for the second exodus began on March 7, 1940, two days after Lavrentiy Beria recommended that Colonel Deszberg be shot. Beria now ordered his minions "to deport by April 15 of this year to the regions of Kazakhstan . . . for the period of 10 years all members of the families of former officers of the Polish Army [and the other condemned prisoners]. Family members include by definition wives [and] children, as well as parents, brothers and sisters if they happen to live in the same location as the rest of the family of the POWs or prisoners."

If we accept the number of Katyn victims as 21,892, and

use five as the number of each man's family, then Beria was ordering the arrest of 109,460 civilians, mostly women and children. They would be dumped in a sparsely populated Soviet republic whose land mass was equal to that of all the nations of Western Europe combined. These were Borodin's "Steppes of Central Asia," originally inhabited by a nomadic people of Mongolian extraction. Under the forced collectivization in the 1930s, half the native Kazakhs were killed, starved to death, or forced to emigrate in search of food. By 1940 there were only 2 million Kazakhs, and they were outnumbered by those whom Stalin had obliged to live there: Russians, Koreans, Germans, Ukrainians, and Poles. And Americans! Hundreds of Ford Motor Company workers had come to Russia in the 1930s to build Model A cars and trucks, and when they had served their purpose were delivered to the Lubyanka in the very "black ravens" they'd assembled.

Kazakhstan was a vital part of the Gulag Archipelago, as Aleksandr Solzhenitsyn would dub Stalin's far-flung system of labor and punishment camps. There were eleven prison camps in the republic, including Karaganda, the worst of the lot; another devoted entirely to the Wives of Traitors to the Motherland; and a third in which Solzhenitsyn himself would slave and hunger.

In Beria's order, the families of the Katyn victims were sentenced to *svobodnayha ssylka*, "free deportation," one of Communism's chilling oxymorons. They'd be scattered across the steppe to survive as best they could, but straying no farther than twenty-five miles from the place where they were set down. In Kazakhstan, as elsewhere in the Gulag, the Marxist boast – "From each according to his ability, to each according to his needs" – had been considerably modified. "He who does not work," the exiles would be told again and again, "neither will he eat." And even a worker did not eat very much.

I am struck by Beria's easy reference to the duration of

their exile: ten years. A "tenner" was the typical sentence for a political prisoner – those who weren't shot – and often enough it was a life sentence. If the prisoner survived his sentence, ten more years might be added. And if he survived *that*, he'd probably be released into the surrounding community, condemned to "live in 'perpetual exile' and never be allowed back into Russia."

As understood in saner nations, a passport – even Basia's gray Travel Document of 1955 – was meant to safeguard a traveler outside his country of residence. But in the Orwellian world of Joseph Stalin, the average citizen couldn't leave the Soviet Union, and his passport controlled travel *within* the country. Even that privilege was denied to the exiles: they had no passports, effectively imprisoning them in the *oblast* (administrative district) where they found themselves. Without the Bluecaps' permission, they couldn't leave the oblast, couldn't come near any large city or national frontier; couldn't visit the oblast capital or an important railroad junction – indeed, couldn't live in a town of any size.

BY APRIL 1940, word of that February deportation had spread on the wing through the eastern borderlands, and every Pole understood that the Bluecaps might come for him without warning. Indeed, the history of Eastern Europe had imbued its residents with the knowledge that their lives were always subject to disruption. Thus, before he went off to fight the Germans, Aunt Krysia's husband hid several gold discs at the bottom of his wife's small compact, containing her rouge. He knew that, whatever happened, his stylish wife would take the vanity case with her and, sooner or later, would find the treasure. Zdzislaw Deszberg also kept gold coins at home in case of a sudden departure.

At 99 Potocki Street, the dreaded hammering at the door came some time after midnight on Saturday, April 13, 1940. Unlike her sister and stepson, Mama had no gold hidden away, nor was she prepared in any other way for the arrival of the NKVD, in Basia's recollection:

She just stood there. That is the conclusion we reached, Lalka and I, when we compared notes much later. It seems that the soldiers who came to deport us, seeing Mama standing there, doing nothing, packed some household things for her and put as many clothes on the two of us as they could. We must have looked like two cocoons on matchsticks.

The Bluecaps knew – none better! – that extra clothing would be priceless in Siberia, that if not needed for warmth it could be bartered for food, and that the only safe place for a spare dress, sweater, or jacket was on one's body, since luggage could be lost or stolen.

But here's the astonishing thing about the men who came to the Deszberg home: I have read a dozen accounts of the deportations, and each of them relates (like Anna Poplewska quoted earlier) how they were shouted at, hurried, and shoved into a sleigh or a lorry with whatever belongings they could snatch in the few minutes allowed to them. But at 99 Potocki Street, Beria's enforcers actually took the time to dress two little girls in the clothes that would mean the difference between misery and a life that was merely difficult.

Fifteen years later, Basia would have an instant and powerful effect on me, but I doubt that as a terrified six-year-old she could have charmed the Bluecaps in that way. Was it the older sister, the poised and pretty Lalka with her hair in plaits? Perhaps, but I suspect the magic was worked by Mama. She may have seemed helpless to her daughters, but at thirty-four she was a beautiful woman, and the NKVD commander was a man, after all. And perhaps he realized, as Basia and Lalka did not, that Mama was four or five months pregnant with her third child. I hope Colonel Deszberg knew that, at the age of sixty-five, he was to become a father for the fifth time. Redoubtable old warrior, it would have warmed his heart in the chill and hunger of that prison in Kiev.

And come to think of it, Mama wasn't just "standing there doing nothing." At a minimum, she gathered up and took with her the following items:

1. The famous chamber pot, about which Basia and I would share a laugh on the road to Italy.

2. Her photo album, or anyhow a handful of family photographs.

3. A copy of *Pan Tadeusz* by Adam Mickiewicz, whose prophetic theme was his love of a nation lost to Russian occupation.

4. Her "treasure box" of mementos, including a letter from her husband, written during one of his annual call-ups before the war, and Tas's note to Basia about the new puppies.

5. A box of sugar cubes.

6. Six crisp new 100-zloty bills, a small fortune in prewar Poland, though now technically valueless.

7. The Shirley Temple doll, though perhaps Basia was the one who had the presence of mind to bring it along.

8. A bar of mildly scented *Savon Benignina*, in its box promising that daily use would maintain a healthy complexion. Mama had bought the soap at great expense and danger during the German bombing of Lwow the previous September.

Beyond those tangible objects, Mama had two assets that would serve her well in this crisis and in the years to come. One was her beauty. If she was a handsome woman at fifty, when I presented myself for her inspection in London, she must have been stunning at thirty-five, with the bloom of motherhood on her. Perhaps as important, she spoke some Russian, as did her sisters. How Mama, Krysia, and Nuna came to learn this language, in a region of Poland that for more than a century had been occupied by Austria, is something of a puzzle. Most likely Mama and her sisters had picked up a working knowledge of Ukrainian, the mother tongue of farmers and tradesmen in their part of Poland. Ukrainian and Russian are similar, on the order of Norwegian and Swedish.

SO MAMA, THE GIRLS, AND A SUITCASE or two were piled into a lorry already crowded with other deportees, and driven to Lwow's handsome, glass-roofed Central Station, from which so many Poles had already been dispatched to prison camp or exile. The glass was gone now, shattered by German bombs, and one set of tracks had been adapted for the wide-gauge undercarriage used in the Soviet Union. (The Russians simply laid a third rail outside those that served the standard European gauge.) On this line, in the freight yard behind the station, a train waited for them, twenty or twenty-five rust-red wagons behind a steam locomotive with a red star on its snout. No doubt there was a baggage car as well, because Beria had specified that boxcars be provided for farm implements and such family treasures as a sewing machine, and at least some exiles managed to bring them. "We were allowed to take every-thing," recalled Zofia Wonka: "clothing, bedding, and cook-ware [and] a 'Singer' sewing machine purchased in 1939." Finally, there were two carriages reserved for the guards.

The standard Russian boxcar – always called a "cattle car" by its unwilling passengers – was fifty feet long and a bit less than ten feet wide, providing 475 square feet of floor space. Beria's order specified that each car should hold thirty passengers, which would have permitted sixteen square feet per person – a bit more than a modern coffin. Typically, though, the exiles speak of allotments of forty, fifty, sixty, or more per car. "In our case," one woman told me, "seventy-two people were crammed into one of those [wagons]. Worse still, if the number seventy-three hap-pened to be a member of your family, tough luck! He or she was shoved into the next one."

The boxcar had an exterior steel frame and was walled with ten-inch boards, laid horizontally inside the frame, and the whole thing painted the color of dried blood. Each side had a sliding door of the same construction, held shut by a steel bar when the train was moving. There was also a tiny window, high up on either end and sometimes barred. The roof was sheathed with tin.

Inside were three-decker sleeping platforms, which the passengers generally assigned to children and the elderly. The upper platform was especially valued, since the windows provided fresh air and a glimpse of the country they were passing through. The toilet was a hole in the floor, eight inches across and rimmed with metal so it couldn't be enlarged for an escape hatch. Into such a compartment, Basia was loaded with thirty or fifty or seventy others:

I don't remember anything except being pushed and shoved and feeling hot, and then I was on the upper sleeping platform. There, it seems, I spent the whole journey, except when squeezing past people to get to the toilet. This was a hole in the floor with a blanket or sheet around it; I remember the cloth as white, so probably it was a sheet. And people would say "dziecko idzie," a child is coming, and the others would let me through.

The only thing that stands out in my mind is people singing the national anthem when the train was crossing the frontier into Russia. Everybody tried to get to the tiny windows for their last look at Poland.

The song was "Dabrowski's Mazurka," a rousing hymn to the exiles who fought under Napoleon's banner at the turn of the 18th Century, after Poland was partitioned and occupied by Russia, Germany, and Austria. The Poles hoped that Napoleon would eventually lead them home to a free and unified country. Toward that end, they fought the Austrians in Italy on behalf of France, in an eerie forecast of Wladyslaw Anders's 2nd Polish Corps that would storm German positions under British command in 1944. Few anthems are as stirring::

> Poland will not perish
> As long as we shall live:
> What those countries took from us,
> We'll reclaim with steel!
> March, march, Dabrowski,
> From Italy to Poland;
> We will follow you
> And win back our nation.

Once Italy was secure, however, Napoleon had no interest in helping the Poles go home, and the Anders Army would get no greater reward.

The Polish-Soviet frontier had supposedly been erased by the plebiscites of October 1939, transforming eastern Poland into Western Ukraine and Western Belarus. In fact, the barriers were still in place and guarded by Red Army soldiers. When the Deszberg women crossed that frontier in April 1940, and the passengers burst into "Dabrowski's Mazurka," its final verse must have set Mama to weeping:

> Her father said to Basia
> With tears in his eyes:
> "Hear our soldiers, child,
> Marching to their drums!"
> March, march, Dabrowski,
> From Italy to Poland. . . .

ACCORDING TO RUSSIAN RECORDS, Basia's train was carrying 1,111 souls from Lwow to Kazakhstan, plus the locomotive crew and a few dozen men of the 13th Convoy Forces Security Division, formed at Kiev in November 1939 for just this task. The guards were commanded by Lieutenant Klikow, his first name not recorded.

Five such trains left Lwow's Central Station that day, April 13, and another train four days later, carrying 9,000 of the city's residents into exile. And forty-five more trains left the same week from other railroad stations in eastern

Poland, for a total migration of 57,936 souls, according to the lists that have come down to us. However much I discount the passengers' recollections – the length of the trains, the numbers jammed into each boxcar – I can't shrink them to this number. Perhaps some trains were omitted from the record, or the numbers aboard them were undercounted.

Lieutenant Klikow's primary duty was to ensure that nobody escaped, and for this purpose a machine gun was mounted atop a guards' carriage behind the locomotive and another on the last car of the train – what Americans call the caboose. As a secondary duty, the guards were also supposed to feed the Poles. Paragraph seven of Beria's instructions was very specific on this point: "Along the journey by rail, the deportees shall receive free hot food and 600 grams of bread per person once every twenty-four hours." Six hundred grams: one pound, five ounces.

The reality was very different. The boxcar doors were sealed for the first day or two, until the train had left Poland. For at least that period of time, the passengers had to depend on what they'd brought from home or what their companions might share with them. Once the train had crossed the prewar frontier, and the Poles less likely to make a run for freedom, the steel bar was removed and the door slid open for food and water. "Then the provisions might consist of black, sour bread, fish soup with heads and entrails in it, or simply hot water (*kipiatok*)." In another account, "Volunteers from each wagon . . . jumped out with jugs, buckets or other containers to bring the millet porridge and black bread – half a kilogram per person – back to the train. The travellers were fed in this way on average once every two or three days." So the bread ration might actually work out to six ounces a day – and note its color! To the Poles, and especially to those from the countryside, bread was the staff of life, and a good Polish loaf was brown, not black. The color of Russian bread seemed proof of Russian backwardness.

Esther Hautzig, who as a young girl made the journey east in June 1940, described her wagon as a literal cattle car, stinking of manure and gouged by hooves. There were forty passengers and the usual tiny windows up high. Once a day they were brought cabbage soup by a soldier carrying "a rusty pail" and another with wooden bowls and spoons. The soup was "an orange liquid where shriveled bits of tomato, carrots, and cabbage floated like refuse," which for the first several days Esther couldn't bring herself to swallow. "At other times, it was possible to buy fresh farmer cheese and black bread at a rural station." The door wasn't opened for these transactions; rather, prisoners poked their heads through one of those tiny windows, bargained desperately with the peasant vendor, threw down the agreed sum, and accepted the food from a child standing on the peasant's shoulders. "Sometimes even a jug of milk made this wobbly trip," Esther recalled.

At one of these stops, Mama was among those who went to collect the meal, such as it was. She found herself in line with Aunt Nuna. Quite apart from the mixed joy of seeing her sister again, this encounter may well have saved the lives of Mama and her daughters, or at the very least eased their time in exile.

The aunts and Zbyszek, like us, were also deported on April 13. We were in different carriages. At midday, more or less, the train would stop and some passengers were given buckets and allowed to queue up for soup. That is how my mother and Aunt Nuna met, and it helped us to find each other later on, in Kazakhstan.

There was very little light coming from the small barred windows. The nights were black, and the days were almost as dark. It felt good when the doors opened wide to let people out to get the soup or water.

The journey was rather painful. Mama was very ill, and we realized later that she had had a miscarriage. She was sure it would have been a boy, finally.

The boxcar had no springs. Neither the floor nor the sleeping platforms had any padding. The boxcar swayed and clattered over uneven tracks, and it slammed against the next car with every change in grade or speed, throwing passengers to the floor or against one another. In such an environment, it's no wonder that Mama lost the baby. She had thought of him as a boy, whom she would name Jan, whether for his grandfather Jan Deshegyi or for his Uncle Jan, who had preceded him into the Gulag.

The delivery would have been attended by the other women in the carriage, many with experience in home birth, but there was no chance that a five-months' infant would survive. How decent a man was Lieutenant Klikow? Alas, probably not very. If he were as amiable as the Blue-caps who'd arrested the Deszberg family, he might have permitted a burial by the railway tracks, as sometimes happened. More likely, as with most deaths among the deportees, the stillborn child was abandoned somewhere along the railroad tracks.

The girls knew none of this, or else banished it from memory. Basia remembers passing the time with her sister, as children do, playing with whatever was at hand:

Lalka and I managed to scrounge a bit of bread, and we made some dice. They kept breaking up and we spent most of the time reshaping them. And Lalka used to tell me stories when we slept next to each other. If I dozed off, she would wake me up and say "I haven't finished yet."

In another boxcar, their fifteen-year-old cousin was also passing the time as best he could:

It happened that a girl from the neighborhood, whom Zbyszek had admired from afar, was also on the train. So, he says, they held hands, he sang to her, and on the third day he kissed her.

Seventy years later, I managed to retrieve Zbyszek's account of the deportation, written as a cadet in the Anders

Army and preserved in a collection at Stanford University. Alas, the youngster in his essay chooses to be very serious, and he does not mention this little romance.

THE TRAIN WAS BOUND for the easternmost region of Kazakhstan, a distance of 3,200 miles – New York to London, say, or London to Athens *and back*. The journey took eighteen days: through the Ukrainian capital of Kiev, where Colonel Deszberg was probably still waiting for execution (he may have heard the train!); through Staro-bilsk, in whose monastery the defenders of Lwow were held; across the Volga River to Kuybyshev in Russia. Then they crossed the Ural Mountains, following the Trans-Siberian Railroad across the limitless steppes to Chelya-binsk, Omsk, and Novosibirsk. They traveled day and night, though with frequent halts for food, to take on coal or water, to give a Moscow-bound train the right of way, or to dispose of those – mostly the very young or very old – who died overnight.

At Novosibirsk (which means, more or less, New Siberian City) the train turned south, leaving Russia for Kazakhstan. South of Semipalatinsk, now a major city and even then a considerable town, it made regular stops along the single-track railway line to Ayagoz, its final destination. At each stop, Lieutenant Klikow parceled out the Poles in lots of 100 or so. Aunt Krysia, Aunt Nuna, and Zbyszek were set down near the town of Georgievka. "On the first of May," as Zbyszek told the story, "we reached a small railway station, around which there were small huts which housed half-savage Kazakhs. All around there were the steppes with an outline of bare, stony mountains. Lorries were already waiting for us, and they took us to neighboring farms. Here we started a new life somewhere in Khazakstan on unwelcoming steppes."

Another passenger saw no trace of civilization whatever when the boxcar door opened upon her destination. "There was no station, it was in the middle of the steppe," she wrote. "They put down some planks of wood and told us to get out. . . . I remember [them saying], 'Now get your things and run into your Poland!' It was a barren steppe. We stood there. It was becoming hot, and it was [only] the beginning of May. And there was a terrible silence."

Like her, Mama and her daughters were deposited at a station that was just a number, with no settlement in sight. By my reckoning, on a wartime map of the line below Semi-palatinsk, this was Station Nine, 100 miles south of the city. As Basia recalls her arrival in the oblast that would be her home for the next two years:

As the train approached our destination, some car-riages were detached. People were put on lorries and driven off – just a few families in each. We drove for a good while through the steppes, with the vehicles in front of us disappearing until there were only two lorries left, with Mama, Lalka and myself in the last one with another family. We were taken to a very desolate place with a little hut standing all on its own. Lalka and I sat on each side of Mama. She put her arms around us and sat still and stiff as a rod while the soldiers negotiated with a Kazakh man standing in front of the hut.

It was now night, warm and calm. The air was green, I remember distinctly. Someone has suggested it might have been the Northern Lights. Is it possible?

Yes, the most common hue for the Northern Lights is an eerie green. And yes, Basia might well have seen the aurora in Kazakhstan, at fifty degrees north latitude, even on the first of May. Joe and I saw the Northern Lights in East Alton that same year, though when snow was on the ground – they were white, as I remember, and in my childish imagination the great ribbon of light seemed to crackle as it wavered.

It was now that Mama's command of Russian would have been priceless. No matter if she had an accent, or perhaps could only speak in the present tense: for the Kazakh too, Russian was an alien tongue, and one he'd been forced to learn; he too would have spoken it roughly. Basia thinks that he was allowed to select his overnight guests from among the Poles still on the lorry, and very likely he picked Mama because they could communicate after a fashion:

He must have chosen us, and we were invited by him into his home. There were four or five people in the little hut, all talking and laughing and making welcoming gestures. They produced a samovar, and Mama produced some sugar cubes. The grownups would tie a cube to a piece of string and pass it round, dipping it into the "tea." It was actually kipiatok – boiled water – with a tang of charcoal. Water from a samovar always tasted of charcoal.

The grownups seemed to have a lot to say, and Mama stayed talking with them well into the night while Lalka and I went to sleep on a platform running round the walls of the hut, planks of wood like bunk beds. What a difference from the train! We slept on animal skins, there was enough room to move, and to add to the strange but marvelous feeling, the wolves howled in the night.

And that was our first night in Kazakhstan. Maybe because of the tedium and discomfort of the journey, sitting on the lorry in the greenish light of the aurora and then being welcomed by the Kazakhs in their little hut was so magical. Whenever I think of Russia I think of the little Kazahk hut, wrapped in the soft, greenish air of Aurora Borealis, and the Kazakhs' readiness to share their home with us.

The next day a lorry arrived and we were taken to a kolkhoz, a collective farm.

CHAPTER SEVEN

La Donna È Mobile
1955

OUR VERY FIRST DRIVER out of Les Abrets was a gallant Frenchman in a gorgeous black Citroën with clamshell fenders and doors that opened to the rear – "suicide doors," they were called by Billy Kenney and Lyle Morrill, the automotive connoisseurs of my high school years. You see such cars in French films of the 1950s: *la police* arrive in them, braying like unhappy donkeys. Rich men drive them, and government officials.

I took the rear bench seat, with the rucksacks, while Basia sat up front with the driver. Even that didn't dim my joy at the way the Frenchman took the winding road to Chambery, showing off the Citroën's front-wheel drive and catlike suspension. Billy and Lyle would have given their front teeth to drive such a car, or even to ride in one. (Like the down-market Deux Chevaux, the shifter was on the dashboard.) No doubt the Frenchman was laying it on a bit, for Basia's benefit. In any event, he got us to Chambery in time for an early lunch, which we ate on a park bench by a stream: bread, cheese, and wine from our common bottle.

Basia would be staying some months in Perugia, so her wardrobe was more extensive than mine, and her pack was smaller, which left me to carry the food and drink. My rucksack had two side pockets, one for the wine and the other for the cheese, while the long French loaf sat crosswise at the top of the pack, secured by the flap, allowing us to tear off a chunk whenever the mood overtook us. I am told that the loaf is properly called a baguette. Whatever the name, those were the finest carbohydrates I have ever consumed, the soft inside and the crisp brown crust.

Having dined, we shouldered our packs and walked

through Chambery, stopping once to refill our wine bottle. As we left the bar-tabac, I saw that it was called *La Savoyarde*, like the bell at the Sacré Coeur in Paris. So we were in Savoy, where that great bell had originated! That was enough local knowledge to satisfy us, and we set off along Route 6 to Modane, the last town before we crossed over the Alps into Italy.

"That automobile," Basia said, "was a *Traction Avant*."

"Drive ahead?" I fancied that I was getting rather good at the language.

"Well – drive *before*, I think."

"Front wheel drive?"

"I suppose so."

I liked my version better, so I cried "Traction avant!" when I found a good place to wait for our next ride. "Drive ahead! On to Italy!" Soon Basia was doing it, too, and we giggled like schoolchildren by the side of the road. And I noticed that she no longer insisted on walking on if we didn't immediately get a ride.

The road tacked south to avoid a mountain, as towering as any I'd ever seen, but here just a foothill to the white peaks in the distance. Then east, then north, then south again. This was done in short hops with families, farmers, and a salesman. Then we came to Saint Michel des Maurienne, squeezed between the River Arc and another *massif*. Alas, an hour or two earlier, this mountain had slid upon the Route d'Italie. A road crew was pecking away at a great pile of rocks and dirt, and the police were guarding a barrier of sawhorses between them and us. Our driver – the salesman – cursed and announced that he was returning to the village for lunch and probably to spend the night.

We thanked him and got out, and Basia fell into deep conversation with a policeman. "We must go back to Chambery," she told me, "and find a different way to Modane."

I unfolded the BP road map. The detour would undo most of what we had accomplished today, and put us on a longer road besides. Basia meanwhile had collected the rest of the police force, three middle-aged men in blue pillbox caps, and a fourth official whose cap read SNCF. It was the railroad man who had a solution: "If we follow the train tracks," Basia said, "we will find a bridge across the river. Then we will be back on the highway and we will walk to Modane."

"How far?"

"Seventeen kilometers," she said after a further consultation.

"Three hours," I said, judging by our hike along the Saône to the youth hostel in Lyon. "We'll be in Modane before dark." (Too late, I didn't add, to venture across the Col du Mont Cenis, meaning another sweet night in a hotel room.) "Traction avant!" I cried, to the wonderment of the police.

We walked along the railroad bridge, really just a trough of steel, which spared us from having to look at the Arc River running wild with snowmelt below us. At first we walked on the wooden ties, but they were too far apart, so we moved to the side, our shoes booming on steel.

And when we were safe on the south bank, we were met by – a bus! A dozen passengers were climbing down, fetching suitcases, and preparing to cross our bridge in the opposite direction. Another bus, it seemed, had been dispatched from Chambery to pick them up, while this one would turn around and go back to Modane. Basia learned this from the driver, who then offered to take us with him. So we clambered into our own private, forty-passenger conveyance, deliciously spread out across the two front seats.

Traction avant!

IT WAS FOUR O'CLOCK when we reached Modane, up the narrow valley of the River Arc, between stupendous snow-topped mountains. The bus driver gave us the news that the Col du Mont Cenis was still unplowed. Cars and trucks had to be loaded onto the *motorail* and taken through the Mont Cenis Tunnel, to Bardonecchia on the Italian side.

I have since explored the Alps on skis, and I marvel at our innocence (to give stupidity its polite name). Did we really imagine that we could hitchhike over a seven-thousand-foot pass in the spring of the year? At the height of land, on April 11, the snow was probably still twenty feet deep.

We went to the little railroad station. Could we buy one-way passage to Bardonecchia? *Mais certainment!* And how much did a second-class ticket cost? *Cents francs.*

Twenty-eight cents! I found a lavender 100-franc note in our common purse, along with five 20-franc coins. Basia exchanged them for two pasteboard tickets, and we sat down to wait for the train, closing our collars against the afternoon chill. The tunnel entrance was like a little fort, built from great gray stones, with a keystone arch over all. "The tunnel," Basia said, relaying what she'd learned at the ticket window, "is fourteen kilometers long." All by itself, that explained why France had long ago electrified its trains. Imagine traveling more than eight miles behind a coal-burning locomotive: the passengers would suffocate.

When we got out on the Italian side, the afternoon was much brighter, for we were now on the southern slope of the Alps. As we stepped down to the platform, a border guard beckoned us over to his kiosk. "*Niente da dichiarare,*" Basia told him. He stamped our passports and gave her an admiring survey, from the top of her head to her calves. He was splendidly uniformed, though his kiosk looked as though it had been knocked together from battlefield debris.

"*Niente —*" I said.

"*— da dichiarare.* Nothing to declare."

I decided that Italian would come easy to me, and I rehearsed this phrase as we walked down the road toward the village. Niente da dichiarare, nothing to declare! Meanwhile I kept checking the road behind, hoping a vehicle would come along. Soon enough, a van did appear, swaying on worn-out springs. I faced about and held up my palm, smiling hugely at the driver.

Yes! He slowed and stopped, beaming at us through the open passenger window. Basia climbed into the cab and slid into the middle of the bench seat, with me close behind. We held our rucksacks in our laps, and I found that the passenger window was not so much open as inoperative. The crank rotated, but the glass stayed hidden, if indeed there was any glass.

Basia fell into animated conversation with the driver, a big-bellied man with a three-day growth of beard. Words poured out of his round face – beautiful words, as much sung as spoken. My high school Spanish helped a little. I caught the word *casa* – that would be a house. And *signorina*, close enough to senorita that I got the hang of it. And *ostello*, which had to mean hostel. *Ostello della gioventu!* Was there ever a prettier phrase for something so homely as a double-decker steel bunk in a dormitory room?

"There's no hostel in Bardonecchia," Basia translated, as the driver negotiated hairpin turns with much squealing of brakes and swaying on the truck's worn springs. "But he invites us to stay at his brother's farm. . . . The house was closed for the winter," she went on. "It has no electricity and no running water. What do you think?"

"What about a hotel?" I had nothing against the truck driver's brother, but neither would I have minded another evening curled up with Basia on a hotel bed.

"No, and he says *Torino* is a hundred kilometers. We'll never get there before dark."

"Okay," I said. "*Mi casa es su casa.*" That got a smile from her, though whether of admiration or pity, I wasn't sure.

The truck driver seemed harmless – rather sweet, in fact, and delighted to do us a favor. This was, I would discover, an Italian characteristic.

The farmhouse was above the village, perched precariously on the sloping land. We carried our rucksacks inside, where our host lit a kerosene lamp and showed us around. The house had a large living room, with a kitchen and a bedroom behind it. He waved us into the bedroom with a flourish, and gallantly announced that it was ours. Basia accepted for herself alone – my grasp of the conversation was good enough for me to know that – and spread her sleeping bag on the mattress. Though bare and far from clean, it was hardly worse than those in the hostels in Paris and Lyon.

I was hugely disappointed, but I didn't want to argue the point in front of our host. As it was, he was looking from one of us to the other with an open mouth: traveling together but sleeping apart?

He carried the lamp into the kitchen, where we dined at a wooden table on the bread and cheese we'd bought in Chambery, washed down with two bottles of white wine that the truck driver produced from a cabinet. The bottles were unlabeled, and the wine seemed sweet after our days of *vin ordinaire*. And it was deliciously cold, as if it had spent the winter in that kitchen. It tasted, as I would write in that letter home, "like heaven in my mouth."

"He says," Basia translated, "that he and his brother make this wine. It's rather good, don't you think? And he says he would cook pasta for us, but there is no stove."

This caused our host to explode into speech. He looked at me – looked at Basia – waved his hands and made great declarations, which ended with laughter. "He says," Basia translated, "if you can't speak Italian, then you must find an Italian girl to teach you. He says she will put her tongue into your mouth and teach you the language."

"I think I'd rather learn Polish," I said.

Well, all right, I probably didn't, and anyhow it wouldn't have been entirely true. Along the road yesterday, during one of those interminable waits, Basia had given me an introductory Polish lesson, consisting of the alphabet from *ah* to *zet*. The seminar had left me slack-jawed. How could twenty-four letters (three letters were missing, and another appeared twice) be pronounced in so many different ways? Italian, by contrast, struck me as a marvelously straightforward and sympathetic language. Signorina! Ostello della gioventu! Niente da dichiarare!

There was a ratty couch in the big room, which would be my bed, and a folding metal cot with a thin mattress, which our host took for himself. For our toilet, we stepped outside in turn and tended to our business in the black night, while the Alpine snow-melt ran down a stream nearby: no doubt I was peeing into the water supply of Bardoneccia. The night was overcast, but I could feel the great bulk of Mont Cenis behind me – *Moncenisio,* I should say – beneath which we'd traveled a few hours before. The chill off the snow-fields was like an open freezer door, and the lights of Bardonecchia were sprinkled prettily below . . . not as many lights as one might imagine! The War was only ten years in the past, and Italy hadn't made particularly good use of its American reconstruction aid.

Then we got into our sleeping bags – or blankets, in the case of the truck driver – and settled down for the night. Before he blew out the kerosene lamp, our host sat up in bed and, with astonishingly graphic hand and mouth gestures, offered to give me oral sex. "No," I said with as much dignity as the situation permitted. *"Solo signorina."* Whether he understood this fractured Italian, I'm not sure, but he took the rebuff good-naturedly, settled back, and extinguished the lamp. (Perhaps, indeed, he was happy to be relieved of the obligation!) Soon he was snoring, and I too composed myself for sleep.

I am somewhat disappointed to find that Basia remembers this evening better than our cuddle at Les Abrets. She also remembers it somewhat differently:

As for the truck driver's hospitality, his wine was not that bad. It was white, and it tasted more like fruit juice than wine, but it must have been strong. After a couple of glasses I got a bit tipsy. In the night I heard loud footsteps, decided it might be him, so I put a chair under the door handle. He did rattle the door but then went off. And tried his luck with you, as you told me later. I hope you are not offended that you were not his first choice.

IN THE MORNING we brushed our teeth with our wine from Chambery, standing on the porch overlooking the village. This proved to be a mistake, red wine mixed with Macleans toothpaste, a taste so appalling that we brushed again at a brook on the walk down to Bardoneccia. We found a tavern, bought a *cafe latte* apiece, and had a more formal wash-up in the toilet room. (The toilet itself was a squatter, two porcelain footrests above a hole in the floor.) We then went shopping for bread. The loaves proved to be short and rather dry on the tongue, much inferior to those glorious French baguettes. Much the same proved to be true of Italian cigarettes, called Nazionale.

And another difference! Whereas French drivers had been content to admire Basia with words alone, keeping their hands off what they assumed was my property, the Italians were much more forthcoming. The drivers who took us to Torino tended to steer with the left hand and gesture with the right, which every once in a while dropped down to pat Basia's knee.

The day had warmed up considerably by the time we walked through the city, so we stepped into a convenient alley and shed our coats. I changed into a polo shirt, then folded my jacket beneath the flap of the rucksack, where the long French loaves had formerly resided. Basia similarly stowed her duffle coat. She also moved her school ring to the third finger of her left hand, and turned it so that the plain gold band was on the outside. Henceforth we would pose as a married couple, in hopes of discouraging amorous drivers.

Our last ride of the day was in a long-haul van whose steering wheel was on the right, as if English built. There were two drivers, who when we climbed aboard placed us between them. This made me wary – whose knee would get patted this time? – but all was in order. The off-duty driver had to sit by the left-hand door, so when they wanted to overtake another vehicle, he could climb out the window – head, shoulders, and torso! – with his feet on the seat, his buttocks on the windowsill, and his fingers holding the top of the door, to see if the oncoming lane were clear of traffic.

Nightfall found us in Alessandria, 200 kilometers east of Bardonecchia, a good day's work compared to yesterday and the day before. The YHA guidebook promised a hostel on the outskirts, but the drivers had a better idea: they planned to spend the night at a relative's house, so we could sleep in the cab of their truck. This seemed a splendid idea, since they'd take us to Genoa in the morning. They worked like the crew of a tramp steamer, picking up cargo in one city and taking it to another, sometimes not returning home for weeks or a month, staying with acquaintances or sleeping in the truck. There was a bunk behind the seat and level with the top of it. Basia climbed up there, rolled out her sleeping bag, and wriggled inside. I did likewise on the bench seat, which smelled of leather, sweat, and something else – garlic, perhaps.

The truck doors banged open before sunrise, and our drivers piled in, coughing and farting and smelling of – yes! – garlic. They drove us to Genoa and left us there, so as to drop off their merchandise and pick up new stuff, with an uncertain destination. So we found a cafe and brushed our teeth at the washbasin in the toilet room. Then we ordered rolls and cafe latte. As with the Italian language, I was already addicted to Italian coffee. It came out of an espresso machine, black as ink, to be mixed with milk that had been infused with steam, so that it was hot and frothy.

Then we headed south along the Mediterranean, with cliffs crowding us on the left, the limitless blue sea on our right – dark blue with a hint of purple, like Basia's eyes – and a driver who made the Sign of the Cross before charging back into traffic. Having ensured that God was on his side, he then cut the corners. Sometimes he worked the horn; usually he didn't; and often enough he chatted to Basia with both hands off the wheel.

The next driver sang to her, like Zbyszek serenading his sweetheart on the train to Kazakhstan. "*La donna è mobile*," Basia explained to me, the hillbilly from New Hampshire. "From *Rigoletto*."

"What does it mean?"

She got him to sing the aria again, while she translated. I tucked the words into memory, rather unfairly associating them with the girl I loved:

> A woman is flighty,
> A feather on the wind,
> Changing her words and her mind.
> Always so friendly,
> With her pretty face,
> She weeps and she smiles,
> And never tells the truth.

"I saw the opera in Beirut," she told me after the driver set us down. "At the cinema. The girls cried when Gilda was killed, and the boys laughed at us, so the manager made us leave."

Meanwhile the upside-down ring worked its magic. No driver since Torino had dropped his hand to Basia's knee, even when the designated *marito* was banished to the back seat with the rucksacks. The ring was her only jewelry, since she'd left the gold bangles with Mama and she never wore earrings. I asked her about that, because most American girls wore them. We discussed the ideal earrings at great length, waiting there by the side of the road while the

Mediterranean stretched off to infinity.

We made good time along the coast, riding between the cliffs and the sea. At every turn, it seemed, a tiny Fiat came charging at us, seemingly headlong.

In time, we caught a ride in one of those same Fiats, whose driver explained that it was called *Topolino*, in honor of Mickey Mouse. This was the comparatively severe Fiat 500 of the 1930s, not the bulbous model of today. I climbed into the back seat, to discover that there was no back seat. I sat crosswise on the floor with my knees drawn up and my feet resting on our rucksacks and the driver's briefcase.

Then it came out that I was an American – and from New Hampshire! The driver pulled to the side of the road, reached back for his briefcase, and showed me the letter-head of an insurance company based in my home state. What, he wanted to know, was *questo*? He pointed to a drawing of the Old Man of the Mountain, the icon of New Hampshire, appearing on road signs, liquor bottles, and stationery. He was an insurance salesman; he'd represented this company since the War, and he'd always wondered about the Old Man. So I had the challenge of explaining the notion of a rock formation on a cliff, which when viewed from a certain angle looked just like the face of a jut-jawed, beetle-browed man; and Basia had the challenge of trans-lating it into Italian.

THE TOPOLINO TOOK US us to La Spezia, on the Gulf of Poets, where Shelley had drowned in a shipwreck. His body washed ashore, to be cremated on the beach. As I learned the story from my English-major friends, Lord Byron danced around the funeral pyre and snatched the heart out of the blazing corpse. Alas for English Department lore, it was a certain Edward Trelawny who'd retrieved Shelley's heart, the same gentleman who taught the poet to swim and hadn't done a very good job of it.

I would have lingered at this enchanted spot, for every

kilometer was bringing us closer to the *Università per Stranieri*. For me, Perugia meant the end of our journey together, while for Basia it was the start of a new adventure, so she was eager to press on. Which we did, catching a ride in another of those tramp steamers of the Italian road. Sitting between the two drivers, in the heat of the afternoon, Basia put her head on my shoulder and fell asleep. I put my arm around her – I was the marito, after all! – and soon I was dozing too. We must have slept the better part of an hour, until a blatting horn awakened me. The land was comparatively flat, the road fairly straight. "*Dove siamo?*" I asked the driver. Where are we?

"Cecina," he said.

That didn't sound right. I consulted our map, and sure enough, we'd passed the turnoff to Florence. I wakened Basia. "We've gone too far," I told her. "We should have gotten off at Livorno and headed inland."

The driver stopped. We got down, crossed the pavement, and begin to flag cars and trucks going north. They ignored us. It's not enough that we make a mistake, but Someone then arranges things so that we can't remedy it.

Then came *la polizia*! They arrived from the north in a U.S. Army jeep with the top down, which made a U-turn and swung onto the verge with us, spitting gravel from its tires. The officer in the front passenger seat had one polished boot propped on the slant of the fender, in the best go-to-hell military posture. There were four of them, in black uniforms, black boots, peaked caps, and pistols on their hips. All except the driver, they sprang out of the jeep to left and right. They were bursting with energy, the officer especially. He marched up to me, hooked his fingers in his white belt, expanded his fine chest, and demanded . . . what?

I turned to Basia, who answered him politely and with the sweetest of smiles. Nevertheless he fired another question at me, and again Basia supplied the answer. I stood there in the hot sun like a ventriloquist's dummy, speaking Italian with a girl's voice. I heard the word *autostop*, first from Basia, then from the policeman. Autostop? Good grief, was hitchhiking against the law in Italy? Such a thing had never occurred to me, child of liberty and the American way of life. Would we be spending tonight in Cecina jail?

The officer's voice softened, and he turned away from me in favor of the pretty girl. Back and forth the sallies went. His fine black eyebrows went up. He smiled! He understood! Then he stepped into the roadway and surveyed the oncoming vehicles, as if planning to purchase one. He stopped a long-haul truck, spoke briefly to the driver, and sent him on his way. Meanwhile his associates gathered by the jeep to share a Nazionale cigarette.

"He will find us a ride," Basia said. "He's looking for someone to set us on the road to *Firenze*."

And by golly he did! After the third or forth attempt – a whole new concept of autostop – the officer was satisfied. He stepped back. The driver got out to make room for us, and Basia climbed into the cab while the driver, the police, and I admired the sweet curve of her pupka. Then . . . the policemen rose to their full height, expanded their chests, and saluted us!

I decided that, of all nations in the world, Italy was the one I loved the best. The language was musical, the music was memorable, the coffee was delicious, the sun was hot, the cops were helpful, and my sweetheart was sitting beside me.

Our driver had no assistant, so Basia and I traded places. She would relay instructions and I would climb out the left window as required, to look for oncoming traffic. It was great sport, and I was sorry when we turned away from the coast and the country opened up, so that my services as lookout were no longer required.

We had wasted two hours on that excursion to Cecina, and it was clear that we wouldn't reach Florence before dark. At five o'clock, our most recent driver set us down on the main street of a fairly substantial town – Pontedera, I think it was, where Vespa motor scooters were manufactured. To my private delight, there was no hostel, and on the main street we found just such a modest hotel as we'd patronized in Les Abrets. So once against we found ourselves in a twin-bedded room on what I regarded as the second floor, but what to everyone else was *il primo piano*. And again we had two nun-like beds, a washbasin with *acqua non potabile*, and a bathroom down the hall.

We dined on pizza. To my astonishment, this was not a pie with cheese so hot it burned the roof of my mouth, such as I had enjoyed with beer as an undergraduate, but a cold cake that we bought by the piece at a nearby shop.

I washed up first, while Basia went for a stroll. If you have been counting, then yes, it was now Wednesday, April 13, five days since that shower at the municipal baths in Paris. It's amazing what one can do at a washbasin with a bit of soap and the corner of a towel.

Stripped to the waist, I found that my face was many shades darker than the rest of me, and that my arms were red from two days in the Italian sun.

When Basia returned from her stroll, she was flushed with pleasure. "The whole town is walking up and down," she said. "You must see them! It's the *passeggiata*, and it's a tradition. Every evening they walk up and down."

While she washed up, I joined the townspeople on the sidewalk outside. They were handsomely dressed, and I drew some stares for my polo shirt, beard, and sunburned arms. I didn't find the promenade as enchanting as Basia had, so I retreated to a bistro across the street.

"*Una bierra, per favore*," I told the proprietor at the counter, full of pride for my mastery of the language. I would drink the beer standing up, assuming that, as in England, there was a price penalty for sitting at one of the little marble-topped tables with their black hoop chairs.

With his right hand, the proprietor put a beer in front of me – *Personi*, it was called, light and bubbly in a glass with a heavy bottom, a slender waist, and a company crest on its side, the whole thing bedecked with dew. Something new to admire about Italians: they knew the value of refrigerating beer! Then, with his left hand, the proprietor added the accessories, a coaster and an ashtray, both advertising Cinzano. Finally he announced the price, which passed me in a blur except that it had a five in it. I pushed a 500-lire note toward him, and he gave me back a reassuring quantity of aluminum coins and filthy 100-lire notes.

Soon I found myself hemmed in by curious townsmen. What was I doing in Pontedera with my beard and my curious inability to understand a simple sentence? On the counter, I placed the Personi glass to represent myself as a hitchhiker, then I drove the Cinzano ashtray down the road toward it. "*La macchina,*" I explained. Then I raised my open palm. "*Autostop!*" I cried, and the saucer stopped and picked me up. I sipped the cold beer triumphantly, but alas they didn't understand. So I went through it again, expanding my explanation with their prodding, until everyone was satisfied. The tables behind me had ceased their conversations, the better to listen to ours. "*Tedesco,*" said a fat woman in black, stroking her chin and looking meaningfully at my beard. "*Si, si,*" agreed her companion, likewise ample and garbed in black: "Tedesco!"

"German," said Basia, when I brought this new word back to her, like a cat depositing a mouse for her admiration. "She thought you were German."

"Germans don't much wear beards, do they?"

"No, but you remember the journeyman carpenters from Lyon, on their wander-year? She probably associates hitchhikers with them."

Then we went back to our kissing game. I was confident that this time I would reach my heart's desire, but I was disappointed: This virtuous maid subdues me quite! So in time I returned to my own chaste bed.

Evidently I was less cheerful than at Les Abrets. When asked about our nights on the road, Basia produces one little gem, which must refer to this evening in Pontedera. I treasure it as an example of the accidental effects we have on other people's lives – throwing off a pronouncement, promptly forgotten by us, while the other party carries it around for the rest of her life. Basia's story doesn't reflect particularly well on me, which no doubt explains why it's not in my own stock of memories:

Oh yes, I do remember the hotel, though I have no idea where it was. Such luxury, and all for a dollar each! And I remember a bit of a conversation we had, that left me rather puzzled. You were in bed, I was standing by the window looking out at the town, and you said, "One of these days you will go on your own way and find that no one is following you." Having thought about it, I turned around to ask what you meant, but you were asleep. Did we have a disagreement about something?

Ouch. I'm sure she's right. The pronouncement sounds just like me or, more accurately, like the Young Artist I fancied myself to be.

But what I like best about this fragment is that I was already asleep!

Ah, youth.

WE WERE IN FLORENCE by ten o'clock next morning, but didn't visit the Uffizi as we had planned. We pressed on to the south, 160 kilometers across the hilly spine of Italy. Each hilltop wore a village or small city, or at the very least a walled farmstead, for defense against invaders or to catch the breeze.

Perugia proved to be one of these hilltop cities, with a view of Assisi to the southeast. I remember a fine cool cathedral in a plaza, with wide steps leading up to the door, and an old man in a black suit sitting on one of the steps.

Indeed, the town itself seemed cool, at least in the shade. We passed a cinema featuring Marlon Brando in *Il Selvaggio*, The Wild One, which I'd seen last year at home. I told Basia that the movie, about motorcyclists terrorizing a small town, was inspired by the annual motorcycle rally in Laconia, New Hampshire, where legions of overweight men and their girlfriends gathered every August to drink beer in the streets. . . . It was curious to think that this custom must seem as exotic in Perugia as Frederico Fellini's *La Strada* had seemed to me, at the Piccadilly Cinema in Manchester.

I don't remember the university at all, though it must have occupied a significant portion of the town. (Perugia was then a town, not the crowded city of today, infamous for the rape and murder of a young Englishwoman – a psychedelic horror beyond Uncle Jan's worst imagining.) At the housing office, Basia was given a mimeographed list of rooms, with many of them already lined out. The first place we investigated was on the third floor of a newish apartment building, downhill from the town center, where an American couple had a room to let, with use of the kitchen and a shelf in the refrigerator. He was writing his doctoral thesis on Perugino, while she was that 1950s institution, the housewife with a liberal arts degree. She introduced herself as Anne, and at Basia's mischievous prompting we settled that I was from New Hampshire and she and her husband from Indiana.

Basia's room had a splendid vista of orchards, shanties, and a stream where women were scrubbing laundry on a corrugated washboard such as Mom had used at the Caretaker's Cottage in East Alton. I leaned out the window and photographed everything. Then Basia peeled off a quantity of 1,000-lire bills as her first month's rent. We left Anne to count them – 10,000 lire, $16.67 – and went off on a passeggiata of our own.

We strolled around a fountain in the vast central plaza. We explored alleys with many steps, though not so many or so steep that they discouraged the Vespas, whose drivers negotiated the steps in a thoughtful manner with their feet out to the sides for balance. Sometimes a girl rode side-saddle behind the driver. She would smile at us, while he stared straight ahead, intent upon his manly balancing act. In these alleys, the shade was so deep that I actually felt a chill, and was glad to come out into the sun again.

Back at Basia's lodging after dark, we found that the hall lights were on a timer. We had to press a button at the top of each flight of stairs, then hurry along to press the next button before the lights went out, leaving us in the dark. We were giggling and a bit out of breath by the time we reached the apartment. Anne smiled fondly as we burst in, but the husband – I think his name was Greg – was working studiously at a desk, and like the Vespa drivers made a point of ignoring us. I followed Basia to her room, picked up my rucksack, and kissed her goodnight. Then I went off to unroll my sleeping bag in an apple orchard nearby. There was no question that I might spend the night in her room. Even if Greg and Anne had been agreeable, Basia wouldn't have invited me, for fear of branding herself a fallen woman. And Greg didn't look as though he were about to offer me a place on the couch.

And that's all I remember of the town where we parted. I would have guessed that I hitchhiked to Rome next morning, but Basia recalls that, like Faust, I lingered for a time:

I think you stayed a few days in Perugia to settle me in, and I did feel rather upset and lonely when you left.

Ah me. If only I'd known that at the time!

CHAPTER EIGHT

Some Miracle from God
1940-1941

"GLANCE ONLY AT A MAP of Soviet Russia!" cried Lenin, awed by the vastness of the country he had seized in 1917. In Europe alone, the workers' paradise sprawled across 2,123,600 square miles, a landmass larger than the Indian subcontinent. On the far side of the Ural Mountains, there was a territory three times again as great – "abysses of space," in Lenin's phrase, "which could contain dozens of large civilized states." His successor, the paranoid Man of Steel, would find a practical use for those abysses.

"The steppe rolls away on all sides like a sea," wrote Zoe Zajdlerowa of Kazakhstan. Irish born, having spent much of her adult life in Poland, she had the European's dread of unfathomable space. "Not a tree or a shrub breaks it verti-cally anywhere. There is almost no life. . . . The sun is an enemy; the habits of the native populations, unaccustomed to life between four walls, primitive and repellent beyond words."

Stalin had herded Kazakh nomads onto collective farms, made them speak Russian, and now obliged them to absorb tens of thousands of Poles, mostly city dwellers with no idea how to milk a cow or shear a sheep. The head man of the kolkhoz might be Kazakh or Russian, but whatever his nationality, he was more annoyed than pleased to have a dozen bewildered women and children quartered upon him. "He who does not work, neither shall he eat!" The rule applied to the farm itself, which had to grow enough food to feed its population plus a considerable tribute to the NKVD, which might seize the seed grain if it didn't meet its quota.

Life on the kolkhoz was an ordeal even for the young and healthy, working twelve and fourteen hours a day on thin gruel and a bit of bread. For children, the old, the sick, and the pregnant, it could be a death sentence. The Kazakhs resented the Poles and mocked their incompetence. Acts of kindness, such as Basia had experienced on her first night in Kazakhstan, were random and unpredictable: the same overseer who today brought you a gift of butter might tomorrow extort or steal your belongings. That, at least, was the recollection of the vast majority of the exiles. Many of them recalled being told upon their arrival: *"Privykniosh – pozhyviosh a nie privykniosh, podehniosh"* – get used to it and survive; otherwise you will die. This was intended, I think, as a bit of useful advice to those like Mama who had previously lived a life of privilege. At the kolkhoz, she had to transform herself into a peasant laborer:

At first she had to milk cows, and they were vicious. She was black and blue all over. The cows also kicked the pails and spilled the milk, so the management gave up on her and she was assigned to sheep dipping. The sheep however were as bad as the cows, and they kicked just as hard. She wasn't much good at that, either, so they finally assigned her to the kitchen. It was just about the best work you could get on the farm.

There were quite a few children. They were not very friendly, maybe because we gave ourselves airs, or perhaps the propaganda in Russia at that time was that Poles were enemies of the Russian people. They must have worked only short hours because most of the time they played in the fields around the farm. Lalka and I didn't work either. I don't know how this came about. Most of the stories I have read about Russia tell how children had to do hard and dangerous work at a very young age, weeding the fields in high summer with temperatures in the forties [100° F] on empty stomachs, or filling traps with poison during a mouse plague.

There were many Kazakhs working on the farm, and I enjoyed watching them. I liked their wise smiles and almond eyes with drooping eyelids. Sometimes of an evening, groups of Kazakhs would sit together eating semichki, *dried sunflower seeds. They would put a handful of seeds into their mouths, chew for a time, then spit out the husks onto their chins, slowly forming a long, black beard. It was a trick I tried to learn but failed.*

I also remember the huge expanse of the steppes and the millions of stars in the blue-black sky.

Mama was credited with a kopek or two for each pail of milk she delivered to the central vat, or for each ewe she sent through its dip of carbolic acid. For a day of this labor, or for twelve hours of making soup and washing pots in the collective kitchen, she might earn a ruble and a half – thirty cents. This was a pathetic sum on the free market, with prices like those that had ruined eastern Poland after the Russian invasion. As a worker, though, Mama could buy from the cooperative at lower prices, and she also received bread coupons according to her productivity, half a kilo of black bread if she were judged a second-class worker.

"The Russians brought us to Siberia," as one exile wrote of Kazakhstan; "they left us there like unwanted puppies and didn't concern themselves with what happened to us." Most of the Poles survived by selling off their belongings, unto the clothes on their backs. "Whenever I was in the market," wrote the same young woman, "I was always asked if I wanted to sell the dress I was wearing."

STALIN WAS PLEASED with the results of the April deportations. As the newspaper *Krasnaya Zviezda*, Red Star, reported on June 15, 1940: "All the most dangerous counter-revolutionaries from Western Ukraine have been arrested and ample evidence has been gathered against them." Basia treasures this description of herself, Lalka, Mama, Zbyszek, and the aunts. Counter-revolutionaries!

Still, one couldn't be too careful. A third wave of deportations was ordered for the end of June, when locomotives, boxcars, and the 13th Convoy Forces Security Division –

presumably including Lieutenant Klikow and his platoon, back from Kazakhstan – could again be assembled at Lwow and other Polish cities and towns. A majority of the June exiles were Jews. Many were urban residents; many were well educated; and some were Communist sympathizers who'd accompanied NKVD troopers to the homes of ethnic Poles, identified them, and helped transport them to the trains. No matter! They too were alien; they too might be counter-revolutionaries; they too must go. They were sent to the north and east of the Soviet Union, on journeys almost as cruel as those that had claimed thousands of lives in February. Instead of freezing to death along the way, they perished from thirst and heat stroke and suffocation, in metal-roofed boxcars under the July sun.

See how luck determines whether we live or die! For Basia to be exiled to Kazakhstan in April was a terrible thing. But to be sent to Archangelesk in February, or to Siberia in July, was worse.

Meanwhile, Hitler and Stalin continued to sweep new nationalities into their separate but similar hells. My brother and I followed their conquests through the pages of *Life* magazine. We were, as I have said, especially taken with the brave resistance of the Finns, who had battled the Russians to a draw, losing a tenth of their country but saving the rest.

In April 1940, while New Hampshire thawed from a particularly hard winter, the Germans seized Denmark and Norway. In May they blitzed through Holland, Belgium, and France, culminating in the fabled evacuation of British, French, and Polish soldiers at Dunkirk. In June, the Red Army marched into Latvia, Lithuania, and Estonia. Thus Stalin took back most of the land that Lenin had been forced to disgorge to Germany in 1917 and to the Polish Republic in 1921.

The Battle of Britain now began. It was an air war for the most part, German bombers pitted against Royal Air

Force fighter planes. The latter included nine squadrons composed mostly of Polish pilots, with 307 Squadron bearing the heraldic name "City of Lvov," as the English spelled Basia's home town. The Poles were regarded as especially effective and ruthless in aerial combat, credited with shooting down 600 German aircraft.

Hitler's war effort was fueled in part by his improbable friend in Moscow. Russia delivered 6,400,000 barrels of oil to Germany (much of it from Poland) along with 1,600,000 tons of grain, 140,000 tons of manganese ore, and foodstuffs, cattle, and timber. In return, Germany supplied weapons, industrial machinery, generators, and locomotives to the Soviet Union.

Three years later, those same Deutsche Reichsbahn locomotives would carry 90,000 German soldiers, captured at Stalingrad, to slave labor in Siberia.

ABOUT THIS TIME, we left East Alton and moved west along Lake Winnipesaukee to the town of Gilford. Far from being a time of terror and loss, as it was for Basia's family and much of Europe, 1940 for us was the beginning of a return to working-class respectability: we graduated from penury to merely being poor. The worst time for us had been the mid-1930s, when Dad was felled by tuberculosis, the Irishman's disease. He spent three years in the sanatorium at Glencliff, in the New Hampshire mountains, while Mom "went on Relief," as welfare was called. She had a credit at the grocery store, and every second Thursday a truck came to our door with flour, raisins, prunes, and dried peas. Americans ate a lot of pea soup during the Great Depression, to the point where it became an expression of disgust among the boys at Alton Central School. A slip on the ice was "*pea soup!*" So was a difficult test.

Like the Fords, the American economy was emerging from the Depression, thanks to the warplanes, tanks, and guns that were ordered first by Finland, then by Belgium,

Holland, and France, and now by Britain, as each in turn armed itself against the greatest war machine the world had ever seen. Poland's agony was America's windfall! European money washed through the United States, allowing the newly wealthy to pay a caretaker $30 or even $35 a week. Mrs. Damon didn't care to match those sums, so we moved to a rented house while Dad built a new Caretaker's Cottage for Mr. Manning, who was developing a summer estate in Lakeport.

These houses – the interim one in Gilford and the new one in Lakeport – boasted electricity and running water, hence were a great step up from life in East Alton. The water was cold, to be sure, and we still bathed only on Saturday evening, from a basin filled with water from the kettle on the Glenwood range. Mom called this a "sponge bath," though we didn't own a sponge.

Dad bought a refrigerator, an RCA console radio, and a Kenmore washing machine, all secondhand but more or less serviceable. Our milk would stay fresh; Joe and I could listen to "Captain Midnight" at five o'clock on weekday afternoons; and Mom no longer had to bend over a scrub board in the sink. Nor did she have to wring out the water afterward: the washing machine had rollers for that. They were turned by hand, but the washing itself was done by an electric motor. It sat on a little platform beneath the tub and powered the agitator by a V-belt, meanwhile dripping oily water upon the kitchen floor.

Dad was careless of flaws like the oil leak, and careless too of school calendars and district boundaries. Thus we moved from Alton to Gilford while classes were in progress, instead of waiting for summer; and by housing us in Gilford while he built the new cottage in Lakeport, he obliged Joe and me to change schools again the following year.

Dad built that cottage entire, with the help of a farmer named Clarence Dame – framed it, enclosed it, wired it, roofed it, and painted it, meanwhile doing the maintenance on the Manning estate. He was very clever with his hands, like most men reared on a farm. I remember him framing a door for Mr. Manning's dining room. Dad drove two nails into the bottom of a wide board, loosely tied a string between them, and drew an elegant curve with a pencil pressed against the string. Not until I studied geometry in high school did I understand that this was half an ellipse, with the nails as its foci and the string as a constant distance from the foci to any point on the outside curve.

The great thing about being a kid is that this weird existence – Alton to Gilford to Lakeport, three schools in as many years – seemed perfectly natural, as did the poverty to which Dad's poor health and itinerant life consigned us. (His bout with TB had left him with chronic asthma, which that summer had him taken off to the hospital in a hearse, since the ambulance was otherwise occupied.) Just about everyone we knew was poor. Our fathers cut our hair and soled our shoes; our mothers put soap scraps in a bottle and added water, which we used to wash our hands at the kitchen sink. Most of my friends bathed once a week, and most of us qualified for free or half-price lunches in the cafeteria of the Lakeport school. There was no paperwork for those lunches: they were entirely at the teacher's discretion. I was in the third grade by this time, taught by a tall lady named Miss Agrafiotis. She adored me because I always had the right answer, so I got my meal ticket at no cost, whereas Joe paid a nickel for his. This was my first hint that life might reward me for knowing the answers.

In little more than a year, my ambition had cycled through a remarkable evolution, from Polish cavalryman to Finnish ski trooper to (I blush to say it!) German tanker to Royal Air Force pilot. I mailed a quarter and the seal from an Ovaltine can to the producers of the Captain Midnight radio drama, and in time received a cardboard instrument panel that I unfolded and tacked to the bureau in our bedroom. Here I sat for hours with an old broom handle for a control stick, diving and jinking, shooting down Messer-schmitts, Stukas, and Heinkels.

BASIA TOO WAS GETTING ALONG with her life, and even enjoying it after a fashion:

The War for me wasn't a calamity. I remember being hungry, very hungry in Russia – and very cold! – but I was too young to imagine a dismal future.

That's the secret, isn't it? Too young to imagine a dismal future! If I had been transformed into one of my heroes – calvalryman, ski trooper, tanker, fighter pilot – I wouldn't have found the life as happy as in my seven-year-old daydreams, rat-ta-ta-tat! As Basia writes:

I remember the War as a series of adventures. Being hungry and cold and having chilblains cannot be called a tragedy. The chilblains hurt and itched. So did the lice! On the collective farm, everyone was engaged nonstop in louse hunting. You would see people jerk, scratch, produce a louse, squeeze it between their thumbs, wipe their hands on their clothes, and go for another one. Mama boiled onion skins from the kitchen and rubbed our hair with them, and after a while rinsed it with the onion water. She was convinced that the onions would get rid of the lice. But all the treatments failed, even having our hair cut or rubbed with petrol.

They lived in a barrack, with the girls running wild from dawn to dusk. At some point, they were sent to school, but that lasted only two days. When Mama learned that her daughters were being taught to parrot hymns to *Batko* Stalin, Daddy Stalin, she put a stop to their education. Instead, she read to them each evening from the book she'd brought from home:

I could read a little before we were deported, but I learned properly on the copy of Pan Tadeusz *that Mama took with her to Kazakhstan. And she probably took it because it was my father's favorite book, and he used to read it to her. So, in a way, it is thanks to my father that I know one of the most beautiful books in the Polish language.*

Alas, I can't read Polish, and the translations I have seen are uniformly awful. But the poem is indeed a marvel, if only because the very first word is "Litwo!" – Lithuania! So the epic is actually about Poles in exile, living under Russian rule. Even though Lithuania was a century and a half removed from Polish governance, and though the poem's author never actually lived in Mama's Poland, her eyes must have clouded with tears when she read:

> Now bear my sorrowing heart home
> To the wooded hills and green meadows
> On the banks of the blue River Niemen.

There's a Good Russian in the story. After a brawl between his troops and the Polish gentry, Captain Rykov expresses his sorrow that the Tsar had sent him to meddle in the affairs of his neighbors:

> What's our business with Poland?
> Russia for the Russians,
> Poland for the Poles!
> But the Tsar doesn't see it that way.

Even less did Daddy Stalin see it that way.

There was a novel, too. *Potop*, the Deluge, deals with an even earlier period of the Polish-Lithuanian Commonwealth. The "deluge" was a Swedish rampage in the 17th Century, a catastrophe that killed one-fourth of the population. Like great novelists through history, Henryk Sienkiewicz personalized the butchery by mingling it with the love story of a handsome rascal named Andrzej and a beautiful maid named Olenka, who through confusions and misunderstandings and bloody happenings are kept apart until the closing pages. Andrzej became Basia's hero, and when she grew sleepy she'd write the latest page number on the barrack wall, for fear she'd fall asleep and Lalka would coax Mama into continuing the story.

Basia doesn't remember how long they were trapped on the collective farm – a few months, perhaps longer. Then the redoubtable Aunt Krysia tracked them down and persuaded the NKVD to let them move into the village of Georgievka, where the aunts and young Zbyszek had managed to settle. Georgievka boasted a hospital, with a Tatar doctor but almost no medicine. It also boasted a pharmacy managed by a large Russian woman named Anna Pavlovna, for whom Aunt Nuna swept and cleaned, and who now hired Mama to wait on customers. Given the level of service in Soviet Russia, I find it hard to believe that this was strictly necessary; more likely, Anna Pavlovna put Mama on the payroll out of the goodness of her heart. She also supplied the sisters with cotton wool, an almost unavailable necessity in the early months of exile, before hard work and scanty food stopped a woman's monthly bleeding. And bars of soap – gifts as precious as gold. Probably Comrade Pavlovna was herself an exile, deported to Kazakhstan for some real or fancied offense. And in the end she annoyed the Bluecaps so much with her generosity to the Poles that she was sent to a labor camp.

Most nights, Mama and Aunt Nuna slept at the pharmacy. They also took their meals there, thus providing more food for Krysia and the girls. This was also a wise arrangement in the winter, when one could become hopelessly lost a few feet from home in a *buran*, a wind-driven snowstorm that left drifts higher than a man's head.

Like the other Poles, Mama and her sisters supplemented their earnings by selling bits and pieces of their clothing. Since there was so little in Soviet Russia, virtually anything could be sold, even rags. "The Poles were perceived as being very wealthy because of the quality of their belongings," writes Halik Kochanski. "A plain shirt or bed sheets were rare commodities costing more than a month's wages. . . ." Lalka's clothes were passed down to Basia, just as I inherited shoes, shirts, and trousers that were too small for Joe. But when Basia outgrew something, it was sold to the highest bidder:

One day Aunt Krysia sent us to the market to sell some old clothes. It was a fiasco, because Lalka fainted. Like Mama in similar circumstances, I just stood there while the people around us revived Lalka and gathered the clothes, giving them all to me. I had to carry them back by myself because every time I told Lalka she should carry some, she threatened to faint again. I told Aunt Krysia that I would never, never again go to the market with Lalka. But I think she regretted the idea anyway. Our things could have so easily been stolen. Stealing was just as widespread in Kazkhstan as catching lice. People were poor and hungry and you stole from the poor because there were no rich people around.

Again I find myself wondering if there was something magical in these little girls, if people shopping for rags would nevertheless return everything Lalka had dropped.

I think Kazakhstan was worse for Lalka. She was weaker than me, often sick, but above all she was older. Those couple of years made a huge difference. She was much more aware of the situation. She was growing out of her clothes, and she probably knew the jewelry brought from Poland by Mama and the aunts was slowly disappearing. And, as she told me much later, all the time in Russia she was scared that "they" would take Mama away, and that she would disappear like our father.

And for Mama, Kazakhstan must have been pure Hell.

THE SISTERS RENTED a *lepianka*, a hut with mud walls and a thatched roof, a ten-minute walk from the pharmacy and the market. Because clay was rare in Kazakhstan, the walls were laid up from *kiziak* – the droppings of cows, sheep, or camels – mixed with earth and straw, cut into blocks, and dried in the sun. These bricks were stacked to head height for a wall; poles and branches were laid across for a roof; and the building was more or less waterproofed with a coating of fresh kiziak. "These huts would only last two or three years before needing to be rebuilt," as one observer writes. "They were breeding grounds for every type of insect and teemed with earwigs, woodlice, fleas, bedbugs and, of course, the ever-present lice."

The lepianka consisted of one small room containing two mattresses, a window, and a kitchen partitioned off from the living space, along with a shed to store dry cow pats to be burned for cooking and heat. There were four or five such huts in a rough semi-circle, and in the center another containing a pit toilet.

There was a tiny, skinny dog in the neighborhood, and I sometimes smuggled some food to him. One day I saw boys beating him up, so I bribed them with Aunt Krysia's powder compact (thankfully, not the rouge compact with the gold in it) to stop torturing him. Later I heard shouting and laughter and when I went out to have a look, the boys were trying to crucify the little thing. They were holding him and hammering a nail into his paw. I didn't want to let them see me cry so I spat at them and went in.

Basia's cousin, the fourteen-year-old Zbyszek, worked several days a week on a collective farm nearby, sleeping and eating there, and occasionally stealing a bag of flour or sack of potatoes for the lepianka. At one point he went off to work on a gang building a road "to China." This was a typical Five Year Plan project to connect Kazakhstan with Xinjiang province and Mongolia, with each kolkhoz supplying a work crew to build a section. As was customary in the workers' paradise, the quotas were impossible to meet and the workers spent much of their time faking the progress they'd made.

Zbyszek was young, strong, and smart. He was a molodec – a "well done!" sort of chap. He was an expert at stealing eggs from an old woman living nearby who kept a couple of hens, and he even initiated Lalka into the business. I was too small.

Aunt Krysia stayed in the lepianka with us, probably because with her charm and ingenuity she was best equipped to do the shopping, a very difficult chore when there was little money and few goods.

In the summer, Lalka and I would go into the fields with a sack and a bucket to collect kiziak. The fresh cow pats went into the bucket, the dry ones into the sack. The raw stuff would be mixed with whitewash and used as a disinfectant for painting walls inside the house, to kill the insects. The dry pats were used for fuel. Often we came back empty-handed. Many children were doing the same thing, and you had to have sharp elbows and fast feet to win out. And our hands were sore after handling raw kiziak.

We kept a piglet in the shed for a while, which Aunt Krysia had managed to buy. Lalka and I looked after it and grew very fond of it, despite the fact that it ate my Shirley Temple doll I'd brought from Poland.

Then we heard the piglet was going to be killed. Mama and Aunt Nuna came home to take part in the killing, and Zbyszek was also there. Lalka and I were told to fetch water from the well, but we stayed in the outer room and listened. The piglet squealed and squealed, until Zbyszek hit it on the head with a hammer. Lalka and I sobbed. When Mama and the aunts came out of the kitchen after the killing, they had tears running down their faces, but they also had a triumphant look. We hated them, but we ate the pork nevertheless.

And once we kept an eaglet in the shed. We fed it with worms, flies, insects, and a mouse or two when we managed to get them. Finally its wings outgrew the shed, and although it was still very young, we had to let it go. I hope it was strong enough to be independent and had a happier fate in the wild than our unfortunate piglet.

THAT WINTER WAS HARD, though perhaps less awful than if they had been out on the steppe, on the collective farm. Temperatures in Kazakhstan can rise to 108° F in summer and plunge to 46° below zero in winter. And the wind blows all day, every day. In the lepianka, Mama and her sisters fashioned a Christmas tree from a twig. December 25, 1940, fell on a Tuesday – a workday like any other. But the exiled Poles, wherever they were, managed to create a simulacrum of Christmas decorations, to sing carols, and to pray.

There was plenty of snow in Georgievka, and Aunt Krysia who was strong on hygiene made us take off our clothes – Lalka and me – and go out and take a bath. She would rub us with snow, we would jump and wriggle and stump and squeal, but after a few minutes it was quite nice and warm. Altogether infinitely better than going to the bania *– the public bath – with the older women with their gray, skeletal bodies, protruding bellies, and breasts hanging down to their knees.*

If the snow lay too long against the lepianka, the mud bricks would soften, so as soon as it was light, Lalka and I had to go out and start clearing the snow away. And the snow kept coming. So we worked practically the whole day, on and off, until it was dark. By the time spring came there was a sort of snow tunnel around the lepianka.

Mama's greatest feat, or at least the one she talked about with greatest pride, was to steal a Communist flag. She dyed it with Anna Pavlovna's help, and made it into two fufayki, *anoraks lined with cotton wool, for Lalka and me to wear that winter.*

And oh, I remember the joy when Aunt Krysia came nearly to the bottom of her rouge compact and discovered the gold coins her husband Adam had put there! They kept us in food for months.

As for the Russians in Georgievka, I was not interested

in them, compared to the Kazakhs on the collective farm. The Russians looked like us; they were not particularly nasty or nice. The only thing remarkable about them was their spitting, at least that's what I thought. They could express a range of emotions, especially when accompanied by appropriate gestures. You might spit just because you needed to, you might spit in anger and contempt, or in merriment. I tried to imitate them but, as with the sunflower seeds, I failed. I don't think it was a lack of talent. You need privacy if you want to learn how to spit, and I did not have any. The other children would laugh at my efforts, and Lalka was always there.

As part of the girls' education, Mama wrote down the hit songs she remembered from hearing them on the radio and on the streets of Lwow before the War. And she sang to them, the pop songs, ballads, and arias from opera:

Mama had a lovely pure soprano. Aunt Krysia was a dramatic soprano, and Aunt Nuna an alto. It was a pleasure listening to the three of them singing together. I still remember and enjoy the Polish prewar hit songs, and the Russian and Yiddish songs that Mama and the aunts sang around the lepianka – Ochi Chernye, *a love song, and* Bublichki, *about a peddler trying to sell the last of his bagels before nightfall.*

And I remember Mama singing Szumia Jodly *– How the Fir Trees Sigh – from the opera by Stanislaw Moniuszko, even though it was a tenor role.*

We were discouraged from learning Russian, though, which was a great pity.

Basia did pick up a serviceable exile's vocabulary, sufficient to deal with the Russian and Kazakh children in the neighborhood and in the fields, and to bargain with the women in the market.

And she learned to write, in a very respectable cursive hand. If I close my eyes, I can see her: a fierce child with blonde plaits, bent over a rough table in that mud hut in

Georgievka. (I am tempted to write "darling girl," but Basia in the spring of 1941 would have been skinny and smudged, with nits in her hair.) She has a pen, an astonishing luxury in Kazakhstan. She has ink! And she has crayons or colored pencils – green, red, and yellow – with which to draw wildflowers to bracket her poem.

With the pen she writes: *Kochana Mamusiu*, Dearest Mummy! The letters are as much drawn as handwritten: *Zycze Ci Mamus – Bys nie chorowala – Bys zowsze us-miech – Na ustach miala – I zeby cos sie stalo – Jakis cud od Boga – Bysmy wracaly – Do naszego Lwowa.* Which is to say:

Dearest Mummy!
I wish that you
Will never be sick,
That you always have a smile
On your lips,
And that something will happen,
Some miracle from God,
So we may go home
To our Lwow.

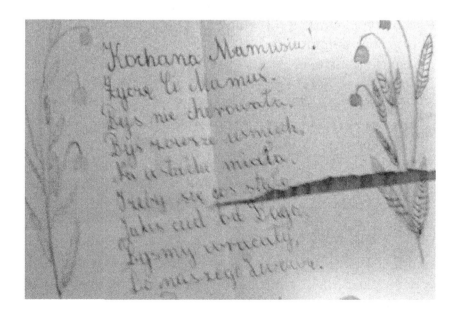

She signs it at the lower left and adds the place and the date: Georgievka, 24 May 1941.

She is seven years old! She has spent a grand total of three days in a schoolroom! I couldn't have composed such an elegy at that age, nor penned it so neatly. As for the sentiments, I'm not sure I could compose such a heart-breaking message now, with all my tired old skill. There is fear in the poem: if Mama's health should fail, what will happen to Basia? There is an understanding that happiness is both necessary and fragile, and above all that the Deszberg women need a miracle to save them.

IF BASIA MEANT HER POEM as a prayer, it was answered by an improbable deity: Adolf Hitler in Berlin. Four weeks after she wrote it, he sent his forces crashing against the Red Army across a front of 1,800 miles. The date was June 22, 1941. If the world had been astonished by the speed and ferocity of Germany's invasion of Poland, Operation Barbarossa was blitz to the third or fourth power – the largest military operation in the history of the world, and arguably the one with the most momentous consequences. The invasion involved 4,500,000 men, mostly German but including sizable contingents from Austria, Romania, Hungary, Czechoslovakia, Italy, Spain, and (on the northern flank, hoping to regain the land lost in the Winter War) Finland.

"In the space of two months," Aleksandr Solzhenitsyn wrote of the Russian debacle, "we abandoned very nearly one-third of our population to the enemy – including all those incompletely destroyed families [their menfolk sent to the Gulag]; including camps with several thousand inmates, who scattered as soon as their guards ran for it; including prisons in the Ukraine and the Baltic States, where smoke still hung in the air after the mass shooting of political prisoners."

One such jail was Brygidki on Kazimierzowska Street in Lwow. The 1st Mountain Division was again the spearhead, supported this time by a battalion of Ukrainian fascists. They were greeted by a stench from the cells and torture rooms of Brygidki, where 1,500 inmates had been murdered by the guards before they bolted. The cleanup was tasked to Jews who had unwisely remained in the city they hoped would be a refuge.

Not all the Bluecaps made it to safety. The 13th Convoy Forces Security Division, which had escorted hundreds of thousand of Poles into exile, was among the units thrown into the defense of Kiev, where *forty-three* Red Army divisions were destroyed in the summer of 1941. Lieutenant Klikow, the commander of Basia's deportation train, would have been one of 600,000 Red Army troops killed or captured in that one stupendous battle. Among the few who escaped the encirclement was the roly-poly Nikita Khrushchev, former political commissar at Lwow and future dictator of the Soviet Union.

Kiev was only one of many such disasters. By the end of 1941, Russian casualties would amount to seven million men. Nearly half were prisoners, penned in barbed wire compounds where two-thirds would die of starvation, disease, and hypothermia. Partly this was the result of German racism: in the demonology of the Third Reich, Slavs were little more valued than Jews. (Indeed, the first inmates to be systematically gassed in the new concentration camp at Auschwitz, near Warsaw, were Russian prisoners of war, not Jews.) And partly it was simple logistics: who could possibly care for so many prisoners? The U.S. Army ground forces, at their height in the Second World War, numbered only 2,753,500 men. Imagine the entire fighting force of the United States, penned in a barbed-wire enclosure!

But mostly it was a reflection of a combat as huge and as savage as any ever waged in the bloody history of mankind.

CHAPTER NINE

We Live in the Castle
1955

AFTER LEAVING PERUGIA, I hitchhiked to Rome and made the obligatory visits to the Sistine Chapel (postcard to Mom) and the Colosseum (postcard to Joe, reporting that it was next to a shantytown and swarming with cats). I also donated an aluminum coin to the Trevi Fountain. After three days of this, I bought a ticket to Venice, in a train so crowded I had to surrender my rucksack before squeezing aboard. The earlier arrivals passed it from hand to hand, to be stacked with other luggage in the toilet, while I stood like a vertical sardine in the vestibule.

Venice was . . . well, *adorable*, just as I'd hoped. Among its virtues – canals, gondolas, fishermen mending their nets – I found a vendor in the Piazza San Marco selling a pair of earrings that, to my eye, exactly matched Basia's description of her ideal. They were silver with a clip fastener and a dangling stone of lapis lazuli, just the color of Basia's eyes. (I did not then know about cornflowers.) Over the course of two days, I drove the price down from 5,000 to 1,500 lire, or $2.50 at the then-rate of exchange. Could Aunt Krysia have done better? I put them in an envelope with some padding and a pretty note. Alas, Italy's postal workers being what they were, my little tribute never reached Perugia.

I hitchhiked to Milano, took a tour of La Scala (postcard to Basia, regretting that *Rigoletto* wasn't on offer), and boarded a train to Paris. I found no illuminated map at Gare de Lyon. To make the connection to Calais, I had to challenge a man with SNCF on his cap: "London?" I asked. "*Choo choo?*"

Manchester seemed a dreary place without Basia, all its possibilities tapped out. Gordon Olson turned up, one night

141

in May, tossing a pebble against Ian Fellowes's window and sending him to wake me. Turning Mr. Olson's check into sterling was a boon to me as well as to Gordon, for the bank put the money in a dollar account.

I then rearranged my future. Unlike the earrings, my letters to Basia did get through, and we agreed to meet in Perugia at the end of June. I canceled my booking to Montreal and made a new one for September, on *RMS Brittanic* to New York. I also wrote my draft board to explain that I'd been unavoidably detained by the press of my studies, but would be sure to present myself for my U.S. Army physical in October. My last letter from Basia told how she'd spilled from a bicycle in one of Perugia's steep alleys, landing first on the steps and then in the hospital. In consequence, just as I had done with Modern European History, she'd stopped going to class. I sent a jocular telegram which, like the earrings, vanished into the black hole of the Italian postal service.

I emptied my bank accounts, taking Senator Fulbright's blocked sterling as one-pound notes, eighty of them, to carry me through a summer on the Continent; and turning Gordon's $100 into traveler's checks to get me home to New Hampshire in September. I stowed the traveler's checks, my typewriter, twenty or thirty Penguin paperbacks, and 140 pages of typescript into my suitcase, along with my Harris tweed jacket and University scarf. I gave my winter coat to Ian Fellowes, who had long admired it. I said goodbye to the gang at Caf and took the train to London, where I checked the suitcase at Euston Station. From there my journey was a straight line to Victoria Station, Dover Marine, *Invicta*, Calais, Gare du Nord, Gare de Lyon, and the night train to Florence.

To my shame, I didn't visit Mama in North Ealing, coming or going. I could at least have sent her a photo of Basia's room!

I didn't sleep much on the journey. The compartment

was jammed, four of us on one side and four facing us, shoulder to shoulder and knee to knee. To doze was to slump upon a neighbor and get elbowed in return. (This gave me a whole new slant on Uncle Jan's fear of letting his niece travel unescorted to Italy.) Every hour or two I got up, paced the corridor, and put my head out the window in defiance of the placard: *Nicht hinauslehnen! Defense de se pencher en dehors! E pericoloso sporgersi!* After midnight we crossed into Switzerland, and two fierce customs officers marched through the carriages, demanding passports and inquiring about cigarettes and whiskey. When daylight came, we rattled over breathlessly tall trestles, through tunnels, and down to Italy. "*Niente da dichiarare,*" I told the Italian official in his splendid uniform, thrilled at my mastery of his language. So many syllables, so many vowels! *Nee-AYN-tay dah DEE-kee-ah-RAH-ray*: nothing to declare!

Next we rattled along the rocky spine of the Appenines. I was entranced by the narrow hilltops, most of them flattened for a vegetable garden. I pitied the farmers who climbed those hills every morning to cultivate their crops, and even more I pitied the soldiers who'd marched up and down them in the winter of 1944-1945. What an awful place to fight a war!

At two o'clock in the afternoon, I emerged somewhat shaken into Stazione Centrale at Florence. I fueled myself with a bowl of spaghetti at the stand-up restaurant, then stepped out into the heat and glare of a summer afternoon. I walked across the Ponte Vecchio, held up my open palm, and managed to reach Perugia before nightfall, to find Basia . . . gone!

"She went off to Capri with Laetitia," said Anne, the landlady. "They'll be back any day now." She smiled at me – grinned, I should say. "Well, *Dan,*" she said, investing my name with great meaning. "Basia told us all about you!"

Really? *All?*

I stayed to chat, in hopes of learning more, and perhaps of being invited to use Basia's room in her absence. Alas, all I got was a cup of coffee and the information that, like her husband, Anne had majored in art history. They married after graduation, then she worked as a typist while he went to graduate school. This was a familiar scenario. My best friends at the University of New Hampshire were in a like situation, Priscilla working as an editor in the publications office while Jim studied Milton, though she was a far better scholar than he.

I unrolled my sleeping bag in the familiar apple orchard, downhill from the apartment house. I slept for ten hours: I'd been traveling, by this time, for the better part of two days. The dew was heavy, and my sleeping bag was soaked in the morning. I stowed it in my pack regardless, and hitchhiked to the east coast to visit the improbably tiny republic of San Marino. I spent the nights at Rimini on the Adriatic. The hostel was a cement-block rectangle like the one in Paris, though freshly whitewashed. A German family arrived shortly after I did – mother, father, and two kids – and dragged mattresses to the flat roof, sleeping there instead of the gender-specific dormitories. (During the day, I used the roof to dry my sleeping bag from its night in the apple orchard.) I taught *Vati*, as the family called him, the English words for hot and cold, and he gave me their German equivalents, against the time when I traveled north. I sent postcards of San Marino, swam in the Adriatic, and walked the long, empty beach, feeling rather sorry for myself. As I'd earlier discovered in Rome and Venice, traveling alone was not nearly so much fun as with Basia.

No doubt I also composed some paragraphs for the novel I was writing at the time. I'd abandoned the story that had occupied my winter mornings, shivering at my typewriter in a bathrobe and fingerless gloves. But the great thing about Stephen Faust was his adaptability. He fit most anywhere, whether debating at the Union, hitchhiking to

Italy, or yearning for a girl who'd promised to meet him but had instead flitted off to Capri: La donna è mobile!

Three days later I was back in Perugia, and – yes! – Basia had returned from the south. The plan, she told me, was to hitchhike to Lerici on the coast, to live in a castle and swim in the Mediterranean. "I have a swimsuit from Capri," she said, "and Laetitia and Giorgio will come with us!" I ought to have been disappointed to find our team doubled in size, but I don't think I was. Youth is a time of winging it, of playing the music of life by ear.

When I first sat down to write about Lerici, I believed that Laetitia too was a student at the *Università per Stranieri*, but evidently not. My brother Joe died last year, bequeathing me a footlocker of mementos from the 1950s. Among them are photographs of Lerici with my captions taped to the back, to accompany an article I'd tried to sell to *Mademoiselle*, at that time one of the most "literary" of American magazines. (I eventually sold an expurgated version to *Boys' Life*.) Thus I find that 1955 was Laetitia's fourth year on the road. God knows how she paid for it! Thieving, probably. Not drugs or prostitution, I'm pretty sure, and she certainly wasn't independently wealthy. These were questions that didn't occur to me at the time. Laetitia was French, heavyset and handsome, with ripe lips, and I found her attractive enough.

As for Giorgio, he was Italian, and he attended the 14th Century *Università degli Studi*, also located in Perugia. He was thin and effeminate, with a triangular face – quite handsome, actually, as I see from those photographs – and Basia introduced him as a *marchese*. I find that a marquis ranks below a duke and above a count, which seems rather elevated company for a university town on a hilltop in Umbria. But Giorgio had an engraved business card to support his claim of nobility, and it actually did bear a coat-of-arms.

No matter! We were young, we were foreigners, and if Giorgio wanted to rank just below Prince Amadeo, Duke of

Aosta and claimant to the Italian throne, we were happy to believe. Supposedly his family had a palazzo in Rome. In Perugia, though, he lived in a *primo piano* flat, where he arranged for me to spend the night in the spare room. Two large ladies presided over the establishment, whom at the time I took for his mother and aunt. Next day Basia explained that Giorgio was only a boarder there, and that I should have left a hundred lire on the bureau to pay for the laundry! And now she adds:

I met him in Perugia, and we became such good friends that people thought I had converted him. Perugia was a small place then. We went to the cinema to see "Madama Butterfly." I always cry at Butterfly's great aria, so Georgio put his arm around me, to comfort me. It was all over Perugia the next day that we were a couple.

Anyway he did maintain that he was a marchese, and he decided I should be a duchess, because then I would be more welcome when we went to visit his family in Rome. Well, I was as much of a duchess as he was a marchese, I think, and we never did go to Rome. I am afraid I did not convert him, either.

He went to Confession every week, never got absolution, and was terribly mortified.

IN THE MORNING WE SET OUT for Lerici, Basia and I in the vanguard. (A band of four hitchhikers stood very little chance of getting a ride.) That gave us time to renew our friendship, and for me to fall in love all over again.

For Basia was transformed. She was a blonde! She wore earrings! (Not mine, alas.) And she had acquired two wide, intricate silver bracelets. But just as in Caf she'd defined female beauty to me, and it mattered not at all what she was wearing or how she wore it, so in Italy I was entirely content to shift my adoration to this blonde with earrings and bracelets.

I told her how I'd found the pair in Venice, bargained

for them, and mailed them to her. "Oh!" said Basia. "I wish I'd known. It would have made a difference!" I pondered that while we walked through Florence and took the opportunity to visit the Uffizi. (Yes, ye tourists of the 21st Century: we walked up to the door, smiled brightly, and were admitted. No reservations, no payment, and indeed I don't think there were any tickets.) What difference could my gift have made in Basia's life? Might it have protected her from whoever had given her the earrings she was wearing now? I decided it was better not to ask.

Basia had acquired a particular interest in Piero della Francesca, inspired by a professor at Perugia. "He would come wheezing down the corridor," she said, her face alight. "And when he arrived there would be silence, absolute silence. And the way he talked about art – magnificent!" I felt a twinge of jealousy toward the asthmatic professor who'd put that glow on my sweetheart's face.

She marched me to Gallery Seven and the twin portraits of the Duke and Duchess of Urbino. (Like Prince Amadeo, the duke would have outranked Giorgio at a dinner party, though just barely.) She talked of perspective, and how the background continued across the two portraits, and how they actually made a single painting as the Duke and Duchess gazed at one another, past the frames and through the centuries. "And the landscape goes on into infinity!"

I tried to share her pleasure, but the Duchess seemed a frump compared to the girl I was with, and the Duke had clearly lost a fight or two in his youth. But Basia admired even the nose with its ninety-degree bend, for she'd broken hers in that bicycle accident. She showed me the scar. I yearned to kiss the tiny white mark, but refrained out of respect for the guard in his glorious uniform. He'd had his eye on us (or perhaps only on Basia) since we entered the gallery. The Italians were great ones for holding hands – even the men held hands! – but they didn't kiss in public.

We reclaimed our rucksacks and got on the road to Pisa

and the coast. While we waited for a ride, I turned the conversation to her landlady, who'd learned *all* about me from Basia. Sure enough, it seemed that Anne had teased out the details of our romps in Les Abrets and Pontedera, kissing and cuddling, bed and breakfast. Blessed woman, she'd told Basia that she ought to have seized the opportunity to lose her virginity between clean sheets, with a trustworthy young man with a hard-on . . . not that Basia referred to the erection as such. "I thought that was your belt buckle!" she said, as merry as when luring Americans into comparing home states. Nor did she say "trustworthy." I'm guessing that it was taken for granted, and that Anne did not go into the deeper and less comfortable truth, that it is never a good idea for a young woman to place her trust in a young man with a hard-on.

Anne also supplied the bottle that turned Basia's hair the color of sunlight, and encouraged her to wear clothes more modish than the duffle coat and black trousers from Manchester. Thus the loose-necked green top Basia was wearing today, and the gray trousers that ended fashionably at mid-calf. She'd had her outfit made to order during her stay on Capri.

"When we arrived, my eyes were still purple from the accident," she said. "So I wore sunglasses and a hat down low on my forehead. Greta Garbo was also staying there, and she also wore sunglasses and a hat. So when people *looked* at me, you know, I would say: 'I vant to be alone!'"

This was a line from *Grand Hotel*, which we'd seen at the Piccadilly Cinema in Manchester. When I watch the film today, I get quite a pang. Except for her plucked eyebrows, Garbo does indeed resemble the young Polish girl of 1955, even to the light accent.

"We thought that was hilarious," Basia said. "We thought everything was hilarious, or interesting or beautiful. Laetitia is great fun."

As with the professor, I felt a twinge of jealousy. Was I

great fun? Probably not. The disadvantage of being in love is that it makes us desperately serious. Laetitia and the professor could put on their little acts for Basia's entertainment, while I wanted something from her: I wanted her to love me in return.

Oh, and her eyes! They'd entirely recovered from their battering. They'd picked up a hint of green, in fact, from the top she was wearing, so that under the hot Italian sun they seemed – what? – *cerulean!*

NOW BASIA TELLS ME a sad story, which I shall insert here, because surely it was on her mind at the time, and because it goes to show how little I really knew about her life:

In April, just before our trip to Italy, Uncle Jan's wife was taken to hospital and diagnosed with cancer of the liver. When the ambulance came to take her, I was left with baby Anna having her nappies changed and Jacek on the pot. Aunt Jadzia did come back from hospital that time, but while I was in Perugia she died.

She never mentioned it at the time, not at Manchester nor on the road to Italy, nor as we hitchhiked to Lerici.

TOWARD FOUR O'CLOCK we reached the Mediterranean and hiked down to the sea-washed harbor of Lerici. The castle towered over the village, a splendid pile of stone, big-shouldered and blocky, high on a cliff over the Gulf of Poets. To seaward, below the castle, a breakwater projected into the bay. This provided a quiet mooring for Lerici's fishermen, their boats tied up in neat rows, facing the village and its promenade. My YHA guidebook told us that the castle was built in stages from 1152 to 1555. The stone masons who finished the job would have been the thirteenth generation on the job. Think of that!

The castle guarded the bay that led up to La Spezia, though a 12th Century cannon could hardly have lofted a ball to the opposite shore, the island of Palmaria, smoky now in the afternoon haze. The castle was shaped like a pentagon, topped with a pentagonal tower – the keep – that widened at the top, the better, no doubt, to pour boiling oil upon besiegers. We had a stiff climb to the entrance, followed by flights of interior stone steps leading up to the courtyard. This was oddly equipped with a line of soapstone sinks, each with a single tap – non potabile, of course. At one sink, a middle-aged man was combing his hair so as to conceal a bald spot. Tee shirts and underclothes were drying on a line. The ramparts weren't quite waist high, an astonishing hazard by today's standards, and indeed in present-day photographs I see that a guardrail has been added to discourage visitors from tumbling over the side.

The manager was a delightful little woman named Madi, who wore a French sailor's shirt with horizontal stripes. We gave her 900 lire, three nights' lodging for the two of us, and in return Madi stamped our YHA cards with an image of the castle that took up two ordinary spaces. "Ask if we can stay longer," I whispered to Basia. If Madi was so proud of her establishment that she'd acquired this elaborate stamp, she might bend the three-night rule for us. Basia translated. Madi patted her hand, gave me a birdlike glance (sguardo!), and invited us into the keep for a glass of wine. Her apartment was up one flight, a cluttered room with piles of magazines and paperback books. Clearly the extension would be granted.

As the conversation rolled along – Basia's Italian was quicker than I remembered, and accompanied by much more in the way of shrugs, finger flicks, and pouts – Madi kept darting those sguardi at me. I had an uneasy feeling that she had a pretty good idea of all that had transpired between Basia and me: the green gloves, the Savoyarde bell, our stroll along the Saône, the quarrel and the cuddle, the lapis earrings, the blonde hair.

When Laetitia and Giorgio caught up with us, I was put

150

in charge of the young marchese. He'd brought a sheet and a pillowcase from his lodgings, but had no notion of how to make up a bed. I showed him how to fold the sheet as a sleeping bag, to spread a ratty hostel blanket over it, and to tuck everything under at the foot. There was no pillow on the mattress he'd chosen, so I stole one from a neighboring bunk. The men's dormitory lay deep in the bowels of the castle, quite cool, with window openings to the south. There was no glass. I could hear the Mediterranean sighing far below, and when I leaned out I could see a cove with narrow white beaches, tight against a cliff.

"I made my bed!" Giorgio boasted to the girls when we climbed the steps to rejoin them.

There was an American girl at the hostel, rather bossy, and I fancied that she was the same young woman who'd led us in Twenty Questions on our April crossing to Calais. There were three boys with her, also Americans, who were competing for her attention. Laetitia was much amused by this quartet. "*La petite bande*," she called them, the little gang.

This was the weekend of the Fourth of July, and the gang was passing around a bottle of Chianti in honor of the day. We had wine bottles of our own, and perhaps we acquired more in the course of the evening. By sunset – a glorious sunset, with great swaths of orange and red, beneath bellying black clouds – the celebration had become quite general, ten or twelve of us talking and drinking and pairing off.

The American girl . . . what was her name? Something Midwestern and competent. Carol and Ethel come to mind but don't quite fit. *Dorrit*. Yes, that's it. "Let's go skinny-dipping!" Dorrit cried when darkness came down, which it did very quickly. The idea of a nude swim was met with great excitement, though not by Basia, who pleaded a headache from her day in the sun – nor by Giorgio, who decided to have dinner in La Spezia.

Laetitia and Basia perched on the rampart of the castle

"He will be looking for American sailors," Laetitia told me as we set out.

"Does Basia really have a headache?"

"Oh, she will never go topless! Those convent girls, they don't even look at their *own* skin!"

We trooped down what must have been two hundred rough-cut steps, past a bistro where some Australian boys and Irish girls were jitterbugging to a scratchy phonograph record. "Glenn Miller!" Dorrit cried, wavering in her plan.

Instead of joining the dancers, though, she invited them to help us celebrate the Founding Fathers, which they did, down more steps to the water. We could have made our way to the beach, but we were more interested in getting our clothes off, so we dropped them in heaps on the rocks – boys on one rock, girls on another, facing in opposite directions – and waded into the sea.

The moon was up and full, just as it had been for Basia and me at the Sacré Coeur, and it was great fun to see those young breasts bobbing in the Mediterranean, even if Basia's weren't among them. But don't imagine that we canoodled, oh no. Even Dorrit, when I swam over to her, bent her knees so the water came up to her collarbone. She was really rather pretty in the moonlight, with her hair wet and slicked to the side of her head. I felt that it was all right to admire her, since my beloved had forsaken me. "By any chance," I said, "were you on *Invicta*, going to Calais in April?"

"No," she said. "I came over on the *Seven Seas*, to Bremen. Is the *Invicta* a student ship?"

"It's the ferry from Dover to Calais."

"Oh, yes, of course," Dorrit said. "You're English, aren't you?"

I was delighted. Americans didn't make the best of impressions in Europe, and anyhow we weren't supposed to hitchhike, but to drive our land yachts with orange license plates: U.S. Forces in Austria. (There were a lot of those in Italy that summer, because in a rare display of comity the Russians agreed to leave their occupation zone if we left ours. The Americans stationed in western Austria had all been deployed to Italy.) What with one thing and another, I much preferred to pass for English.

When we dressed and climbed the steps again, we found the bistro closed for the night. "Oh dear!" cried one of the Irish girls. "It's gone eleven and we're late for curfew!" To be sure, the courtyard was empty when we reached it, and

Madi's window in the castle keep was dark. The resourceful Dorrit found another bottle of wine, and we continued the party on the ramparts, with the sea sighing in the moonlight, far below us. I sat with Laetitia, and after a bit I put my arm around her strong shoulders and kissed her on the mouth. Though it doesn't reflect great credit upon me, I distinctly remember this small infidelity. When my lips met Laetitia's, I felt such a jolt of electricity – an actual *spark*, it seemed – that I pulled back. *Il don è mobile!*

Madi ended this little game. She exploded from the keep with a flashlight and a blizzard of Italian. Most of the revelers escaped, but we did not. The flashlight was in my face from the first moment, and to make matters worse I made the mistake of laughing at the sight of tiny Madi in her nightgown.

In the morning, Laetitia and I went on punishment detail, along with Dorrit and an Australian who introduced himself as Tich, which was somehow short for Richard. We swept the courtyard and weeded the scraggly vegetable garden, while Basia sunned herself in a white swimsuit, chatting with Giorgio and giving us pitying smiles from time to time.

SOME OF THE VAGABONDI celebrating the Fourth of July turned out to be German, husky lads who were bicycling through Europe. Their English was excellent, and at my request they gave me a tutorial while I swept the courtyard, to add to what *Vati* had taught me at Rimini. Please, thank you, excuse me, good morning, goodbye. Sausage with potato salad. *Eine bier, bitte.* How much does that cost? Where are you going? Where is the youth hostel? Go left, right, straight ahead. . . . German, to my tongue, came more easily than Italian, and much easier than French. I could now find a youth hostel in four languages, an accomplishment that, in the summer of 1955, seemed much more significant than a long essay on the birth and death of the

Roman Republic in 1848-49.

We also acquired a companion in the person of Enrico, a young fisherman who more or less adopted us. He was in his twenties, tall for the time and well built; he evidently made it a practice to visit the castle every weekend and hit on the foreign girls, on the no doubt well-founded theory that their morals were looser than those of the maidens of Lerici. Further, I judged that when the girls didn't co-operate, he switched his attention to their boyfriends.

Enrico kept his skiff on a mooring in the harbor, from which one afternoon he rowed us past the seawall and the castle, past the cliff from which the German bicyclists liked to dive into the Mediterranean. He wanted to show us the *Grotta Azzurra*, blue grotto, which he promised was more handsome than the famous one at Capri.

The southern cove is guarded on its far side by the Maralunga peninsula, with a rocky escarpment on the sea-ward edge and on the coast beyond. Somewhere along here is the *Tana del Brigantino*, the pirate's cave, not really a grotto but more of a passage through the rock, open at both ends. I have no way of comparing it to Capri's Blue Grotto, and if Basia and Laetitia didn't agree with Enrico's assessment, they were too polite to say so.

But for beauty it will serve, silent in the limpid after-noon, water drip-dripping from Enrico's oars, the cave's walls and ceiling a flickering blue indeed, the sunlight reflected by the sandy bottom to dance upon the stone. It was one of those enchanting reversals, as when that warm breeze caressed us in Lyon. Here, the water contained more light than the air, so it was our primary illumination . . . and we were young and would never die!

On the row back to Lerici, Laetitia began to ruminate upon chest hair. Enrico's fine pelt, curly and black, im-pressed her as particularly handsome, compared to mine, which she judged to be too sparse and too brown – a brown, moreover, that was blonding daily under the sun. As for Giorgio, his chest was quite bare, as hairless as the girl he would have liked to be.

Enrico smiled sweetly, understanding that, whatever we were talking about, it had something to do with him. To change the subject, he took a pack of Nazionale from his trouser pocket and handed it around. We each took a cigarette except Giorgio, who didn't smoke. Enrico smiled even more sweetly and said: "Will you take one from my lips?" (Basia translated this foreplay for me.) Without waiting for an answer, he put a Nazionale between his own lips, lit it, took a drag, and passed it to Giorgio. Thus was the marchese seduced into smoking his first cigarette.

What was Enrico's experience during the War? I didn't ask, and not because we didn't have a language in common – Basia would have been our go between. He would have been a youngster in 1945, but boys did their share in the War, on both sides. (That Polish boy in shorts, digging an air-raid trench in the summer of 1939!) Nor had his pretty homeland been spared. Not far north of Lerici, on the Ligurian coast, there's a village I came to know fairly well in later years, Vernazza by name. No road goes through it, though Mussolini had a railway track built along the shore, so Vernazza has had train service since the 1930s. Hard by the railroad station there's a plaque with the names of villagers killed during the War: twenty or so young men lost in North Africa; about the same number *caduti in Russia* (and what a shock those frozen winters on the Eastern Front must have been, to fishermen from the Mediterranean!); and twenty or so killed in the Resistance, on one side or another. Enrico must have experienced some of that, if only at second hand.

Then there was Madi. In my brother's footlocker, I find two photographs of her. In one, she is leaning out the window on the castle keep, her hair white, full, and shoulder length, and her arms folded on the windowsill. My typewritten caption reads: "Madi, Queen of the Vagabonds.

Tiny and shrill-voiced, she likes to keep her castle full of men, and she rules them from her window up on the castle wall." In the other photo, she is greeting two newcomers, the boy with a student cap and squared-off pack, the girl bareheaded. Madi is shaking hands with the young man while holding a broom in her left hand, and she's looking at me, or more likely at my absurd Speed Graphic press camera. Her face surprises me. Where my memory holds an image of an ancient crone, the photograph shows me a middle-aged woman with a handsome, almost masculine face. She even grins like a man. My caption: "Madi greets two Danish hitchhikers. She divides the world into Vagabondi and Capitalisti, and only the former find a warm welcome at her castle."

English hostels were idealistic enterprises, run for the betterment of young people, meaning someone under twenty-five and traveling by foot, bicycle, or public transport. Hitchhikers were tolerated, but if you drove up to an English hostel in an automobile you'd be quickly turned away. This was not the case in Italy, as I knew from my stay at Rimini, with the Volkswagen parked out front and the German family camped on the roof. Italian hostels were private establishments – capitalistic, one might say – that provided the manager with a livelihood. The rules were arbitrarily enforced, or not enforced at all, at the hostel keeper's pleasure.

I find that her name was Maddalena di Carlo, and that she was locally famous as a *comunista e partigiana*, Communist and guerrilla fighter, who each year carried the Red Flag in Lerici's May Day parade. I can find no one to tell me, however, what her career as a partisan amounted to. Did she blow up German troop trains, pack supplies into the mountains, turn the crank on a mimeograph machine, or merely curse the Fascists?

After the War, Madi became *custode amata del castello di Lerici*, the castle's beloved custodian, until the hostel was shut down in 1974. The citizens of Lerici decided that Madi could no longer provide "an effective and hygienic management," so they voted her out. By that time, it is true, the onetime gamine had become a crone indeed, all but sexless in her cropped gray hair, lean face, and cast-off clothing. But I suspect that the real reason for closing the hostel was the hope of attracting older, fatter, and richer tourists. Our castle is now a museum of paleaontology!

She was fifty, give or take a year, when we stayed at Lerici. Indeed, she must have been just about the same age as Basia's mother, though without Mama's comforting warmth of face and body. And, like Mama, she must have had a fascinating life. I don't know; I didn't ask, any more than I asked Mama about her life in Poland, Kazakhstan, Persia, and Lebanon.

When we are young, we don't have a great deal of interest in those who came before us. At twenty-two, the entire setup – the mountains and the seas, the languages and the national boundaries, and especially anyone past the age of thirty – seems just a stage for us to play our roles upon.

Last Boat to Pahlevi
1941-1942

FOR THE POLES IN CAPTIVITY, the German onslaught changed everything. Once again I find myself struggling with the fact that a disaster for some can be a blessing for others, and I am not alone. "This event, cataclysmic for millions, proved to be salvation for the Polish exiles," in the words of Halik Kochanski.

The change began at the hellhole of Moscow's Lubyanka, where the tattered and emaciated Wladyslaw Anders was ushered into the presence of Lavrentiy Beria, the NKVD chief. General Anders was cleaned up, allowed to communicate with the exile government in London, and told to create an army out of Polish prisoners of war being held in camps or assigned to work gangs in Soviet Russia. Partly to advance this project, British troops marched into Persia on August 25, 1941, deposing the old Shah in favor of his son, Mohammed Pahlevi. They occupied the southern half of the country we now call Iran, while Russians occupied the north. The improbable allies now had a common frontier, across which supplies could flow to the beleaguered Red Army and its new Polish legion.

LIFE CHANGED FOR JOE AND ME as well. That June, in our five o'clock rendezvous with Captain Midnight and his Secret Squadron, our heroes had been chasing "the most rascally and dangerous criminal in the world . . . an evil genius such as the world has never known before." His nationality was never specified, but it was obvious from his name: *Ivan Shark*. Though the United States clung to a facade of neutrality, our support for Britain was never in doubt. Now that Russia had become Britain's ally, Captain Midnight's story line had to change. Ivan Shark was killed off in an airplane crash, to be replaced by the odious Gestapo agent, Baron Kurt von Karp.

And when Joe and I returned to school in September, we each received a booklet into which, every Monday, we were supposed to paste a red stamp bearing the image of the Minute Man of Concord, Massachusetts. The stamp cost ten cents, a considerable sum at the time, but I don't know of any child in my fourth-grade class who failed to come up with the dime. When we'd filled it, we would exchange our booklet for a $25 War Bond, though I don't think anyone believed that the War could possibly last that long.

THE GERMANS MADE THEMSELVES at home in their newly conquered *lebensraum* in eastern Poland. (A somewhat deceptive term: they didn't view the country as a "living space" but as an agricultural colony, with Slavs to become slaves again.) In Lwow, the Gestapo took over the central police station, where earlier the Bluecaps had strutted. And Brygidki Prison, once cleared of its corpses, resumed its routine of interrogation, torture, and murder, though with a particular focus on Jews. Within a year, most of the city's 110,000 Jews would be dead, along with a nearly equal number who'd fled the Germans in September 1939 and taken refuge in Lwow.

Not that life was comfortable for the uncircumcised. Lwow under occupation was a "chaotic, half-empty city, a rubbish-strewn landscape without moral order." As was their wont, however, the Germans did establish their own peculiar sort of order. Thus Basia's street, which had formerly honored Count Andrzej Potocki, was renamed for the goofy hero of Wagner's epic *Der Ring des Nibelungen*. So if Mama and the girls were now to return, they'd find themselves lodged at 99 Siegfried Strasse.

Basia, at least, was safer in Kazakhstan. Even as they brutalized the population, the Germans made an exception for blonde and blue-eyed children, kidnapping 200,000 youngsters under a program called *Lebensborn*, Fountain of Life, to be reared as German. Lalka might be disqualified by her brown eyes, but Basia – blue-eyed Basia! – would have made an exemplary Aryan child.

THE POLISH EXILE GOVERNMENT had granted another star to General Anders, building an army from the men being released from jails, prison camps, and labor colonies. "Most of them had no boots or shirts," he would write in *An Army in Exile*, "and all were in rags, often the tattered relics of old Polish uniforms. There was not a man who was not an emaciated skeleton and most of them were covered with ulcers, resulting from semi-starvation, but to the great astonishment of the Russians . . . they were all well shaved and showed a fine soldierly bearing."

According to Red Army records, 8,000 Polish officers had been taken prisoner in September 1939, and 2,000 more were arrested in the December roundup. Yet fewer than 500 emerged from the Gulag. Most came from a single small camp, Grazovec, where they'd been sent after a selection process similar to the one that saved the life of Anders himself: they spoke Russian, or they seemed sympathetic to Communism, or they had some other characteristic that might be put to use in a postwar Poland under Moscow's sway. A few others had survived by passing themselves off as enlisted men, wisely expecting that officers would be brutalized by the Bluecaps.

Where was the rest of the officer corps, more than 9,500 men? To add to the mystery, many of the freed men reported seeing familiar faces in the camps, who now could not be found. These included Anders's own adjutant and chief of staff, captured with him in September 1939. When the Russians were pressed about these men, the answers were "vague, uncooperative, and worrisome." By the time he was done, Anders compiled the names of 4,000 officers who had been captured but could not be found, a list that he knew was far from complete.

The Poles were given a training camp at Buzuluk, halfway between Moscow and the capital of Kazakhstan. Here General Anders formed his ragged recruits into the Polish 5th Division, the name of a prewar unit. The British would send uniforms for them, to be brought in through Persia; the Russians would supply food and weapons.

The Russians also granted an amnesty "to all Polish citizens on Soviet territory at present deprived of their freedom as prisoners or on other adequate grounds." That word – amnesty – implying a crime committed but now forgiven, infuriated the Poles in 1941 and still rankles the Polish diaspora today.

Halik Kochanski estimates that, in the summer of 1941, 616,000 Poles were in Soviet Russia as prisoners of war, deportees, slave laborers, and Red Army conscripts. As usual, Moscow's count was much smaller and curiously precise: 387,982. Part of the problem lay in how the Russians defined Polish citizenship: the Red Army conscripts were certainly omitted, along with many or most of those whose native language was Hebrew, Yiddish, Ukrainian, or Belarusian.

And, after all, what did amnesty mean in the fall of 1941? The Germans occupied all of Poland, Ukraine, and Belarus, along with European Russia almost to the gates of Moscow. The Poles couldn't go home! In theory, they were now free to move around the Soviet Union. They were given *udostovierenya*, travel documents, and the Polish government was allowed to establish offices in cities and at railroad stations to help the exiles on their way, the money to come from the gold reserves spirited out of Warsaw in September 1939. For their part, the British sent freighters around the top of Scandinavia to Murmansk with supplies for them – *SS Atlantic*, for example, carrying 159 tons of blankets, 76 tons of footwear, 247 tons of clothing, 10 tons of canned milk, 30 tons of medicines, 8 tons of chocolate, and 2 tons of Bovril, a beef extract popular with English workmen as a sandwich filler. Some but certainly not all of this bounty reached the Polish *delegatura*, distribution centers, staffed by Poles from England and by the exiles themselves.

But where were the amnestied Poles to go? Millions of Russians were fleeing before the German advance; entire factories and their workers were moving to safety beyond the Ural Mountains; and millions of troops were being rushed in the other direction, to the front. Lazar Kaganovich's rail network, which had been strained by the task of deporting a few hundred thousand Poles in 1940, was stressed to the point of collapse by "this great avalanche of transmigration." Many of the exiles decided to stay put, preferring the harshness of their settled existence to the perils of a new railway journey, the risk of capture by the Germans or imprisonment by the NKVD, or of sickness and death en route.

And some regarded themselves as forever cut off from home. These were the women who'd entered marriages – formal or informal, voluntary or forced – with Russian or Kazakh men, or who otherwise felt sullied by their trip through the Gulag. The women who did escape to Persia almost never referred to rape, prostitution, pregnancy, and abortion. But one male survivor recalled that in his camp a Polish woman, married and the mother of two, "had a third child with a Russian, the head of the cafeteria. It happened undoubtedly in order to ensure her subsistence." Another told how female prisoners "were treated like 'goods' to be used, traded for a piece of bread. If one didn't want to have a 'protector' – a so-called 'camp husband' – then she was ill-treated, her life made disgusting. . . ."

Those accounts were unearthed by the American feminist scholar Katherine Jolluck, who also found letters from two Polish women to their husbands, confessing that they'd been forced to take up with local men. "My life here is hell," one woman wrote, "but I have not had the courage to kill myself. . . . One day some herdsmen, more than a dozen, one after the other took advantage of me. As one of them showed a desire to keep me close to him I preferred that. I serve him as a wife. I carry a child in my womb. . . . I beg you, forget me forever, remake your life."

Other exiles weren't told they were free, or were forced to stay by overseers determined to keep them. Or amnesty came too late for them: "One hundred and eighty-six Poles were released from Zolotisty," Solzhenitsyn writes of a gold-mining camp in northern Russia, "out of 2,100 brought there a year before."

But tens of thousands did set out to find the rumored Polish army. "I saw arriving from all parts of the boundless Russian territory a flood of thousands and dozens of thousands of prisoners of war and imprisoned or deported civilians," as General Anders recalled the human wave that descended upon Buzuluk.

BASIA THINKS IT WAS MAMA'S brother – the ladies' man and perpetual engineering student, captured when he tried to escape into Romania in 1939 – who brought the news of the amnesty to Georgievka:

Uncle Jan was in a labor camp, and he had quite a privileged position there since he knew a lot about building roads and bridges. He joined the Anders Army when he was released from the camp, and then he set out to find us. I remember seeing him for a very short time in Georgievka. He arrived with his boots tied around his neck and his feet wrapped in newspapers and scraps of cloth. Boots were very valuable in Russia, and they were apt to be stolen from your feet if you fell asleep on a train.

Jan brought with him the necessary papers, tickets, and instructions. And it was probably he who told us to go to Semipalatinsk, where the other Deszbergs were.

Then there was fifteen-year-old Zbyszek, Aunt Krysia's

son. To rescue as many civilians as he could, General Anders organized a cadet corps for teenage boys and girls. Ostensibly they were military auxiliaries, though their duty in most cases was simply to put on weight, regain their health, and resume their interrupted education. Zbyszek was a natural for the *juniaki*, as it was called. Basia remembers how he joined:

A Polish officer, dressed in an English uniform, came to our area to recruit young people into the cadets. Zbyszek was off like a shot. Then the rest of us moved to Semipalatinsk, towards the end of 1941.

One hundred miles north of Georgievka, Semey (as it is called today) was a railway junction with a population of 100,000 – for Kazakhstan, a considerable metropolis. Among its residents was Basia's half-brother, the banker Zdzislaw Deszberg, along with his wife and baby boy. Like Mama, Waleria was pregnant when the Bluecaps came for them on April 17, 1940, four days after emptying the flat at 99 Potocki Street. Zdzislaw had been foresighted enough to keep a stash of gold at home, and in the confusion of their arrest, Waleria managed to hide the coins in her hair.

They too were bound for the steppes of Kazakhstan, but Zdzislaw persuaded the Bluecaps that he'd had medical training, so they granted him privileges unavailable to most of the deportees. Thus he and his wife were living in Semey in November 1940, when the baby Janusz was born. The fortunate Deszbergs! Many Polish families were decimated by their exile, but the Deszbergs not only survived but actually increased their number. The two families now joined forces, combining their talents and increasing their chances of surviving a second winter in Kazakhstan. Very likely, indeed, Zdzislaw had been tapped for the Polish *delegatura* in Semey, charged with aiding refugees.

BY OCTOBER 1941, General Anders had 40,000 men in uniform, enough for two divisions, though only a minority actually carried weapons. Nor were rifles the only items they had to share: the soldiers divided their already-scanty rations with about the same number of civilians, clustered miserably around the training camps. Eventually the army numbered 75,000 men, women, and "cadets." Perhaps half were veterans of the prewar Polish army. The rest had no previous military training, including Uncle Jan and a young man named Menachem Begin, the future prime minister of Israel.

Stalin wanted to throw these half-starved men into combat under Russian command. As with the brutality of the NKVD, this wasn't simply the dictator's hatred of the Poles: he was as careless of Russian lives as those from the conscripted nations. The Red Army version of blitzkrieg called for massive numbers of tanks, close air support, and the spilling of stupendous quantities of blood: 26 million of Stalin's subjects would die before the War was over.

General Anders wanted his men to recover their health and train as a cohesive force – a Polish Legion, like the one that had fought under Napoleon's banner in Italy. In London, meanwhile, Winston Churchill sensed an opportunity: if he could bring the Poles out of Russia, they'd reinforce the British Army in its seesaw battle against German and Italian forces in North Africa. Toward this end, the exiled Polish prime minister, Wladyslaw Sikorski, made his roundabout way to Moscow in December to argue the point with Stalin himself. (Sikorski was brother to the defender of Lwow who had been murdered in the Katyn massacres.) He pleaded for Churchill's solution: let the Anders Army move to Persia, where food was plentiful and the men could more easily be supplied. Stalin was outraged. "If the Poles do not want to fight," he snapped at Sikorski, "then let them go."

It was never wise to annoy the dictator. Unknown to the Polish delegation – and perhaps to Stalin himself – the price was paid at a gold-mining camp on the Arctic island of Kolyma. "Sikorski displeased Stalin," Solzhenitsyn writes of this incident, "and in one night they seized thirty Polish women at Elgen and took them off and shot them."

WHILE SIKORSKI AND STALIN were arguing, Japanese bombers devastated the U.S. Pacific Fleet in Hawaii. We happened to be visiting Mrs. Damon in East Alton that Sunday afternoon – December 7, 1941. No doubt Dad wanted to show off his new prosperity, which included a 1934 Chevrolet truck. Joe and I rode in back, wrapped in a blanket and sitting against the cab.

We were astonished to find that Mrs. Damon had sold her shorefront home and moved into the Caretaker's Cottage on Chestnut Cove Road. Our once-drafty house had been painted, insulated, and equipped with electric lights, running water, and an oil furnace. So we sat in our former living room and basked in warmth that didn't come from a fireplace and was evenly spread around the room. By the front door stood a grandfather's clock that had stopped ticking; Dad had it running in short order. "It needs a drop of oil once or twice a month," he instructed Mrs. Damon.

"On the first and the fifteenth," she agreed, and wrote the information on a filing card that she tucked inside the door of the clock, where the pendulum now swung in obedience to Dad's tinkering, tick tock. I was impressed alike by my father's limitless knowledge and by Mrs. Damon's brisk sense of order.

In the dusk, we drove home along Lake Winnipesaukee, Joe and I blanket-wrapped in back. It was dark by the time Dad turned onto the road to Mr. Manning's estate, where we were greeted by his secretary, a formidable lady named Miss Duckworth. She had a flashlight, with which she signaled Dad to stop. "The Japanese have bombed Pearl Harbor," she announced. "We're at war."

I whispered to Joe: "What's Pearl Harbor?" He didn't know. Neither did Dad, and probably Miss Duckworth didn't know either. No matter. We were at war! I was thrilled, though the most immediate change was Admiral Ito Himakito, now added to Captain Midnight's roster of villains. Dad got an "A" ration for the truck – four gallons a week, enough to take us to the First National store on Friday night and to Mass on Sunday morning. In time we'd also get ration books for food, and especially for sugar, coffee, meat, and butter.

We had the occasional blackout, against the possibility that the Germans might decide to bomb Lakeport. Clarence Dame, the farmer who'd helped Dad build our house, was our Air Raid Warden, and he came around with a steel helmet and a flashlight to make sure no light showed from our windows. He also gave Joe and me a card with the silhouettes of German and American warplanes, so we could be aircraft spotters.

NEGOTIATIONS OVER THE Anders Army, bitter at times, lasted through the winter, while the soldiers and their encircling civilians shivered and starved in tents and dugouts. Not until March 1942 did the first ship leave the Russian port of Krasnovodsk with 1,387 Polish sailors and airmen aboard. They crossed the Caspian Sea overnight, reaching the port of Pahlevi (named for the young Shah) the next afternoon, arriving within hours of the Indian Army ambulance unit that had been sent to prepare a camp for them. The flood of refugees continued for more than a week, with thousands of Polish soldiers and civilians living under canvas in the rain (and snow, in the first few days).

Over the course of a month, 43,597 Poles were dumped onto the sandy shore of Persia, nearly a third of them civilians. They were louse-ridden, starving, and sick. "Exhausted by hard labor, disease and starvation – barely recognizable as human beings," as one refugee recalled, "we disembarked at the port of Pahlevi. . . . There, we knelt down together in our thousands along the sandy shoreline to kiss the soil of Persia. We had escaped Siberia, and were free at last. We had reached our longed-for Promised Land."

The British were appalled to see the civilians coming ashore. What did they know of caring for women and children? The newcomers had to be fed, clothed, and provided with cots and tents. And they needed medical care! British and Indian doctors became pediatricians and gynecologists overnight, and British and Indian soldiers became barbers, cropping the head, armpits, and groin of every Pole past the age of puberty, as part of the delousing procedure.

"Are we going to get nothing but women and children?" Winston Churchill groused to his foreign secretary, when he learned about the civilians. *"We must have the men."* Worse, there were rumors that 50,000 children might be next. Richard Casey, representing the British government in the Middle East, wanted the exodus stopped until better facilities were in place. "To put matters brutally," he telegraphed London, "if these Poles die in Russia the war effort will not be affected. If they . . . pass into Persia, we, unlike the Russians, will not be able to allow them to die and our war effort will be gravely impaired."

That first wave came mostly from the Polish training camps, a thousand miles north of Krasnovodsk. Those from Archangelsk, Siberia, and the steppes of Kazakhstan had a longer and more arduous journey. The Russians directed the refugees south to Uzbekistan, and from there they had to make their way to Krasnovodsk. Many were pulled off their trains and forced into collective farms for the summer harvest, and some of these would never be allowed to continue their trek.

The rail journeys were often as terrible as those that had carried them into exile. They were no longer under NKVD guard, but by the same token no longer got the occasional meal of thin soup or black bread. Hundreds, perhaps thousands, died along the way or were left behind when they went to forage for food and the train started without warning. Motherless children were sent to Russian orphanages that were little more than warehouses, or with luck were informally adopted by a Polish adult.

WHO TOOK THE LEAD for the Deszberg women? Perhaps it was Uncle Jan, the newly minted officer in the Anders Army, or Zdzislaw Deszberg, the banker who'd passed himself off as a medical man. Or perhaps Mama and the aunts managed for themselves. In any event, they made their way south, 550 miles to the Kazakh capital of Alma Ata, then east in a 500-mile zigzag to Tashkent in Uzbekistan, and northeast again 1,100 miles to Krasnovodsk in Russia. That 2,150 miles is a crow's-flight distance: by train, the journey was much longer, and it seems to have taken them most of the summer.

As to when they reached the Caspian Sea, Basia got a clue years later when she and Lalka worked at Radio Free Europe in Munich. Among the RFE executives was Kazimierz Zamorski, who recognized the Deszberg girls from the boat that took them from Krasnovodsk to Pahlevi. He'd been in charge of the final transport, he told them, and they were on it.

The last boat to Pahlevi! If you missed the last transport, 250 miles across the Caspian Sea, you'd spend the rest of the War in Soviet Russia, and perhaps the rest of your life. Uzbekistan, now an independent state, recently opened its archives to the Polish government. At least 100,000 Poles came onto its territory in 1942, those records show, and "[m]any of them remained in the Uzbek soil forever."

Mama, the girls, and the aunts must have reached Krasnovodsk toward the end of August, to be on the last transport. This was the oil tanker *Kaganovich*, named for the same "Iron Lazar" who'd co-signed the Katyn Order and arranged for Basia's deportation in 1940.

"The empty tanker was sitting high in the water," as a

young Polish soldier recalled what it was like, boarding *Kaganovich* in the scorching sun. "Soldiers and civilians, loaded with all their belongings, edged up and up the steep gangways. We had to balance between the ship's rusty hull and the long drop to the dock below. . . . The flimsy rope handrail was of no use as we carried something in each hand and could not even wipe the sweat trickling into our eyes. Everything had to be taken on board at one go. There was no return from the ship."

By my best reckoning, 1,275 Poles were jammed aboard *Kaganovich*, most of them soldiers of the 5th Infantry Division but including 181 women and 311 children. As Basia remembers the journey:

I remember people around me shouting, pushing, and crying because not everyone was allowed onto the boat. As the boat started to leave, I saw a man clinging to the shore lines, and as the rope was pulled in, he just kept on walking into the sea. I don't know what happened to him – whether he got back to the shore or was drowned in the sea – but I remember his contorted face. That was my last sight of Russia.

The crossing must have been rough, because people around us were retching and crying and praying, in fear I suppose of the boat capsizing.

The conditions were as miserable as any the exiles had yet experienced, and their bodies were weaker. They had no food except what they'd brought with them, almost no water, and no latrine except for a board perched over the rail – and many were afflicted with diarrhea. The sun fried a steel deck so crowded that each person had to negotiate with his neighbor if he wanted to stretch his legs. If someone died, the body was passed from hand to hand to the rail, where it was dropped without ceremony into the Caspian Sea.

The crossing took the rest of that day, all night, and much of the next day, September 1, 1942. Because *Kagan-*

ovich had a deep draft, the passengers had to clamber onto tugboats to be brought to shore. (The soldier quoted above was stuffed into a tugboat's engine room, up against the boilers.) As Basia recalls her arrival in Persia:

But then the joy of reaching the shore and the sight of stalls full of food. Just imagine – food! It was so colorful, the fruit and food the Persians had prepared for us. They had intended to sell it, I suppose, but when they found we had no money, they simply gave it to us. They were such warm and friendly people, the Persians. And because I was thin – painfully so, as far as they were concerned – they would always insist on feeding me.

The weather was beautiful, and in the stalls all those fat and juicy fruits shone in the sunlight. We could have had a feast, Lalka and I, but after a few bites we were dragged away by Mama and the aunts. They were right, of course. The lavatories in the camp were full that night, and Aunt Krysia was one of the sufferers.

A night in the latrine was the least of it: 639 Poles died of disease and starvation upon reaching safety. They are buried in a bedraggled cemetery in Pahlevi, its name now changed to Bandar Anzali. More hundreds – thousands, perhaps – died elsewhere in the country, after moving on from the tent camps on the shore of the Caspian Sea. Typhus was the big killer, followed by malaria and pellagra. Most of the gravestones bear the same year of death – 1942 – and most seem to mark the graves of children. Basia and Lalka were luckier:

And then we were taken to a camp near Tehran. Life was great. We slept under tents and had school lessons under the trees, and American gifts arrived for us. Some were just right, some not quite – a child might be given a man's boots, which he then had to exchange with someone else.

Mama managed to enroll Lalka and me in a boarding school run by the Sisters of Santo Spirito in Tehran. So one morning we said goodbye to her, the aunts, and our camp friends, and we were driven to the convent. We saw a huge wall and a wooden gate, studded with iron. We asked the driver to take us back to the camp. Too late! A nun came out, took us firmly by the hand, and led us inside. The gate shut behind us with an awful finality.

And that was the beginning of my war.

Many of the Polish women moved into the city, and some married Persian men, never to leave. But Mama and the aunts chose to stay in the camp. As she had done in Georgievka, Aunt Krysia maintained the tent that was their home: she was the shrewdest shopper, and she could earn a bit of money by making facial creams for the other women and eventually for affluent Persians. Aunt Nuna cleaned house for Persian families. Mama got a job as a cook and sometime waitress at the "O Club" where U.S. Army officers ate and drank. There were by this time several thousand American servicemen in Persia, headquartered at Camp Amirabad on the outskirts of Tehran. Their job was to speed the flow of military equipment to Russia, including 15 million pairs of boots and 250,000 pounds of *tushonka*, the Red Army staple of tinned pork and lard.

As an officer's wife, Mama was granted a stipend by the Polish government: 256 Persian rials a month, the equivalent of two pounds sterling or $9.60 at the wartime rate of exchange. (Probably by no coincidence, £2 was a month's pay for a British Army private.) From this, and from her earnings at the O Club, Mama managed to pay for Basia's and Lalka's education at the convent school, while most Polish children had to settle for those impromptu lessons beneath a tree in the camp.

Where had Mama come by her devotion to education? She herself would have had little formal education. Schooling wasn't a priority for girls in prewar Poland, nor was it in most countries of Europe, including England. But she was determined to educate her daughters. "Mama's idea was to get all the education you can," Basia says now. "If you had it in your head, it was yours forever, and it was safe."

THE DESZBERG GIRLS were the only European children at Santo Spirito. The others were Persian, including a lad rumored to be the illegitimate son of the old Shah. They spoke Farsi among themselves, while the nuns conducted classes in Italian. Thus Basia, by her ninth birthday in December 1942, spoke Polish with her sister, Farsi with her classmates, and Italian in class.

After two feral years in Kazakhstan, Santo Spirito seemed to her as little better than a prison:

It was hard, being shut up in the convent. The school was small, with a little concrete courtyard and many children. There was no place where one could be alone, even for a short while. After the steppes of Kazakhstan, I hated to be closed in. And the school was all very haphazard, though there was a bell, so there must have been some kind of formal program. I remember three nuns in particular whom I liked. One was slightly mad; I really liked her.

Those Italian nuns! They were very human. We were bambini *to them. They would cuff us on the head, not in the masterly fashion of schoolmasters here in England, but a gentle slap. Then they would hug us and tell us that Jesus loved us. "You're a good girl; you're going to be good forever and ever."*

They used to call me "Bascina." I cried when I left them. I love that "Bascina" – a diminutive of a diminutive!

The convent meals ("frightful soup – water with rice") were short on the nutrients needed by the Deszberg girls, half-starved after two years in Soviet Russia. Basia was soon felled by the hallucinations, disorientation, and scorching fevers of malaria, probably from a mosquito bite on the beach at Pahlevi. She was sent to a hospital (so huge

174

that she got lost when she decided to go for a walk) where she was treated with a bitter brew of quinine. Back at the convent, the nuns set out to build her up by administering one raw egg daily, cracked into a glass of wine.

She also suffered from the maddening itch of chilblains, in Tehran and for years afterward, from feet soaked in melted snow in the Kazakh springtime. Thirteen-year-old Lalka suffered from her customary ailment:

On Sundays, we went to High Mass in Tehran's big Catholic church and sat in the choir. The choir loft was hot and stuffy, and Lalka developed her habit of fainting. The nuns would take her to a side room, give her coffee, and fuss over her, while I had to stick it out to the end.

Then Lalka announced that she was going to become a nun. The sisters were pleased; I was disgusted. It was all a sham, I was sure, like Aunt Krysia whom I could see sitting in the front pew every Sunday, wearing her best hat and pretending to be pious because she admired the Monsignore who was celebrating Mass. He was, I admit, very good looking.

The castle as seen from the south, with the sandy path sweeping down in a long zigzag. At far left, the launch pad for the German bicyclists, from which they dove into the Gulf of Poets. At far right, the path ends in a precipitous set of rough stone steps. I took this photo from the beach where we spent most afternoons. Alas, it has since been obliterated by rocks and earth fallen from the cliffs above.

CHAPTER ELEVEN
I Knew So Little of Love
1955

DORRIT AND HER ADMIRERS moved on, to be replaced by other *vagabondi* and *capitalisti*. (Madi had no doubt classified the *petite bande* as capitalists, for they were only with us the regulation three nights.) Australians were particularly numerous on the Continent that summer. They had a tradition of spending a few months in the mother country after graduating from "Uni." Then they hitchhiked through Europe with their wonderful accents, their unflagging enthusiasm, and their awful jars of Vegemite.

There were many Irish girls as well. They traveled in pairs, but split up during the day so as to hitchhike with a boy they'd met at the hostel – an Australian, often enough. A boy and a girl would catch rides faster than two boys alone; and a girl with a male companion was less likely to be pawed by truck drivers. This was an understandable error on the part of the drivers: Italy had a class of hitchhiking prostitutes, who catered to long-distance trucks with that convenient bunk behind the seat. They did their business at forty miles an hour!

Indeed, Basia tells me that she and Laetitia were once given a ride by two lads who took them for working girls:

They got a bit too amorous, so we told them to stop the car and we got out. It was a lonely country road, with almost no traffic, so we set out to walk to the nearest village. Then the two young men came back for us. They apologized and invited us to a circus. We all had dinner with the circus people including the Fattest Woman in the World.

One of the young men explained the mistake to me: "How would a woman feel if the men did not express admiration for her bellezza?*" After that I stopped being disconcerted at the way Italian men looked at me.*

DORRIT HAD WORN A TWO-PIECE bathing suit, in the tradition of Dorothy Lamour and other Hollywood pinups, but Basia kept her midriff covered. The souvenir swimsuit from Capri was white, and it was strapless, which I found infinitely alluring – what lovely shoulders she had! There was a zipper down the back, which interested me also, as did the fine curve of her pupka. As for me, I wore my wool trunks from home, where I'd learn to swim in Lake Winnipesaukee, colder and less buoyant than the Gulf of Poets.

Every morning at seven, the two of us met in the castle courtyard, brushed our teeth at the soapstone sinks, and trotted down the sloping path behind the castle – down the stone steps – past the little bistro, now closed – and across the rocks to the beach beyond. We struck out for the Maralunga point of land, where we arrived quite out of breath. After recovering, we swam at a more leisurely pace along the curve of the shore, to complete what we fondly believed was a one-mile circuit, though it was probably only half that. Basia favored the breaststroke, like the other Europeans, whereas the Australians and I used an overhand stroke. (They were much amused to hear that in the United States this was known as the Australian crawl, whereas to them it was the *American* crawl.) Back at the bistro, we dried ourselves in the eight o'clock sun and shared a Nazionale from the pack I'd hidden in my shoes.

The Germans by this time were beginning to prance on their shelf of rock, above us and to seaward, daring one another to make the dive. Finally someone took the plunge – fifty or sixty feet, as it seemed to me, though like our morning swim it was probably less. The diver leapt straight out, as if meaning to reach Isla Palmaria, misty in the morning on the far side of the bay. Then gravity caught him and he swung his arms out to the side, so that his leap became a swan dive. He barely cleared the face of the cliff –

the closer the better, evidently. At the very last moment, he joined his hands above his head, and – splash! – sliced into the water. There followed a breathless interval, during which we were sure he'd cracked his skull on the bottom. But no, he bobbed to the surface, brimming with joy and testosterone, shouting insults at his friends above. Then they had to follow him, one by one.

One day a diver did scrape the cliff on his way down. Luckily the encounter didn't throw him off his dive, but it did give him a chest full of long gray splinters. Giorgio spent a happy hour on the battlement, extracting the slivers of stone with Laetitia's tweezers.

By the time Basia and I trekked up to the castle again, we were dry enough to put on our trousers and tops. Then down to the village – God, what mountain goats we were, trotting up and down that cliff all day! Lerici had a shop where we could buy the materials for breakfast, and eat them too, grocery store and restaurant in one. *Signora* sold us each an egg at retail price, then fried it at no extra charge. She served it on a tiny white plate at an outside table that not only boasted a Cinzano ashtray, but a matching umbrella as well. (I'd asked Basia to quiz Signora about Cinzano, so we knew it was an *aperitivo*. "It stimulates the appetite," as Basia translated Signora's explanation. "Like hunger, I suppose," she added. We thought it hilarious that people might actually need to have their appetite stimulated.) Signora also sold us each an Italian roll, ten grams of butter on a piece of waxed paper, and a cup of coffee. We had, by this time, switched our affection to *cappuccino*, with cocoa flecks on the foam that rose like a meringue above the rim of the cup.

The tab for the two of us came to 300 lire. The same sum – fifty cents – bought twenty Nazionale in a red and white pack. Cigarettes were expensive in Europe, and that's why the Germans didn't smoke, the largest group of young people I'd encountered who were so abstemious. (They weren't worried about their health: it was sex, not smoking, that we'd been taught was dangerous.) I had budgeted my money at two dollars a day, to ensure I didn't run out before reaching London. To the Germans – indeed, to most Europeans in those lean years after the War – two dollars was a considerable sum. And if they did have money left over at the end of the day, they splurged on huge plates of pasta, for the calories they needed to pedal their bicycles along the autostrada and over the Alps.

Giorgio and Laetitia were slower to start the day, so it was mid-morning before our full team assembled. That too was usually in the cove beyond the castle, as Basia recalls:

As I remember it, rough-hewn steps led down to a very deserted beach with golden warm sand and surrounded by cliffs. Sometimes we would spend the whole day on the beach, just a few of us. And there was a contraption made of wood, hanging on for dear life to the rock, with huge gaps between the floorboards showing the sea underneath. At night there was loud music and flashing lights. I wonder what the locals thought of the unkempt backpackers descending on their castle and spending the nights laughing and singing! Well, we danced the evenings away, but only till 10:50 precisely, to be back at the castle on time and avoid Madi's wrath. I don't know if it could be called a cafe or a bistro or by any other name. Do you remember?

Alas, I don't remember the gaps in the floor, though I do remember the music, the scratchy Glenn Miller record from our first night at the castle, along with "Tennessee Waltz" and "Goodnight, Irene" from the Hit Parade a few years earlier. There was also a record Dorrit had donated to the bistro's collection: "Rock Around the Clock" by Haley and the Comets. She'd delivered an earnest tutorial about rock-and-roll – the latest thing, she explained, on the University of Michigan campus. She tried to teach me, but gave it up as a bad job. So after she left Lerici, none of us really knew what to do with Mr. Haley's music.

I also fondly remember the Personi beer at the bistro, one glass of which we would nurse for the entire evening.

LESS OFTEN, ENRICO ROWED us to that grotto on the Maralunga peninsula, or to the beach at San Terenzo to the north. And once we treated ourselves to a *gelato*. Before we laid our money down, Basia interrogated the vendor at great length. We finally settled for what he promised was a Lerician specialty, caramel with pine nuts and bits of chocolate, as superior to English ice cream as our morning cappucino was to the slippery stuff we used to drink in Caf.

Or we'd buy a paper cone of *semi salati*, roast sunflower seeds, which we ate walking along the waterfront promenade, splitting the seeds between our incisors, eating the kernel, and spitting out the husk. Basia told me about eating *semichki* in Kazakhstan, and trying to make a beard of the husks. So we had a contest, failing utterly, even though I already had a foundation to which they could have stuck.

BUT MOST OF ALL, WE WERE HAPPY! The sky is always blue in my memory of Lerici – the sunset is always glorious – the moon is always full – and the tide is always high. Sunrise or sunset, Lerici was *nostro pezzo del cielo caduto in terra*, our piece of heaven fallen to earth.

What a distance Basia and I had traveled, from Piccadilly Gardens in the March rain! At Lerici, we lived in an eternal Now, suspended in time and space. Our castle was the center of the universe – and not just *our* universe, either, but the center of the entire, star-spangled, infinitely expanding cosmos. The sun rose each morning for a single purpose, to light the castle's ancient stones, to bronze our shoulders, and to warm the sand beneath our feet.

Like the sun, and like the castle, this month of July in the year 1955 was the moment toward which evolution had

181

been trending since the earth had cooled. History had reached stasis, with us as its intended end. In some remote corner of our minds, I suppose we understood that this wasn't really the case – that Madi hadn't been put on earth to mind the Castello di Lerici, nor Enrico to row us to the Grotta Azzurra. Perhaps Basia, with her history of war and exile, understood that better than most of us – understood that the earth had a crust as thin as an eggshell, that might crack at any moment and plunge us into the abyss. A first-hand brush against catastrophe is a great asset when it comes to understanding the precariousness of human existence.

And perhaps I – the American unmarked by the War, who indeed had profited from it – understood this less than the others, even the Australian lads and the Irish girls, for whom the War had come almost close enough to touch. But all of us, I think, believed that the world was created for our enjoyment. Even Basia believed that! The whole point of being twenty or twenty-one or twenty-two years old is to ride the cusp of history, with children and old people as bit players in the drama of our lives.

We lived like Odysseus on Calypso's Island, or Hans Castorp on his Magic Mountain. The days melted into weeks, and the weeks, if we weren't careful, might whirl themselves into years. Laetitia was a cautionary example: she'd left home four years ago! In truth, I couldn't have spent more than a fortnight in the castle, perhaps just a week or ten days, though in my memory it seems to stretch on forever.

And I don't know why I left! Looking back, I realize there was a gulf between us, Basia and me, a misunder-standing as wide as the Gulf of Poets. Almost certainly this had to do with my longing to kiss and cuddle, as on those evenings at Les Abrets and Pontederra. I don't remember that this was an issue, but no doubt it was. We were generally in a mob – our own *petite bande* – and Basia would have found it easy to avoid pairing off with me. I was happy enough in her company, but it must have occurred to me that I'd never be more than a friend to her, that I was no less and no more dear to her than Laetitia or Giorgio. We were pals, not lovers, and was there ever a less congenial role for a lad of twenty-two? I decided to emulate Odysseus and move on. The German bicyclists were also ready to push off. They volunteered to find me a ride at the entrance to the Autostrada Azzurra, the fast route to Milano.

So, one morning in July, I said my farewells. Did I even kiss Basia goodbye? I don't remember, but she does. She tells me that we walked together, down the castle steps to the waterfront promenade:

There was another beach, on the village side of the castle, where Enrico and other fishermen kept their boats. That beach was more open to the public, what there was of it. (Mostly villagers, I think. The Italians couldn't afford to go on vacation to the shore.) That was where we said goodbye – we did say goodbye! But no, we didn't kiss.

I shouldered my rucksack and walked with the bicyclists to the entrance to the autostrada northbound. With intent, smiling faces, the Germans walked among the cars stopping at the tollgate, chatting up the drivers, until they found one bound for Milano who was willing to take me along. What a great way to hitchhike! I waved goodbye to them, and in my heart I said goodbye to Basia, whom I had every reason to believe I would never see again. I could have sung, like the troubador:

> Alas! I thought I knew so much of love,
> And I know so little,
> Because I cannot cease from loving her
> From whom I obtained no favor.
> She took my heart entire, myself entire,
> Took herself and the whole world,
> And left me with nothing but desire
> And a yearning heart!

I paused in Milano to pay my respects to *The Last Supper* in a dark, damp room at the monastery of Santa Maria della Grazia. (The mural was dark, too. Like the Sistine Chapel, like the University of Manchester – like Europe itself! – it has since been cleaned, brightened, and climate-controlled.) Next day I hitchhiked to Menaggio, halfway up the west bank of Lake Como. Vagabond wisdom held that Menaggio was a finer place – more *authentic*, in the word of the 1960s – than the more famous resort of Como. Menaggio, we were told, was patronized by Italians, not affluent foreigners. Anyhow, it had a hostel and I'm not sure Como did, so that's where I spent my last two nights in Italy. It was a pretty place, but I was lonely there, and not at all looking forward to a month on my own in German-speaking countries.

It ought to have been an easy jaunt to Lugano in Switzerland, thirteen miles along a country road. What I didn't appreciate was how scarce the traffic would be. Local drivers had no reason to cross the frontier, and I ended by hiking the entire distance. Toward noon, I found myself walking along the shore of a lake, which I fancied was the one over which Lieutenant Henry had rowed Nurse Barkley, that stormy night when they bade their Farewell to Arms. (I was wrong about that. They were on Lake Maggiore to the west, and their row actually covered a greater distance than my walk.) The afternoon was hot, and after a few more miles I was so thirsty that I climbed over a fence and into a cow pasture, where I drank from a clear-seeming brook. A mistake! I was queasy by the time I reached the hostel in Lugano, and sick at intervals through the night. So I stayed put next day, sleeping on the grass behind the hostel until it opened again in the afternoon.

I sprang back to life on the second morning and set out for the Alps. It was slow work, and by noon I had made it only as far as Bellizona, scarcely farther than I had walked the other day. Unlike the Italians, the Swiss didn't seem to grasp the concept of sharing their vehicles with young travelers. I stood by the side of the road for a very long time in the noonday sun. At last a small black Ford Anglia slowed for me, then drove on. It stopped a few hundred meters beyond. The driver stuck his head out the window and called to me in a wondering voice: "Dan?"

Antony Bolcover, yes! I ran down the road, overcome by nostalgia – for Manchester, for Caf, and of course for Basia. I was delighted to see Antony's smooth round face, beaming skeptically at me as only an Englishman can do. He was wearing a jacket and tie despite the heat. I climbed into the back seat, the fourth passenger in a very crowded automobile.

Antony was on a Continental tour with two friends, neither of whom I'd met before. They gave me a lift over the St. Gotthard Pass, on the climb to which the Ford's engine suffered a vapor lock, so we had to turn the little car around and roll it back toward Italy again, until Antony popped the clutch and the engine farted into life. We made it to the top on the second attempt, and took a break at the height-of-land to photograph one another, swapping cameras so we'd each come home with his own portrait. Mine shows a very serious young man with a high forehead and a handsome beard, streaked blond from a month in the Italian sun.

I rode with them to Luzern, where Antony dropped me at an information booth. (They were bound for France, to be back in England in one week's time, whereas I meant to tack east to Austria.) I marched up to the woman at the kiosk and asked: "*Wo ist die Jugendherberge, bitte?*"

"*Was is das?*" she said.

"*Die Jugendherberge, bitte.*"

"*Was?*"

Again I pleaded for the hostel, and this time an impatient smile flitted across her face. "*Ach,*" she said. "*Die JUGENDherberge!*" She brought out a map and a pencil, drew a line from here to there, and handed the map across

185

the counter. *"Sedel Strasse zwölf,"* she said.

"Dankeschön," I said.

"Bitteschön," she replied, just as the bicyclists had promised. I shouldered my rucksack and trudged off toward Number 12, Sedel Steet.

Italy – and Basia – were well and truly behind me now.

Portrait of the artist as a serious young man

THE HOSTEL HAD NO BUNKS, just a concrete floor with a bag of straw for a mattress. After a bit, the straw shifted to the sides and I was more or less sleeping on the concrete. I was awake for much of the night, wondering – as I have sometimes wondered since – what would have happened if I hadn't been so quick to leave Lerici. What if I'd said to the fleeting hour: "Stop a while, you are so fair!"

What if those earrings hadn't disappeared in the post office of Venice, or elsewhere on their journey to Perugia?

What if Basia had been steadier on that bike, hadn't been hospitalized, hadn't quit going to class, hadn't flitted off to Capri with Laetitia?

What if they'd returned to Perugia a few days earlier, or I'd arrived a few days later, so that Basia was there to greet me? I would have been in a finer mood, and people do pick up on moods and respond to them. . . .

More to the point, perhaps, what if I hadn't been so prickly – what if *she* hadn't been so prickly? We were each the second-born child, who'd grown up with fast feet and sharp elbows.

Maybe it would have made no difference. As I finish these chapters, I email them to Basia, and she is surprised at what a romantic fool they make me out to be:

Although I must have been a bit of a romantic, too, I think I was basically a realist. Living in the clouds has its limits, and one needs a bit of grit. I was upset when you left, and no we didn't kiss. But you were certainly not like Laetitia or Giorgio, and I didn't forget you. The others fleeted in my memory from time to time but you were always there.

The way you write about our trip, it seems that all you tried to do was to get me into bed. That was not how it was. It was not an Abelard and Heloise story, but it was not so ordinary, either. I think of it as a bit of friendship and a bit of fancy that had no chance to develop in such a short space of time. It was like a hazy morning with the promise of sunshine. It gave me a glow which spread to everything I saw and thought. It also gave me a feeling of apprehension, of something new that was thrilling but dangerous.

Oh Basia, if you had only known! You could have held me in Lerici with the crook of your little finger.

What if I had told her outright that I loved her? I've always found such declarations difficult, perhaps because love was seldom mentioned at home, and never between Mom and Dad. I'd have been much more comfortable with one of those Jane Austen declarations: "Miss Deszberg, I have come to esteem you greatly!"

What, indeed, if I'd asked her to marry me? That wasn't likely, because I was familiar with the maxim that a writer's muse flies out at the window when his wife comes in at the door. . . . Not that the muse and the bride are rivals, necessarily, but that few writers can afford to support both of them.

If I could now take myself back in time, from autumnal New Hampshire to the sunny ramparts of the castle at Lerici, with Basia Deszberg at my side, could I bring myself to say those words, and to hell with the muse? No doubt, but only because when we play games with the past, it is the present self who rolls the dice. We take our wisdom – which is to say: the intervening years – with us. But of course that can't be. It wouldn't be our young self that we take back to our own springtime, but the wiser and less interesting person we have become. We are given only the one life to lead. That life made us what we are today, so to unspool the years would be futile even if it could be done.

I ENJOYED HITCHHIKING through Switzerland, Liechtenstein (I walked through the principality in the middle of the night, waking the border guard at Feldkirch to get my passport stamped), Austria, and Germany, and in the end I managed to pronounce *Jugendherberge* correctly. I had an especially good time in Munich, where I fell in with some Americans for an evening of beer and song at the Hofbräuhaus. I also picked up a package of mail at the American Express office, forwarded by my landlady at Mauldeth Road West. Among the letters was one from Jim and Priscilla, my friends from home, saying they were sailing to England at the end of August. Jim proposed that we stand at the entrance to Piccadilly Underground at ten o'clock every morning until we met.

There was also a letter from Joe, who wrote: "I saw Clarence Dame the other day. It seems he got a postcard from you. He said, 'I see he's to hell and gone,' by which I presume he meant Italy." This inspired me to send another batch of postcards from Munich. You people are still *there*, and I'm to hell and gone!

Alas, it wasn't the same. Going down the Rhine on a passenger ferry, from Weisbaden to Koblenz, while a beery Bavarian played sad tunes on a piano accordion, I formulated a rule of travel that has held true over the years: What matters is the person you're traveling with. Second to that is what you're doing, and a distant third is where in the world you happen to be.

Back in London, I retrieved my suitcase from Euston Station, and I rented a room at Mr. Hussein's in Finsbury Park. "All races welcome," he promised in his notice on the bulletin board at Piccadilly Circus, so I reasoned that it would be cheap. Malcolm Hopson visited me at Finsbury Park, and so did Jim and Priscilla. Rather than a stakeout at Piccadilly Underground, I checked the Southampton arrivals in the *Telegraph*, and I went to Victoria Station at ten o'clock on the morning their boat was due. I met a dozen or so trains and scanned a thousand or so faces, but eventually they emerged, looking very clean and bright with their rucksacks and a suitcase. It's remarkable how often such youthful arrangements work out, which adults would never dream of attempting.

And in mid-September, I sailed from Liverpool in *RMS Brittanic* of the White Star Line, to fulfill my long-deferred date with the U.S. Army. For once it wasn't raining, and I was put in mind of a ballad my mother used to sing, while accompanying herself on the squeezebox accordion:

> Oh the sun is on the harbor, love,
> And I wish I could remain,
> For it will be a long, long time,
> Before we two meet again.
> It's not the leaving of Liverpool that grieves me,
> But my darling when I think of thee!

Two years of military service were then required of every reasonably fit young American male – and every English male, for that matter. And French. And German, starting in 1956. And Russian and Polish, of course. It was a time when, if one thought about it (as one seldom did), the Third World War might have broken upon us at any moment. No doubt that knowledge had influenced our happy life at Lerici. There were no Russian vagabonds on European roads, but if there had been, we'd have gotten along splendidly, just as we got along with the Germans, mortal enemies just ten years earlier.

I speak only for myself. I'm not so sure about Basia. Russians had murdered her father and brother, sent her filthy and hungry into Kazakhstan, and stolen her homeland to secure its own borders. Germans by contrast had rescued her from exile by their ill-considered invasion of Soviet Russia in June 1941.

Displaced Person
1943-1952

THE GERMANS MADE THEMSELVES at home in Russia, just as they'd done in Poland. At Goat Hills in the Katyn Forest, on the Dnieper River outside Smolensk, that NKVD "rest and recreation" area became the headquarters for the 537th Signal Regiment under Colonel Friedrich Ahrens. Early in 1943, the colonel learned that a wolf had dug up some human bones in the woods nearby, and he ordered the site to be excavated as soon as the ground thawed.

In a gigantic, L-shaped grave, the Germans uncovered what they believed to be 3,000 bodies, each marred by a bullet hole at the base of the skull. The corpses wore Polish uniforms, knee boots, and greatcoats, and their pockets contained Polish coins, letters and diaries, and propaganda newspapers from the prison camps. From the memorabilia, from the decay of the bodies, and from the growth rings on trees planted over the graves, the Germans concluded that the massacre had taken place three years before, meaning that the Poles had been murdered by their Russian captors.

This was a propaganda coup, and one that might shake the Western alliance. Civilians from others countries were invited to inspect the site, along with American and British prisoners of war, as the body count continued to climb.

Radio Berlin broke the story on April 13, 1943. In London and Washington, the first reaction was to ignore it, which allowed Moscow to brand it as a lie. "In launching this monstrous invention," spluttered the Soviet Information Bureau, "the German-Fascist scoundrels did not hesitate at the most unscrupulous and base lies, in their attempts to cover up crimes which, as has now become evident, were perpetrated by themselves." Not for another two days did the *New York Times* pick up the story, giving it two well-hedged sentences on page four: "The latest German attempt to sow discord between the Allies is a story of the alleged finding of graves of 10,000 Polish officers in a forest near Smolensk. In broadcast accounts the Germans suggest that these officers, taken prisoner during the invasion of Poland in the Winter of 1939-40, had been shot in the Spring of 1940."

The Russians went further, branding the Sikorski government in London as "Hitler's Polish Collaborators" for endorsing the German account. The Communist-funded *Daily Worker* in New York and *Morning Star* in London echoed this charge. In Washington, the Roosevelt administration was well salted with leftists, ready to take Moscow's view over that of the Poles. The same was true in Hollywood, where a reflexive anti-Polish bias can be seen in wartime films and for decades afterward. Even *Life* magazine followed the Communist line, putting Stalin on its cover, assuring us that Lenin was "perhaps the greatest man of modern times," and explaining that the NKVD was "a national police similar to the F.B.I."

Winston Churchill had a more realistic view of the evils inherent in Soviet Russia, but what was he to do? Poland had contributed some thousands of men to the British war effort – most of them not yet in action – while the Red Army had *millions* in bloody combat. "Alas, the German revelations are probably true," the prime minister admitted at a lunch with General Sikorski at 10 Downing Street. "The Bolsheviks can be very cruel." But he urged the Poles not to make an issue of the murders. "If they are dead," he said, "nothing you can do will bring them back." He was even more blunt in public. Asked about the Katyn controversy in the House of Commons, Churchill waved the question away: "The less said about that the better."

When it came to a choice between the London Poles (who had nowhere else to go) and Stalin (who'd collaborated with Hitler in 1939 and might do so again), Churchill had no choice. Whatever the cost – even if he had to betray the country on whose behalf Britain had gone to war – he must keep the Russians happy. He said as much to the Soviet ambassador: "We have got to beat Hitler, and this is no time for quarrels and charges."

IN TEHRAN, MAMA had no doubt about the perpetrators of the Katyn atrocity, and she assumed (what else could explain his long silence?) that her husband's body was among those uncovered by the Germans. As Basia says:

Until then, I hadn't thought much about my father's absence. I just knew he would be back! And most of my friends in our wanderings were Polish, and they didn't have fathers either. It seemed natural not to have one. It was only with the news of Katyn – and rumors about prisoners having been beaten, having their nails pulled out and tortured – that I started to have nightmares. And understood that he would not be coming back.

Like everyone in the spring of 1943, the Deszbergs vastly underestimated the scale of the atrocity. The bodies uncovered at Goat Hills were those of officers from a single camp, the converted monastery at Kozelsk, near Moscow. Basia's brother Jurek was probably among them, but sixty-nine years would pass before the "Ukraine list" revealed that her father was probably shot in Kiev and buried nearby at Bykivnia.

IN NOVEMBER 1943, the "Big Three" Western leaders met for the first time. The site was Tehran, not far from the convent of Santo Spirito. At Stalin's suggestion, Roosevelt moved himself and his entourage into the Russian embassy for the conference. The British embassy was nearby, while the U.S. establishment was on the other side of the city, so this arrangement provided security and convenience for the American president. It was also a convenience for the NKVD, greatly simplifying the task of bugging Roosevelt's quarters.

And it signaled to Churchill that he was now the outsider. Two years after the Germans first entered Soviet Russia, the Red Army had turned the tide of the War, not only stopping the onslaught but driving the invader back almost to the prewar Polish frontier. Just as the "alignment of forces" obliged Churchill to favor the Russians over the Poles, it now prompted Roosevelt to favor Stalin over Churchill (who, like the Poles, had nowhere else to go). Still, did he have to be so obvious about it? As Stalin's biographer Simon Montefiore described an early exchange: "Roosevelt winked at Stalin, the start of his gauche flirtation that greatly enhanced [Stalin's] position as arbiter of the Grand Alliance."

Roosevelt's naivete was best expressed by the president himself. In August 1943 he was warned by William Bullitt, his first ambassador to the Soviet Union, that Stalin would impose a Communist government upon any country he managed to occupy. "I just have a hunch that Stalin is not that kind of man," Roosevelt replied. "I think that if I give him everything I possibly can and ask for nothing from him in return, noblesse oblige, he won't try to annex anything and will work with me for a world of democracy and peace."

The conference's first priority was to coordinate a Russian drive into Poland with the Anglo-American invasion of France. Roosevelt and Churchill desperately wanted an offensive on the Eastern Front, to prevent the Germans from reinforcing their divisions in the west. Stalin was equally anxious for the D-Day invasion, which likewise would take pressure off the Red Army. (Toward that end, his agents in Britain and America had been demanding "Second Front Now!" for the past two years.) But he didn't let his eagerness show: "Stalin was the master negotiator," as Robert Gellately says of the Soviet dictator, "tireless, shrewd, and with deep knowledge that he could use as needed."

And he held the ace! No military force had ever attempted anything like the invasion of France, with 150,000 British, American, and Canadian troops coming ashore on five beaches backed by high cliffs that the Germans had been fortifying since 1940. Once on the shore of France, the western Allies must literally do or die, for failure would mean the massacre of those troops. In the east, however, Stalin could start or stop his war effort at will. There were no all-or-nothing ventures on the Eastern Front, but only a bloody slog across open plains.

Having agreed upon a date in May 1944 (later advanced to June), the Big Three turned to the question of Poland's postwar frontiers. With Roosevelt eager to curry favor, and with Churchill constrained by geopolitics, there was no hope that they could stand up to Stalin. Poland would become "the country on roller skates," as we called it after the War. Its eastern half would be incorporated into Soviet Russia, and the Warsaw government would be compensated by a nearly equal slice of Germany. As a result, Poland would shift 135 miles to the west.

It was Churchill who put the idea into words. "I thought Poland might move westward," he wrote after the War, "like soldiers taking two steps [left]. . . . I demonstrated with the help of three matches my idea of Poland moving westward. This pleased Stalin. . . ."

Certainly it did! The new frontiers greatly improved Russia's postwar position, putting the German frontier 135 miles farther from Moscow. Along with a puppet government in Warsaw, this would ensure that Germany never again contemplated an invasion of Russia.

For a time, Basia's home town was in play. Churchill expected Lwow to remain Polish, since Poles had been a clear majority of its prewar population. Stalin, humiliated at Lwow in 1920, was determined that it be incorporated into Soviet Russia. Faced with Stalin's rocklike solidity, Churchill threw in the towel. He was "not prepared to make a great squawk" about Basia's birthplace.

In later years, during his nightlong drinking bouts with his Kremlin toadies, Stalin would tell a little joke about how he had established the postwar borders of Eastern Europe. He'd gone hunting with Churchill and Roosevelt, he said, and together they bagged a bear. The American president wanted the skin as a souvenir rug, but Churchill had the same idea. So they turned to Stalin and asked him to decide: how should they divide the bear? Stalin smiled: *he* would get the skin, and the carcass too. "The bear belongs to me," he said; "after all, I killed it."

BASIA AND LALKA remained at Santo Spirito for the rest of the War. On Friday or Sunday (there was no school on the holy days, Friday for the Persians, Sunday for the nuns and the Deszberg girls) they might be rescued by Mama or Aunt Krysia and taken for an adventure in the city. Less often, Mama's friend from the O Club took them for a treat:

Tom would take us somewhere to have an ice or fruit juice at a restaurant or cafe. That was exciting for us – to have everything nicely served! And it was also exciting because we were out of the school. Tom was really good to us but of course our conversation was always limited.

I don't know if there was anything between Tom and Mama. I hope so, after the frightening and hard times she had been through. And it couldn't have been any easier for him either, being so far from home. Anyway their friendship did not take anything away from my father, who was always a hero with not a bit of clay in his feet.

I have a particular fondness for Tom. Perhaps he found himself in a position with Mama rather like the one I would experience with her daughter: *desire / and a yearning heart!* And his outings with the Deszberg women paved the way for me to hitchhike to Italy, eleven years later, with the youngest of them.

MEANWHILE, THE FORDS were moving on. From Lakeport we moved briefly to Rochester, then to Concord, Massachusetts, where Dad became the live-in manager for the Laughlin estate – or farm, as it now purported to be. Mr. Laughlin had cleverly purchased two gorgeous black Lincoln Continental convertibles, the last that were built in Detroit before the Willow Run plant switched over to the production of B-24 Liberator bombers. To keep the Continentals' twelve-cylinder engines supplied with gasoline, Mr. Laughlin became a farmer, the work to be done by Dad, two day laborers, and Joe and me. We boys earned thirty cents an hour in July and August, weeding vegetables and pitching hay.

And I became best friends with Gordon Olson. There were several Norwegian families in Concord, and an even larger colony of Italians, who grew vegetables and sold them at the market in Boston's North End. Indeed, one family was so very Italian that the sons were named Primo, Secondo, and Terzo, with Secondo in my class at Peter Buckley School. As proof of the internationalism of children – or our ignorance – it never occurred to us that Secondo's name was anything out of the ordinary, or that his parents until recently had been "enemy aliens."

THOUGH NOT MUCH REMEMBERED, compared to the bloodletting on the Eastern Front or the wonderfully satisfying invasion of France, the Allied slog through Italy was a tortuous affair. The countryside I admired in July 1955 – peak after peak, leveled and tamed for agriculture – was the worst possible terrain for an advancing army. By the same token, it was easy to defend, and no more stubborn soldier ever shouldered a rifle than the German *landser* of the Second World War.

The iconic battle of the Italian campaign was the struggle for Monte Cassino Abbey, a Benedictine monastery on a rocky ridge south of Rome. The Americans fought to exhaustion at Monte Cassino, as did the Indian troops who relieved them in the spring of 1944. It wasn't until May 11 that the Anders Army – now designated 2nd Polish Corps – stormed the ridge and conquered it in four days of hand-to-hand fighting.

The Poles lost 11,379 men in the Italian campaign – 2,301 killed, 8,543 wounded, and 535 missing in action – a quarter of those whom General Anders had brought out of Russia. The Monte Cassino dead remain there today, under a Polish flag and an epitaph modeled on Simonides' tribute to the Spartans who fell at Thermopylae: "Passer-by, tell Poland that we fell faithful to her service."

Like Dabrowski's Legionnaires who'd fought in Italy at the turn of the 19th Century, few of the survivors would ever go home. The Red Army crossed the Polish frontier on June 1, 1944, and – true to Ambassador Bullitt's warning to Roosevelt – promptly began to eliminate anyone who might object to Soviet rule. In Lwow, the Polish Home Army rose up against the Germans, taking control of the central train station and the southern part of the city, including Basia's home on what was now Siegfried Strasse. They were joined by units of the Red Army 10th Tank Corps. Poles and Russians fought side by side, but only until the Germans surrendered. Then the NKVD took over, as in September 1939, and 5,000 men and boys of the Home Army were sent into the Gulag. The rest were conscripted into the Red Army.

The Russians then advanced upon Warsaw, where the outcome was even more cruel. Moscow radio called upon the capital to rise: "There is not a moment to lose!" As in Lwow, the Poles were initially successful, but this time they got no support from the Russians. Under the command of General Konstantin Rokossovsky – born in Warsaw but a Russian officer since the Bolshevik revolution of 1917 – the Red Army remained motionless on the outskirts for more than five months. The Germans meanwhile razed the capital and massacred its defenders, using "a ghoulish crew of SS fanatics, convicts and Russian renegades to slaughter 225,000 civilians in one merciless inferno."

The British and Americans pleaded for landing rights in Soviet-controlled territory, so they could drop supplies into Warsaw, refuel at Russian airfields, and return to bases in Italy. Stalin refused most such missions. Two million Red Army troops were on Polish soil during the last three months of 1944, but they busied themselves with setting up a Communist government at Lublin, arresting Polish Home Army fighters, and raping girls as young as nine and women as old as eighty. In the words of Robert Gellately: "The Poles were sickened and revolted by the Red Army's campaign of rape, which left behind venereal diseases of epidemic proportions."

Not until January 1945 did General Rokossovsky advance into Warsaw, by then a depopulated ruin. Two weeks later, the Red Army crossed the prewar German frontier. In the west, the Anglo-American armies (including 1st Polish Corps) had likewise entered Germany, so that after three and a half years of combat and the loss of millions of lives, the country was reduced once more to its 1918 frontiers. The race was now to Berlin – a race that the British hoped to win. "I decided, however," General Dwight Eisenhower wrote, "that [Berlin] was not the logical or more desirable objective for the forces of the Western Allies." The German capital had already been assigned to the Russian zone of occupation, and the genial but apolitical American commander saw no point in wasting lives on it. Winston Churchill protested to Washington, but President Roosevelt was dying, and the question was probably never brought to his attention. If it had been, he would almost certainly have agreed with Eisenhower: let Stalin have the glory, noblesse oblige!

On April 12, Roosevelt died of a cerebral hemorrhage. At Peter Buckley School, the principal called us out to the playground to tell us the news, then gave us the day off. Roosevelt was the only president we had ever known – he'd been in the White House for longer than most of us had been alive. We really did need a day off, to grasp the enormity of his death, and to accept that the president was now the unprepossessing Harry Truman.

THE SCALE OF THE RUSSIAN assault on Berlin was almost beyond comprehension: 2,500,000 soldiers and airmen, 41,600 cannon, 6,250 tanks, 7,500 aircraft . . . proof, if any be needed, that it was indeed Joseph Stalin who killed the bear. On April 30, 1945, with enemy soldiers virtually standing upon his underground bunker, Adolf Hitler shot himself with a Walther PPK like those used to murder the Katyn Forest victims. "So that's the end of the bastard," Stalin said when an aide awakened him with news of his onetime ally's death. Ten days later, the German army, navy, and air force surrendered to the Allies in Berlin. The Second World War in Europe was over.

Unlike the Americans, Winston Churchill understood Stalin's intentions for the nations overrun by the Red Army. He asked his chief of staff to draw up plans for "Operation Unthinkable," to assess what would be needed if British, American, and German – yes, German! – troops were to roll back the Russians and secure "a square deal for Poland." The plan that came back called for 650,000 men to advance on two fronts against a Red Army three times as large. This noble but lunatic scheme was promptly shot down by the Americans. Harry Truman cabled that the U.S. would abide by the occupation zones already agreed upon, and that was the end of Unthinkable. As Max Hastings has written, "The prime minister was obliged to recognize that there was not the slightest possibility that the Americans would lead an attempt to drive the Russians from Poland by force, nor even threaten Moscow that they might do so."

This left Stalin free to install a puppet government in

Warsaw, with his own General Rokossovsky as its minister of defense, and to send a new wave of Poles into the Gulag. Poland lost its eastern half and in return got a piece of Germany, with both territories ethnically cleansed – Poles expelled from the eastern provinces, Germans from the new land in the west. Lwow thus became a Ukrainian city, its spelling changed to Lviv. And Potocki Street, temporarily Siegfried Strasse, would henceforth honor Taras Chuprynka, a Ukrainian nationalist.

While I can remember Roosevelt's death, and I can picture the glaring black headline on the *Boston Record* when Hiroshima was destroyed, I have no memory of the surrenders, V-E Day in May or V-J Day in August. Perhaps I was disappointed that the War had ended before I was able to join it! In any event, the advent of peace inspired Dad to change jobs yet again, and he became janitor of St. Aidan's Church in a suburb of Boston. I was, for about a year, a thoroughgoing juvenile delinquent, palling about with a policeman's son with the unlikely name of Danny Goode. I came out of it all right: Danny and I were only once caught by the police, and his father got us released without being booked. Meanwhile, like Lalka and Basia, Joe and I went to school with the nuns. I value this experience, for I mastered English grammar and a bit of Latin under the tutelage of Sister Maria. We paid rapt attention to Sister Maria, for she taught with a ruler, which she used to slap the palm of an inattentive girl but applied – edge-on! – to the knuckles of us boys.

I can't imagine why Dad thought he'd be happy as a janitor, and he wasn't. In another year we moved back to New Hampshire – to Wolfeboro this time, not far from the Caretaker's Cottage in East Alton. He got a job as a carpenter for a dollar an hour, forty-eight hours a week; he acquired a 1936 Plymouth sedan that wouldn't start in cold weather; and for $2,700 he bought a little house on Pine Hill Road, the first time in my recollection that we lived in our own home.

This was my seventh school in nine years, and the last. And the best! Brewster Academy was a combination of public and private school, with its students divided about equally between local kids and dormitory students. The boarders in turn were divided between youngsters, mostly dumped there while their parents got divorced, and War veterans prepping for college on the GI Bill. We read Homer, Caesar, and Shakespeare; we were taught Latin and a modern language. The teachers took it for granted that, if we had any brains at all, we'd go to college, and half of us did. If it hadn't been for Brewster, I don't know what would have become of me, but I doubt that I would have been a Fulbright scholar at the Victoria University of Manchester in the Lenten term of 1955.

BASIA'S HALF-BROTHER, the talented Zdzislaw, worked at the Polish embassy in Tehran, which again enabled him to improve the family's fortunes. He invested in Persian rugs, and he advised Mama to do the same. She bought a geometric Kashkuli that she promised to Lalka, and a floral Kashan that would be Basia's. The Kashan was still in North Ealing in 1955; I must have walked on its rich colors when I spent the night at Mama's house, before Basia and I set out for Paris. She also bought the gold bangles that adorned Basia's wrist when I met her at Manchester.

Zdzislaw was also able to decide where the refugees would go next, with the War over and the Persians anxious for them to be gone. Poland was still out of reach, as was England, its housing stock depleted by German bombs and its troopships bringing home millions of servicemen from around the world. So the Poles – "displaced persons" in the language of the day – would be settled temporarily in India, Africa, New Zealand, Mexico, and the Middle East. Zdzislaw put the Deszberg clan (increased by the birth of his second son in Tehran) on the list for Lebanon, as the closest to home. They traveled overland by British Army convoy, through Persia, Iraq, and Syria, until they reached the Mediterranean at Beirut:

We lived in a ramshackle house where we rented two rooms from an Arab family. We all lived together more or less, the Arabs and we. Our larger room had three beds, a huge wardrobe, a piano, a main table, and a smaller table that served as our kitchen. The doors and windows were usually open, and we took part in great occasions of the house, such as weddings or funerals. The roof was flat, and I spent a lot of time up there, eating red melons and pomegranates. The house shook when there was a storm, and sometimes a brown cloud of locusts came through an open window, flew across the room, and left through another window. There were also many cats roaming about, trying to steal food. They could even steal a hot cutlet from a frying pan.

Our cat was Ca ne fait rien *or Never Mind. (He was called by both names from the time I started English lessons from an old Polish lady.) He was completely unmoved by any of the goings on, even when other cats stole his food. When he was a kitten, Never Mind's mother didn't want him. So Lalka and I fed him and bathed him in the essence of all kinds of flowers. He seemed to be on the way out, so we decided to let him alone. Free of our ministrations, he got better and grew up into a beautiful, long-haired cat with a thick bushy tail. He was my very special friend, and it was a great tragedy when we left Lebanon and had to leave him behind.*

As always, the Poles set up schools for the children. Lalka went to a proper school, but Basia's classes were in the evening, enabling her and a dozen others to spend their days on the beach or at the cinema. Among other films, they saw *Rigoletto*, with Tito Gobbi as the hunchbacked jester. That was the occasion when the girls cried, the boys laughed at them, the manager threw them out, and Basia first heard the lyrics of "La donna è mobile."

That was too good to last. As soon as Mama got some money together, I was sent to a French school – with the nuns again, though it was not so bad as Tehran because it was only a day school. Lalka and I also went to the American University to study piano and ballet. She was supposed to play nine hours a day, because she was "gifted," and I was supposed to play for two hours. In fact, she practiced for two hours and I for thirty minutes, except when Aunt Nuna bribed me to play a bit longer. Never Mind would sit on the piano and look offended when we stopped playing.

Aunt Krysia was adventurous and wanted to see everything. So when she saved enough money, she and I went to see the Cedars of Lebanon in the mountains. And we went to Syria, to visit the mosque in Damascus.

Sometimes an ancient woman would visit our house, gather the neighborhood children around her, and build a barbecue out of bricks. She would mix the dough, then throw it from hand to hand until it was round and paper-thin. Then she put it on a sort of a huge wok turned upside down, and we all got a piece when it was ready. She told us stories too, half in French, half in Arabic. House members and neighbors soon joined in. There was singing and laughter, and it was very pleasant to sit and listen in the twilight. That is how I remember the Arabs, happy and gracious.

MORE THAN TWO YEARS AFTER the war ended, Basia and the others were finally allowed to emigrate to England. Evidently this was arranged by her half-brother Zdzislaw, who joined the British Army in order to qualify his extended family for emigration. They went first to Egypt, where they were housed at Qassassin, halfway between Cairo and the Suez Canal, living in a tent city that had once belonged to the Anders Army. Aunt Krysia and Basia took the opportunity to visit Cairo and the Pyramids. Then, toward the end of March 1948, they were taken to Port Said, where they walked up the gangplank of the Cunard liner *Franconia*, still in service as a troopship. Hundreds of Polish soldiers were below decks as *Franconia* steamed through the Mediterranean and up the Bay of Biscay, while the civilians were housed in the former first-class cabins:

The English did us proud. I have never since traveled in such luxury. I especially remember the table, which was beautifully laid. Lalka and I had no idea what to do with all the cutlery. I was so busy watching how the others used the many knives and forks and spoons that I don't remember what the food was like. . . . There was a storm, a very bad one, in the Bay of Biscay.

And finally we came to England, and it was raining.

Waleria Deszberg and her two little boys (though not the resourceful Zdzislaw) were also aboard *Franconia* when tugboats brought the ship to dock in Liverpool. The day was April 14, 1948. The Deszbergs were sent to an abandoned Royal Air Force base at Keevil, near Bristol in the southwest of England, where they were housed in a prefabricated Nissen Hut – what Americans called a Quonset.

The hut was a sort of half-barrel barrack made of galvanized steel, divided by curtains to accommodate two or three families. The sky was all shades of gray; the air was gray; and the rain kept rattling on the tin roof.

I missed Never Mind.

Lalka and Basia went to school in Trowbridge nearby, where for the third time they began classes in an alien tongue. By accident or design, Basia's introduction to English literature was an essay by Joseph Conrad, born Jozef Korzeniowski in a town that, like Lwow, had once belonged to Poland but now was part of Soviet Russia.

I suspect that these transitions were harder on Lalka than on her younger sister, as was the case with the Ford boys. Joe graduated in 1948 after little more than a year at

Brewster Academy; Dad gave him the keys to the Plymouth and himself boarded a Greyhound bus to Arizona, on the theory that the desert would be good for his lungs, afflicted first by TB and then by asthma. While Joe clerked in the First National store, I benefited from another two years at Brewster. Similarly, Lalka was packed off to art school in London that fall, living with the aunts and Aunt Kyrsia's husband, back from prison camp in Germany. Zdzislaw also settled in London, selling his Persian carpets for money to start a business, while he and his family lived four to a rented room in Chiswick.

Mama stayed at Keevil camp and worked as a cleaning woman in Trowbridge hospital, to save money for a house of her own. The girls' school expenses were paid by the Polish exile government in London, a government now recognized only by Ireland, Spain, and the Vatican. So Basia was able to transfer to Holy Trinity Convent School in Kidderminster, 100 miles north. Here she found herself in a tall Victorian building, set back from the Birmingham Road, with playing fields behind and St. Ambrose church down the street. Counting her brief flurries in Poland and Kazakhstan, and the makeshift classes in Persia and Lebanon, this was her eighth school, so she was actually one school ahead of me.

Holy Trinity was similar to Santo Spirito in that it had a high wall and a gate. But it had beautiful grounds, with a hockey field and a tennis court. There was no bustle, and the nuns did not run around cuffing and hugging the children; instead, they walked straight and severe. They were a French order. We called them Madame and curt-sied every time we passed them.

We too had to walk tall. "Heads up!" they would remind us. "Chest out, tummy in!" Once I was repri-manded for running in the hall, and I must have glared because the nun told me: "Smile, Barbara! Nobody is interested in your misery." It was good advice that I did not appreciate at the time, just as I did not appreciate anything they did for me. And they did a lot.

Holy Trinity was in many ways a traditional English boarding school, with a morning wash with cold water, and a bath once a week. We went to early Mass, we took Communion every day, and we prayed before every hockey game. We had a dance once, a ball. We invited boys, and the nuns went around the dance floor, and if any of us got too close they came between us and separated us. We also produced an opera, Il Trovatore – *in English, though, and they changed the plot so that Leonora and the Count and the Troubador were all brothers and sisters.*

For field hockey, Basia wore a white blouse and voluminous shorts. Otherwise she wore the blouse with a sleeveless wool dress, a tie, school blazer, and sensible shoes. Except for the tunic, this was the same outfit she would wear during her first year at Manchester. Young people did not own many clothes in the 1950s; the English owned fewer than Americans did, and the Poles had less than anyone.

There was a military school next door and sometimes when the young men were playing football and the ball came over the wall, we threw it back but were told by the nuns not to speak to those half-naked individuals. As we were always supervised, we didn't. So I don't know anything about our neighbors.

Holy Trinity is now a secular day school, with boys admitted in the lower grades. When I asked about the 1950s, the principal put me in touch with one of Basia's classmates, who sent me a photograph of their field hockey team. In it, Basia's face has filled out nicely, and for the first time a photograph suggests the adult she will become. Her hair is more blonde than brown, and she wears it in two thick plaits. She is a good-looking girl, but I suspect that if she'd turned up at Brewster Academy – she'd have been two grades behind me – I wouldn't have paid particular attention. To be sure, the photo is a machine copy, in black and white. . . . Perhaps if I could see her eyes as the blue of cornflowers, that infinite dark blue?

In June 1951, she passed her O Levels, the school leaving exams that English youngsters take at fifteen or sixteen. Most girls left Holy Trinity at that point, because they didn't aspire to university; they would become shop girls, bank tellers, secretaries, wives. Obedient to Mama's devotion to schooling, Basia applied for an additional two years, to prepare for her A Levels. She was granted one year.

I'd already had elocution and extra English lessons from Madame Marie, a very old teacher who lived in the convent. She plunged me into Macbeth *to give me a feel for the beauty of the language. It is still one of my favorite plays. Then, when I had to do a two-year A Level course in one year, I had more lessons in English and Latin. Madame Marie even listened with me to a BBC broadcast of the* Aeneid, *though she blushed at the goings-on between Dido and Aeneas.*

By the spring of 1952, Basia's accent had all but vanished, and she was deemed an acceptable candidate for the University of Manchester, where I would meet her in Caf and judge her the most enchanting young woman I had ever known.

CHAPTER THIRTEEN
We Meet Again
1956-2012

I WROTE BASIA a time or two after *RMS Brittanic* deposited me at Pier 54, and she replied, though I remember only one of her letters. I was a raw recruit at Fort Dix, New Jersey, getting run off my feet by Korean War vets who had learned the hard way that soldiers are worthless who weren't rigorously trained. Basia wrote that she'd seen Ian Fellowes, my boon companion from Mauldeth Road West, come into Caf wearing my plaid winter jacket. "It gave my heart quite a jump," she wrote.

And that was the last I heard from her, or so I believed until recently. But it seems there was another exchange. Basia married in June 1956, just after graduating from the University of Manchester. The wedding was at St. Benedict's in Ealing, a mile from Mama's house. It was an elegant affair, with the bride in a gown, veil, and train, attended by little Polish girls with plaits and crowns of flowers.

By this time I was stationed at Fort Bragg, North Carolina, where I was assigned to Smoke Bomb Hill and a weird combination of Green Beret commandos and Psychological Warfare specialists. I don't remember Basia's letter, but she remembers my reply:

You wrote to me: "I hope you have many daughters, and I hope they bring as much happiness to the world as you have brought to me." It was the nicest gift I got for my wedding.

It was indeed a pretty response, though like those green gloves it seems a bit out of character. Perhaps I was making myself more lovable in the novel I was writing at the time. (Private Stephen Faust?) Forgetting something as elemental as a sweetheart's marriage can't be an accident: it suggests a bruised ego protecting itself. I was crushed – I must have been! I was educated, reasonably cultured for the 1950s, well read for any decade, and admirably well traveled. For all that, it wasn't I who bedded the convent girl. No doubt I envisioned my replacement as Marlon Brando in his wife-beater undershirt, playing Stanley Kowalski in *A Streetcar Named Desire.*

Looking back, though, I'm relieved to know about Basia's wedding, because it solves a puzzle that has long bothered me: Why didn't I look her up when I had the chance? Not many months after, I found myself in France, in Orléans, living in a redbrick caserne formerly occupied by German soldiers, and by French soldiers (including Private Marcel Proust) before that.

We lived a privileged life at Coligny Caserne, French cooks and waitresses to feed us and Polish Labor Service guards to protect us. I sometimes went drinking with the Poles, in a tavern on the Faubourg Bannier. Their evenings began with joy and laughter but progressed in stages to dancing, brawling, and finally tears as they wept for their homeland. The jukebox was a turntable under a glass cover with a hole in it, through which one reached to select a scratched record:

> March, march, Dabrowski,
> From Italy to Poland;
> We will follow you,
> And win back our nation!

I enjoyed those men but never quite made the connection between them and Basia. They were older, and they treated me more like a nephew than a buddy. If I missed curfew or had too much to drink, they'd smuggle me into the caserne through their own guardhouse, to keep me safe from the Military Police.

What stories they could have told! – of the armies that stormed into Poland; of conscription by Germany or Soviet Russia; of escape, desertion, or surrender to the West; of enlisting in the British Army; and (for some of them, their fifth uniform) of working for the Americans in France. Basia's half-brother Jurek might have been one of these men, if fate and his lieutenant's epaulettes hadn't directed him to a mass grave in the Katyn Forest.

One weekend I got a three-day pass and took the ferry to England, to rendezvous with Malcolm Hopson. I could have found Basia as easily! I could have taken the Piccadilly line to North Ealing, walked a few blocks to Boileau Road, knocked on the door, and asked for her address. But I didn't, knowing then what I later forgot: that our last exchange of letters had been on the occasion of her wedding.

Was that terrible of me? Should I have modeled myself on the loyal family friend, a stock character in English fiction, who hangs around for years, doggedly and silently in love with the young wife and mother? That wasn't my style, so I did a fair job of shriving my heart of Basia, though I'm afraid I never stopped talking about her – about our winter at Caf, our spring on the road to Italy, and our summer idyll at the castle of Lerici.

SO SHE LIVED HER LIFE, and I lived mine, and for the most part on different continents. I married late but happily. I never did become my generation's Hemingway, but with Sally's help I wrote some books that still bring me pleasure.

And we did a lot of skiing, an activity that often took us west on Route 4, through the little town of Northwood Narrows, New Hampshire. Here we passed a replica of the Trojan Horse, large enough to conceal Odysseus and his companions, or indeed the Kremlin troika of Stalin, Beria, and Kaganovich, the bastards. The horse stood over a mock graveyard, with ten white crosses representing East Germany; the Baltic nations of Latvia, Lithuania, and Estonia; and Bulgaria, Romania, Hungary, Albania, Czechoslovakia – and Poland!

Like the eccentric anti-Communist in Northwood Narrows, the Polish exile government remained faithful to its mission throughout the Cold War, regularly electing a president, prime minister, and cabinet that met twice a month in London. These rituals ended in 1990, when Poland astonished the world by throwing out its rulers and declaring itself a republic. The London Poles returned the symbols of office that had been smuggled out of the country in September 1939: the presidential banner and sash, the state seal, and the prewar constitution. So the prophecy of Dabrowski's Mazurka was fulfilled, not by steel but by masses of people who turned their backs on Soviet Russia and walked away from Communism:

> Her father said to Basia
> With tears in his eyes:
> "Hear our soldiers, child,
> Marching to their drums!"

A year later, the Soviet Union itself fell apart. Kazakhstan became a nation in its own right, as did Ukraine, with Lviv – the former Lwow – as its second-largest city, as it had once been Poland's.

So Basia's nation was free again, though her birthplace wasn't part of it. Among Poland's new liberties was the ability to probe that great ache in the Polish heart, the murder of 21,892 soldiers, policemen, officials, and professionals in the Katyn massacres. In April 2010, a Russian-built Tupelev airliner took off from Warsaw with ninety-six passengers including Poland's president, the last leader of the exile government in London, other officials, military officers, businessmen, clergy, and relatives of the Katyn victims, bound for Smolensk and the seventieth anniversary of the Katyn murders. It crashed while landing in heavy fog. Since it was their airspace, the Russians conducted the investigation, and they laid the blame – where else? – on the Polish Air Force pilot. So a gesture meant to salve a national grief instead became the source of yet more grief.

That tragedy inspired me to view the Polish feature film, *Katyn*. It opens with a young woman and her child crossing a bridge with a mass of refugees, fleeing the German invasion. They meet another mass of refugees coming from the east, trying to escape the Red Army. Movies seldom make me weep, but this one did: that child might have been my friend from Caf, and that woman might have been Mama, caught between opposing and malevolent armies.

I wrote to the University of Manchester, which told me that for some years mail to Barbara Deszberg had been returned, addressee unknown. However, the family name is an unusual one, and a Google search led me to a typewritten list of refugees who'd reached Tehran in 1942. Six of them were Deszbergs, including Barbara (Basia), Maria (Lalka), and Zuzanna (Mama). Of the other three, Janusz had a birth year of 1940, so I went in search of him, reckoning that he was certainly a relative, and that if Basia had found her way to England, he might have done the same. So it proved. I found an address for him, wrote to him, and learned that he was Colonel Deszberg's grandson – the lad born in Semipalatinsk, Basia's half-nephew. He gave me her email address.

I was skiing in Colorado when her reply came up on my iPhone. What a curious experience, to be riding the Silver Queen gondola to the top of Aspen Mountain, and to catch up with her life – my life! – after fifty-six years:

Hallo Dan, what a surprise! I'm chuffed. I meant to write immediately, but was celebrating my name day in Polish fashion, with people coming and going. What a lovely gift from you on the eve of my name day.

About me: got married, had two children, taught French and Latin, got divorced after fifteen years, and went off to Munich to work at Radio Free Europe, an American radio station broadcasting to Eastern Europe. Now I am here in England for good.

I phoned her and was astonished to find that she had a

distinct Polish accent. To be sure, the telephone emphasizes any oddity of speech, since one can't see the lips or the eyes that also talk to us, and often more eloquently. Growing up, my friends would comment about my mother's Irish brogue, which was inaudible to me until the first time I spoke to her on the telephone, as a freshman at the University of New Hampshire.

Then too, Basia had married a countryman and reared two Polish-speaking children. Later, in Germany, she lived with Lalka and *her* Polish-speaking husband and child, so that was the language she spoke at home and at work. I'd known her at the height of her immersion in English culture, Trowbridge to Kidderminster to Manchester. Her years as an English schoolgirl actually lasted no longer than her odyssey through Soviet Russia and the Middle East.

We emailed often that winter. "You must write this story," Sally said, after reading those messages. That was my thought, too, though I was reluctant to mention it to Basia. She might say no! Worse, she might agree but start to compose her emails as literature, instead of the wry, easy messages she'd been sending.

But it worked out, and in time Sally and I flew to London to meet her.

SO I AM SITTING BESIDE HER for the first time since leaving her at the sun-drenched promenade at Lerici. We are on the couch, at a coffee table with Sally sitting across from us. Beneath our feet is the floral Kashan that Mama bought in Tehran, and that graced the breakfast room in Earling in 1955. On a side table is an open book, the masterwork of one of my youthful heroes, James Joyce. I've read *Ulysses*, though never in one go, start to finish. But here was Basia reading it alternately in English and in Polish!

She is no longer the girl of twenty-one, and no longer speaks the flawless English (with a hint of something foreign) that enchanted me in Caf, that gray, chill winter when we were students together at Manchester. Yet the accent recedes as the week goes by. Perhaps the truth of the matter is that, just as Basia in 1955 defined for me the perfection of female beauty, her voice too became the ideal form of human speech. Perhaps she was never as fluent as I thought!

I can see now, as I didn't at the time, that she is a very spunky woman, opinionated and quick to judgment. I share these characteristics, so it's a wonder we didn't clash more often than we did on the road to Italy.

But here's the thing! Her eyes are the same impossible blue, that cornflower blue, nearly violet at times, but tending toward green when she wears a green blouse, as she does this morning (and as she did at Lerici long ago). More than once, as we talk about Kidderminister or Georgievka, I feel my heart make its slow, sweet cartwheel, as it was wont to do at Caf and on the road. There is no fool like an old fool, unless it be the young fool who gave rise to him.

We talked every day for a week, as I asked the questions I should have asked in 1955. One evening the three of us went to Covent Garden, to see *Macbeth* in honor of Madame Marie at Kidderminster. (Our driver was from Afghanistan. He was very proud of his adopted city, and he detoured along the Embankment, to show us Big Ben and the Houses of Parliament lit up and golden, cleansed like everything else in Europe of the grime of 1955.) We met her children; we met her niece, Lalka's daughter; and we met Uncle Jan's daughter, whom I'd have known as a toddler in Manchester if Basia had dared bring me home from the University.

One afternoon, John Deszberg – as Janusz calls himself now – took me to the Sikorski Museum and the Hearth Club in Kensington. Both institutions are going strong, twenty-odd years after the Iron Curtain rusted away. Not only can the exiles of 1940 visit Warsaw and Gdansk for holidays and dental care (cheaper and more efficient there than in England), but with their European Union passports young Poles can work in London. The secretary at the museum and the bartender at the social club both immigrated from the new Poland. To my ear, they speak a different language than the wartime exiles and their children. It's a more lively tongue – lilting – as if Italians had taken up the Polish language.

WELL, I HAVE GIVEN YOU the love story, such as it was, which brings me to the history lesson that was my other purpose in writing this book.

History happens to one person at a time! If 60 million people died as a result of the Second World War ("prematurely," as historians delicately say), and if thrice that number were wounded, raped, exiled, widowed, or orphaned, that's a total of 240 million victims, more people than lived in the United States at the time. That is, however, just a statistic, as Stalin himself is supposed to have said. The important figure is 240 million *times one*. Like Colonel Deszberg and his son, murdered in the Katyn Forest massacres – like Basia herself – each victim had a history, a family, and a promised future, and each had that life forever altered. I have tried in this book to tell how a child named Barbara Deszberg experienced the Second World War. Now that you've reached the end of the story, consider that you'd have to read 240 million such books to know the full tragedy of the War that began when Germany invaded Poland in September 1939.

The more extended grief was borne by the survivors. Of Basia's family in exile, Uncle Jan was the first to die, in 1963. His daughter was brought up by Aunt Kyrsia and Aunt Nuna in London, while his son followed the traditional English route through boarding schools. Aunt Kyrsia's husband Adam, who'd survived nearly six years as a prisoner of war in Germany, died not long after Jan.

The women fared better, perhaps because they had each other to lean on. Krysia and Nuna were always together, while Mama was more independent. She stayed at Keevil camp when the others bought a house in London, and when she finally made the move, it was to her own place, the semi-detached house in Ealing. Says Basia of her mother:

I think Katyn was always lying there, half dead. Mama was always saying, "I've got to live!" Lalka would have an examination, or I did, or something else was happening in our lives. Even when we were grown up, she worried about me because I was getting divorced, and worried about Lalka because she couldn't have a child. Lalka went on about the child, and I went on about the divorce. When I think of it, Mama never had a decent time in her life! It was first of all the War, and then Lalka and me.

I'm not so sure. Mama, who'd had servants to scrub her floors in Lwow, was obliged to become a scrub woman in England. But at the same time, thanks to her devotion to her daughters' education, she saw one of them graduate from art college and the other from one of the great English universities. She must have been very proud of them. And she surely found joy in her grandchildren.

Alas, she didn't live to see Lalka's child, or to see Poland freed from Stalin's yoke. She always kept the treasures she'd taken with her on that terrible journey to Kazakhstan, and on the equally awful trek to Persia. Basia has them now: 600 zloty in almost new bills, some letters and photographs, and that mildly scented bar of Savon Benignina, bought during the bombing of Lwow in September 1939.

In London, Mama wrote in a firm hand on that box of soap: "Through Russia, Persia, Lebanon, Egypt, England – to Poland, so help us God!" Life did not oblige. Mama died in 1968, when she was only sixty-two. By any humane reckoning, she too was a casualty of the Second World War.

Of the family members who were adults in 1939, the aunts came closest to living a normal span. I have a feeling that I know Nuna, because she reminds me of an Irish woman I knew as a boy, a sort of freelance Sister of Charity. Whenever Mom was sick, Breda would take the bus from Boston and stay with us for a week or two, to keep house, do the laundry, and make coarse meals, her specialty being creamed codfish over boiled potatoes. Something like this was Nuna's life. From Geogievka on, she lived with her older sister, going off to work while Krysia stayed home and mixed her beauty lotions for sale. Nuna died in 1982.

That left only Krysia – the eldest of the sisters. All her life, she urged Basia to dress more fashionably:

I paid very little attention to my clothes. I wore mostly cast-offs, including a long duffle coat that was bought for Uncle Jan's son, then passed on to me. Aunt Kyrsia bought me a Dior coat, but I preferred the duffle. It was more comfortable.

Aunt Krysia was beautiful and could charm the birds off the trees. She was the decision-maker and commander in chief and a tyrant. She tied huge ribbons to my hair, and later to Uncle Jan's daughter, much to our disgust. My first lipstick – that was Aunt Krysia. My first party dress – Aunt Krysia made it.

She made me promise that I would be properly dressed at her funeral. I was.

That was in 1986, when Krysia was eighty years old, give or take a year or two.

LALKA MARRIED A COUNTRYMAN, as Polish women seemed to do. She'd met Wojtek at the Hearth Club, at one of the weekly dances whose function was to match up young people, within the religion and within the language. His story is worth telling:

Wojtek's family lived in Warsaw during the War. His grandmother spoke German, so the family worked in the Resistance, printing subversive newsletters and posters on a printing press in their cellar. When discovered, they were sent to Oswiecim – the grandmother, mother, Wojtek, and his brother Leszek. The Germans left an aunt to look after their dog.

Think of that! Those SS troopers must have talked it over. They had a problem, you see: if they took the whole family, the dog would starve or be eaten. So they spared the aunt, to care for it. The kindness done, they loaded the others into a lorry and drove them to the railroad station, to be delivered to the most infamous of the camps in Hitler's Thousand Year Reich.

Both the grandmother and mother were killed in Oswiecim. Wojtek and Leszek survived because they could play some musical instruments and were assigned to the camp orchestra.

We tend to think of Auschwitz (as the Germans spelled Oswiecim) as a death camp, but its primary purpose was slave labor for the Reich. The weak and sick were quickly worked to death or killed outright, but the strong and lucky survived, which is why we know so much about it. As human skeletons in filthy striped pajamas, Wojtek and his brother were freed by the Red Army in January 1945. They joined the great waves of human flotsam, fleeing west across devastated Europe, and made their way to the American zone of Germany. To the end of his life, Wojtek could not bear to listen to the jolly march he'd been required to play at Auschwitz, when the *Lagerorchester* greeted new arrivals at the train siding.

He was hired by Radio Free Europe in Munich. Lalka too went to work for RFE, as did Basia after her divorce, translating Russian newspapers and television broadcasts for news to be broadcast to Poland, once every hour, seven days a week from 5 a.m. to midnight.

By this time, Lalka had given birth to a baby daughter. That should have been a joy for her, and for Mama as well, but life is not always as pretty as it should be. Mama died before the little girl came along; Wojtek died when she was thirteen, and Lalka died four years later. To be sure, life is a terminal illness, but who is to say that the War did not kill Wojtek and Lalka in the end? He was scarred by Auschwitz, and her ailments – the fainting spells, the aching bones, the trouble conceiving – were probably caused by malnutrition in Kazakhstan, when she was an adolescent.

Thank God for aunts! The girl moved in with Basia, and in time returned with her to London.

Then there was Zbyszek, the "well done!" chap, Aunt Krysia's son. He emigrated to America after the War and, when I spoke to him on the phone, was thriving at the age of eighty-four.

TOWARD THE END OF OUR VISIT, Basia takes Sally and me to Gunnersbury Cemetery, to pay our respects to London's Katyn monument. Buried there is a bucket of soil from the gravesite near Smolensk. As impressive as the monument itself are the tall conifers behind it, echoing those planted by the Bluecaps to cover up their crime.

Afterward, Basia drives us to Mama's house in Ealing. Standing there on the sidewalk, in the weak sunlight of an English noon, I feel the years fall away. I am sure that the white door will open at any moment to let the two young vagabonds out, the lad in his Harris tweed jacket, the lass in her duffle coat, bound for Italy with their rucksacks, their optimism, and their innocence. Is Mama standing in the doorway as we walk down the street to North Ealing Underground? If not, as I know from my own experience as a parent, she certainly kept us in sight from the window. Basia realizes it too:

I was on a beach once, in Italy, and I met an old woman pushing a pram. I said to her, "A grandchild, how lovely!" And she said, "Once you have a child, you just push that pram, and push that pram!" And that's true. Even if the children are away and happy, one never stops worrying about them.

Especially if the child is heading off to Italy with a bearded American with not a word of Polish and no obvious prospects for the future!

Speaking of children, here's an odd thing about those London Poles of the next generation: they have no children of their own. They grew up in England as ideal Poles, ideal Catholics, and there the line has stopped. I am at a loss to guess what has caused the families to die out, but I suspect it is connected with being "displaced persons" in England rather than a country with a stronger tradition of immigration and assimilation. One can immigrate to Britain, more easily than to the United States, but assimilation is a different matter. Basia recalls riding in a taxi whose driver had to brake suddenly to avoid a jaywalker in a turban. "Bloody British passport!" he shouted, referring to the law that any citizen of the Commonwealth could settle in the mother country.

"I'm a British passport, too," Basia pointed out.

"Yes, love," he said. "But you're different."

Yes. She was young, she was pretty, she was white, and her English was excellent, so she was different. But she was not English either, and never would be.

Mama always felt she was not where she belonged. As for me, after my years at the University of Manchester, and especially after a holiday in Poland in the 1960s, I adopted England. Poland then was poor, miserable, and not at all like the country I was told about when growing up. When we came back to London, my children said, "Oh, see the red bus!"

Poland was so gray in the Communist times, the grayness of poverty. Terrible. I could never have lived in the Poland of those years, or even the Poland of today. I am too "English" for that, although I don't feel completely at home here, either. It was great to hear Polish spoken everywhere and to see the advertisements and signs in Polish. I suppose that language is one's home.

And in September 2012 she finally visited Lwow, with her daughter and Janusz Deszberg. They admired the lions for which the city was named. They visited 99 Generala Chuprynka, as Potocki Street is now known, and decided that the building there must be a postwar construction, not the one where Basia lived until April 1940. It was, nevertheless, a very satisfactory experience:

Lwow is beautiful. It is strange, but in today's Poland I feel English and in England I feel Polish. But in Lwow I felt just right. It was wonderful to feel at home, even knowing that I can never live there.

I ADMIRE THEM UNRESERVEDLY: Basia, Mama, Aunt Krysia, and the others. England would be poorer if this family hadn't settled there – which is to say, if the War had never happened. I would be poorer if I hadn't taken the train to New York in September 1954, hadn't set out to study Modern European History at the University of Manchester. What interested me was precisely what the dons didn't regard as history: the Second World War, 1939-1945. By the time I met Basia, I thought that I had nothing more to learn in Manchester. She changed that. From her I began to learn about the 20th Century, and about myself as well. When I left Lerici in July, I thought my courtship of her had been futile, when it was one of the most rewarding things I've ever done – loving her, hitchhiking with her to Italy, and hearing the stories of her childhood, her loss, and her exile.

Which brings me back to the conundrum with which I began this book: without the War, I wouldn't have met her! It's impossible for me to regret our friendship, so how can I regret the events that brought it about? My life made me what I am, and the War is part of me, just as it is part of Basia. War and exile robbed her of everything except herself, her mother, her sister, and her aunts. Yet it gave her that astonishing range of languages and experiences:

visiting the Pyramids with Krysia, playing the piano at the American University in Beirut, an honours degree in Italian and French, and a career at Radio Free Europe.

The conundrum goes on. Hitler went down to hell in 1945, but Stalin's paranoia turned the Second World War into the Cold War that lasted nearly half a century. Because of Stalin, Basia couldn't go home. Because of Stalin, the U.S. spent billions for the reconstruction of Europe, and England repaid the debt in part by allowing me to spend a year at Manchester. And because of Stalin, military conscription was reinstituted in the United States, obliging me to serve two years in olive green, which gave me the background to write my books – about the War, about Vietnam, about the Irish rebellion – about Basia! There is very little in my life that wasn't shaped by the Second World War and its aftermath.

I read a lot, and think a lot, about the War. As time goes on, I see it being reinterpreted, and some of that is admirable. I like, for example, the argument that our particular War was just one campaign in a Long War that began in August 1914 and ended with the collapse of the Soviet Union in 1991. Other interpretations are less admirable: for example, that Stalin wasn't entirely a monster, and if he was, well, Roosevelt and Churchill weren't a whole lot better. Only a college professor or a journalist could be so blinkered as to think that. Yet such perversions are increasingly accepted, as those who actually remember the War become an elderly minority – Basia and I among them. The War is another country, and we were citizens of it. (She a better-traveled citizen than I, to be sure.) We knew that country as natives, while the professor and the journalist will always be tourists.

History happens to one person at a time. History makes us what we are. We live the lives meted out by our time and place – *nor all your piety nor wit shall lure it back to cancel half a line, nor all your tears wash out a word of it!*

Notes and Sources

1 – We Meet in Caf

Just as I let "England" stand for those larger geographies, Britain and the United Kingdom, so does "Soviet Russia" stand for the Soviet Union, and "Siberia" for all the territories of the Gulag Archipelago. That's how we used the terms at the time. As for money, the exchange rate in 1955 was $2.80 to the pound, so a shilling was worth 14 U.S. cents and a penny a bit more than 1 cent. I never had occasion to own a £5 note during my Fulbright year. For undergraduate life in the 1950s, see Ferdynande Zweig, *The Student in the Age of Anxiety: A Survey of Oxford and Manchester Students* (Heinemann 1963), and specifically p. 133 on the matter of sexual mores. Also see David Kynaston's massive studies: *Austerity Britain, 1945-1951* and *Family Britain, 1951-1957* (Walker 2008, 2009).

My most treasured resource has been Basia, who in hundreds of emails, phone calls, and interviews over the course of three years shared her memories of the war years and our friendship in Manchester and on the Continent. 60 million deaths: indeed, the fatalities probably were higher, with Wikipedia giving a range of 60,669,200-84,589,300. Of Poland's 1939 population, one out of five perished in the War, 3 million Jews and the same number of Christians.

Ne'er shed a clout: in Yorkshire, the farmers disfavored changing one's winter clothing before the first of June, and they felt that two times zero ought to amount to *something*.

One day someone: from Basia's email dated 3 Aug 2011. As for her name, she explains (18 Dec 2011): "It is pronounced with a soft s, which is spelt with a sort of an apostrophe over the s or else as *si*. To pronounce: you put the back of your tongue against the palate and the sound that comes out is a soft s. The two a's are short. The same goes for Krysia." Which, I'm afraid, leaves me no wiser than before! *I did logic for a year*: email 3 Mar 2011. *Oh, it's my sister*: from our talks at her home near London, 16-22 Jun 2011. *I am glad we didn't meet*: email 7 Apr 2011. *Okay, if you are sure*: 5 Mar 2011. *I went to great length:* 10 Jan 2011, 4 Jun 2012. *What a funny face*: La Strada (Trans Lux 1954). The heroine was played by Frederico Fellini's wife, Giulietta Masina.

While verifying the quote, I was tickled to find it echoed in *The Pink Panther* (MGM Columbia 2006): "A woman is like an artichoke; you must work hard to get to her heart."

2 – War Comes to Potocki Street

I render Polish words without diacritical marks, and for place names I favor the spelling used in the 1930s. *Our hearts are with you*: Arthur Greenwood quoted in Halik Kochanski, *The Eagle Unbowed: Poland and the Poles in the Second World War* (Harvard Univ. 2012), p. 64. *Universal feast of death:* Thomas Mann, *The Magic Mountain*, (tr. H. T. Lowe-Porter, Secker & Warburg 1927), final sentence. For the roots of blitzkrieg, see Daniel Ford, *A Vision So Noble: John Boyd, the OODA Loop, and America's War on Terror* (Createspace 2010).

All along the road: Bruno Shatyn, *A Private War: Surviving in Poland on False Papers, 1941-1945* (Wayne State Univ. 1985), p. 115. I have taken many of the details of the 98th Mountain Regiment's advance from a German soldier's photo album at collections.yadvashem.org (seen 22 Feb 2011). *Golden-skinned Poles*: Rosa Bailly, *A City Fights for Freedom: The Rising of Lwow in 1918-1919* (Publishing Committee Leopolis 1956), p. 30. *Lwow was a Polish*: Halik Kochanski, p. 9. *Fantastic wooded gorges* etc: Joseph Wittlin, *Moj Lwow*, tinyurl.com/wittlin (seen 23 Feb 2013). Here and elsewhere, I put the text into English with the help of Google Translate and my understanding of the original. *The capital of the largest*: *Salt of the Earth* (Stackpole 1970) p. 306.

Col. Deszberg's birth date and military service from the *Rocznik Oficerski Rezerw* (Reserve Officers Annual) of 1935, p. 381, and his military records at the Central Military Archives in Warsaw. I am indebted to Janusz Lukasiak for pointing me to the former; to Boguslaw Stachula for retrieving the latter; and to Elizabeth Olsson and Janusz Deszberg for translating them. I am grateful also to members of the Kresy-Siberia email group who helped me sort out Polish military terms. I reconstructed the family's history from street directories, medals, reserve officer lists, and family recollections; some of it is an educated guess.

20,000-25,000 Polish-Americans, mostly recent immigrants, joined Haller's Army in France and later served in the Russo-Polish War: Halik Kochanski, p. 5. *Over the corpse of Poland*: Tukhachevsky's order of the day, 2 Jul 1920; my translation. Stalin at the opera: Simon Montefiore, *Stalin: The Court of the*

Red Tsar (Vintage 2003), p. 207. *There can be no doubt*: quoted in Robert Pastor, ed., *A Century's Journey* (Political Science 1999), p. 175. *Largely determined*: A. J. P. Taylor in Norman Davies, *White Eagle, Red Star: The Polish-Soviet War, 1919-20* (Macdonald 1972), p. ix. Also see Davies's concluding chapter, pp. 264-278; *Army officers occupied*: p. 271. *It's a Europe of hatred*: John Merriman, "History 202 European Civilization, 1648-1945," Yale lecture on YouTube (seen 2 Feb 2012). Tukhachevsky was arrested, tortured, tried, and shot in Stalin's purge of the Red Army in 1937.

Mama was always blonde: Basia's comment on my draft manuscript, 2012. *One sinner in the family*: interviews Jun 2011. "Chabrus" is pronounced, more or less, as *habrs*. For "Group Portrait of Women With Cornflowers" (1914), see Graber biography on Wikipedia. Most renderings of "cornflower blue" are of lighter hue. *Lalka was a socialite*: telephone interview, 16 Feb 2011.

Like placenames, Polish personal names are daunting for a foreigner; I was fortunate to meet a girl with a name as manageable as Barbara Deszberg. Worse, a baptismal name and pet name are often very different, so in most cases I have used only the latter. Jurek Deszberg's first name was Jerzy; Aunt Krysia's was Kyrstyna; Aunt Nuna's was Franceska; and Zbyszek's was Zbigniew.

Years later, Waleria: email 18 Dec 2011. *We used to spend August*: emails 6 Feb and 1 Mar 2011. With her approval, I have sometimes joined passages from two or more of Basia's emails as in this case. Janusz Deszberg also provided details of life in Lwow, as he heard them from his family. Jurek's military career from the memorial book *Katyn* (Rada Ochrony Pamieci Walk i Meczenstwa, Warsaw 2000).

I remember the snow: email 16 Dec 2011. *Tas was thirteen*: 3 Feb 2012, and her comment on my draft manuscript. The boy's name was Stanislaw, shortened to Staszek, which was too much for Basia to pronounce when she first met him. So he became Tas (11 Feb 2012). *A prestige and status symbol* etc: Janusz Zawodny, *Death in the Forest: The Story of the Katyn Forest Massacre* (Notre Dame 1962), p. 85.

Polish army records don't show call-up dates for the Deszberg men: the war moved too fast for that. *My father would usually*: 1 Mar 2011. 98th Mountain Regiment's siege of Lwow: photo album at Yad Vashem cited earlier. The defense of Lwow is usually credited to General Wladyslaw Langner, who took over from Sikorski some time after 7 Sep 1939. *To render immediate assistance*: "Order no. 005 of the Military Council of the Belarusian Front," in Anna Cienciala et al, eds., *Katyn: A Crime Without Punishment* (Yale Univ. 2007), p. 43.

3 – I Kiss Your Hand

I am astonished to find that the Speed Graphic is still sold on eBay and discussed on photography forums. The design was old even in 1955. My practice lesson in the kissing of hands, and my visit to Mama's house are Basia's memories, from our talks of Jun 2011. I checked my memories of Paris against Arthur Frommer, *Europe on 5 Dollars a Day: A Guide to Inexpensive Travel* (Frommer 1957).

He learned English: email 6 Feb 2011. *I was offered*: 3 Aug, 17 Aug 2011. *You wouldn't have*: interviews Jun 2011. *When we lived in Tehran*: Basia actually said *Ciocia* rather than *Aunt*, and at first I thought she was saying "Sister Krysia." I have used the English word throughout.

Instead of 25 cents a night, hostels today charge $30 or so, though with more amenities. Breakfast is generally included, and hostelers complain if they have to climb stairs or do without internet. "They should call it a hostel for old people and not for young," said one traveler of the *Auberge Internationale des Jeunes* in Paris, because "they shut down wi-fi at 11:30 pm!" (tinyurl.com/AIJparis, seen 23 Mar 2013).

And instead of the 80% market share they commanded in 1955, Gauloises became so marginal that in the French factory closed in 2005 and the cigarettes have since been imported from Spain. Long before that happened, however, I had quit smoking.

In 1957 I was turned down for a job at the *Herald-Trib* and settled for the *Overseas Weekly* in Frankfurt, Germany.

4 – A Death in the Forest

At that time: Aleksandr Solzhenitsyn, *The Gulag Archipelago 1918-1956: An Experiment in Literary Investigation* (Harper & Row 1975), vol. 2, pp. 19, 75. *Poland never will*: "Germany: Seven Years' War?" in *Time*, 2 Oct 1939. *One swift blow*: quoted in Jan Gross, *Revolution From Abroad: The Soviet Conquest of Poland's Western Ukraine and Western Belarusia* (Princeton Univ. 2002), p. 12; "bastard offspring" is the translation used by Halik Kochanski in *Eagle Unbowed* (cited ch. 2), p. 96. The once-German port of Danzig is now Gdansk. The "Polish Corridor" that in the interwar years separated Danzig from Germany was a creature of the Versailles Treaty and a prime cause of the Second World War.

German methods: Kochanski, p. 119. *The men of the Russian:* Tadeusz Komorowski, *The Secret Army* (Gollandz 1950), p. 47. *During the first try*: Timothy Snyder, *Bloodlands: Europe Between Hitler and Stalin* (Basic 2010), pp. 205-206. The Austrian policeman is describing an *aktion* in October 1941, after Germany invaded the Soviet Union. On the transformation of ordinary men into genocidal killers, no better account has ever been written than Hannah Arendt's *Eichmann in Jerusalem: A Report on the Banality of Evil* (Viking 1963). Daniel Goldhagen made this notion the foundation of his controversial *Hitler's Willing Executioners: Ordinary Germans and the Holocaust* (Knopf 1996). Both authors were concerned with the massacre of Europe's Jews, to the number of nearly 6 million, but of course the same fate befell more than twice that number of Christians, done to death on behalf of Nazi Germany and Soviet Russia. For that broader and bloodier canvas, the necessary account is Snyder's magisterial *Bloodlands*.

I saw a ragged line etc: Bruno Shatyn, *A Private War* (cited ch. 2), pp. 121-122. *For the non-German*: quoted in Kochanski, p. 99. *Whole convoys of common cabbages* and *A pair of second-hand*: Zoe Zajdlerowa, *The Dark Side of the Moon* (Scribner's 1947), pp. 46, 47. The author did not put her name to this searing memoir, presumably fearing for the safety of her family in Poland. Russian words are subject to different spellings when rendered into the roman alphabet, and I sometimes change an unusual version ("roubles" in this case) to one that is more familiar. The actual exchange rate in 1939 was 4 zloty to the U.S. dollar, but in purchasing power they were more nearly equal.

Soldiers ran and *Torn uniforms*: Gross, *Revolution From Abroad*, pp. 47, 45, 28-29. *As a result*: Shatyn, p. 139. *The whole infinitely costly*: Zajdlerowa, p. 57. *But it is precisely*: see Gross's epilog, pp. 225-240, for an extended treatment of this argument. *A sad city* and *Though the winter*: Wladyslaw Anders, *An Army in Exile: The Story of the Second Polish Corps* (Macmillan 1949), pp. 22-23.

I have a very few: emails 16 Dec 2010, 6 Feb 2011. *Lorries with a dozen*: Zbigniew Falimirski, untitled essay (circa 1942) in the collection *Prace Egipskie or prace Palestynskie*, Hoover

Institution, Stanford University, translated by Basia. *When my mother*: email 1 Apr 2011. *The arrested include*: Serov to Beria, 14 Dec 1939, in Cienciala et al, *Katyn* (cited ch. 2), p. 226. *At first he waged*: Solzhenitsyn, *Gulag Archipelago*, vol. 1, p. 113; Russian PWs as traitors, p. 77.

People talk of Prussian: Norman Davies, *Vanished Kingdoms* (Viking 2011), p. 372. *Officers, officials, landowners* and *all hardened, irremediable*: Beria to Stalin, 5 Mar 1940, in Cienciala et al, p. 119. *An ugly, shapeless toad*: Tatiana Okunevskaya, quoted by Simon Montefiore, *Stalin* (cited ch. 2), p. 507.

Fate of the prisoners from eastern Poland: In 2012 a document emerged from the Russian archives with the names of 1,996 Polish men and women shot at Minsk in the spring of 1940. Their graves are still unknown. See "'Belarusian List' of Katyn Victims Found" at tinyurl.com/belalist, "Presidents of Ukraine and Poland Begin" at tinyurl.com/Bykivnia, "Soviet Murders Concealed" at tinyurl.com/sovmurders, "A Voice from the Grave" at warbirdforum.com/comb.htm (all seen 12 Oct 2012). I am indebted also to Mark Turkewicz, email 20 Sep 2012.

In September 2012, the presidents of Poland and Ukraine formally dedicated the Bykivnia site as a memorial to the victims of the NKVD. The location is 50 28 28 N, 30 41 29 E. Together, the Belarusian and Ukraine lists account for only half the prisoners arrested in December 1939.

The overwhelming majority: Nekhoroshev to Merkulov, 22 Apr 1940, in Cienciala et al, p. 181. *Though they could not have known*: Snyder, *Bloodlands*, p. 138. See Snyder's map p. 136 for the flow of prisoners to the principal killing fields. *A few minutes before five*: Cienciala et al, p. 130. A detailed account of what is known about the Katyn executions follows, pp. 130-135. PPK: *Polizeipistole Kriminalmodel*, Police Detective's Pistol. In later years, it was favored by the U.S. Office of Strategic Services and by Ian Fleming's secret agent James Bond. Geco cartridges: Zawodny, *Death in the Forest* (cited ch. 2), p. 23.

It was their social status: Benjamin Fischer: "The Katyn Controversy," in *Studies in Intelligence*, Winter 1999-2000. The number of victims will probably never be determined; I take my figure from Snyder, *Bloodlands*, p. 137; it is in the range commonly cited, though far above what was believed in the immediate postwar years. Indeed, the killings seemed to have continued after April 1940. Fischer estimates that the figure may have reached 27,000 by June 1941.

5 – The Road to Italy

I'd had no experience and *Seriously, Dan*: emails 12 Sep 2011, 13 Feb 2011, 5 Feb 2012. *The new clerk-typist*: Daniel Ford, *Incident at Muc Wa* (Doubleday 1967), p. 166. Back in Manchester, I typed an account of hitchhiking to Italy (dated 27 Apr 1955) with multiple carbon copies, to mail to friends and family at home. My mother kept her copy and in time returned it to me, and my wife has preserved it all these years. It enabled me to check my memories, including standing forlornly on the Avenue Franklin D. Roosevelt in Lyon. I can't find the street today, and I think that FDR's name has been supplanted by that of Charles de Gaulle.

Volare, oh oh: my translation. I can't find the *TNY* cartoon, nor could the magazine's staff. Louann Brizendine supports my notion of how a young man's brain is organized: men, she writes, have two and a half times as much brain space devoted to sexual pursuit as women do (*The Female Brain* 2007, *The Male Brain* 2011, Three Rivers Press). *If I should say*: *Faust* part 1, scene 5 (my translation). *I was eighteen*: email 4 Aug 2011.

6 – The Sky Was Green

Key to understanding the Soviet prison system is the word *Labor* in the ministry's name. "During the war," writes Jean Bingle in *Labor for Bread: The Exploitation of Polish Labor in the Soviet Union During World War II* (Ph.D dissertation, West Virginia Univ. 1999), pp. 12-13, "the camps and collective farms run by the NKVD contributed considerably to the general war effort, at times producing up to ten percent of the non-agricultural production and thirteen percent of the volume of capital investment in the country."

During the night: unpublished memoir by Anna Poplewska, transcribed by Stanislaw Dabrowski and translated by Peter Gessner and Wanda Slawinska, in my collection. I am assured that there could never be a train five kilometers long, since the weight of the following cars would capsize those in the center when rounding a curve. For the deportation trains, see "Gurjanov Transports" at tinyurl.com/deport1940 (seen 15 Apr 2011). *Siberyaki* is the Russian word; the Polish equivalent is *sybiracy*.

A sober and cautious: Janusz Zawodny, *Death in the Forest* (cited ch. 2), p. 5. For the revisionist figures, see Piotr Zaronin in Stanislaw Ciesielski & Antoni Kuczynski, eds., *Polacy w Kazachstanie* (Wroclaw Univ. 1996), and Piotr Eberhardt, *Political Migrations in Poland 1939-1948* (Warsaw Institute of Geography and Spatial Organization 2008). *It now seems likely*: Kochanski, *Eagle Unbowed* (cited ch. 2), p. 138. For its part, the Polish emigre community advocates for 1.7 million or more.

To deport by April 15: Beria to Serov, 7 Mar 1939, in "Katyn-Siberia Documents 1939-1941," p. 12, at tinyurl.com/katyndoc (seen 9 Mar 2011). *57,936*: my calculation, from the numbers in Gurjanov Transports above. Eberhardt (cited above) uses the figure 61,000, p. 19. Kazakh population from Anne Peck, *Economic Development in Kazakhstan* (Routledge 2004), p. 55. It was not until 1987 that Kazaks again outnumbered Russians in Kazakhstan. The story of the Ford workers is told by Tim Tzouliadis in *The Forsaken: An American Tragedy in Stalin's Russia* (Penguin 2008).

Svobodnayha ssylka: Allen Paul, *Katyn: Stalin's Massacre and the Triumph of Truth* (Northern Illinois Univ. 2010), p. 193. *From each according*: Karl Marx, "Critique of the Gotha Program" (1875). *He who does not work*: 1936 Constitution of the USSR, Article 12. For the "tenner," see Solzhenitsyn, *Gulag Archipelago* (cited ch. 4), vol. 1, p. 38. *Live in perpetual exile*: Robert Gellately, *Stalin's Curse: Battling for Communism in War and Cold War* (Knopf 2013, Kindle edition), loc. 7885.

She just stood there: email 13 May 2011. In June 2011, I was able to see and hold the contents of Mama's treasure box. *We were allowed*: Zofia Wonka, "Wspomnienia z Kazachstanu" (Memories of Kazakhstan), p. 3, at tinyurl.com/singsew (seen 12 May 2012). I am grateful to Janusz Lukasiak for pointing me to this account and others like it, and for suggesting how Mama might have managed to speak Russian.

In our case: email 21 Apr 2011. Still fearful of retribution after all these years, the writer requested anonymity. I calculated the boxcar dimensions from a photograph supplied by the same individual; they are much the same as those of an American boxcar of the time. Convoy dates, passengers, and guards from "Gurjanov Transports" cited above.

I don't remember: email 13 May 2011. *Poland will not perish*: tinyurl.com/polandhasnot (seen 20 May 2011), my translation. *Along the journey*: Beria memo, 10 Apr 1940, in Cienciala et al, *Katyn* (cited ch. 2), p. 172. *Then the provisions* and *Volunteers from each wagon*: Keith Sword, *Deportation and Exile: Poles in the Soviet Union, 1939-48* (St. Martin's Press 1994), pp. 19-20. For the importance of bread to the Poles, see Monica Janowski, "Food in Traumatic Times: Women, Foodways and 'Polishness'

During a Wartime 'Odyssey',” School of Oriental and African Studies, Univ. of London 2012. *A rusty pail*, etc: Esther Hautzig, *The Endless Steppe: Growing up in Siberia* (HarperTrophy 1987), pp. 29-31.

The aunts and Zbyszek: emails 6 Feb and 17 May 2011. *Lalka and I managed*: 18 May 2011. *It happened that a girl*: 6 Feb 2011. The route of their journey is depicted in Allen Paul, *Katyn* cited above, p. 147. From point to point, the straight-line distance is 3,050 miles, to which I add ten percent. *On the first of May*: Zbigniew Falimirski essay (cited ch. 4). *There was no station*: from the documentary film *Zapomniana Odyseja* ("Forgotten Odyssey," Wielka Brytania 2000). *As the train approached* and *He must have chosen:* 6 Feb and 4 Jul 2011. Like 1940, 2011 was a time of great solar activity, and the Northern Lights were seen as far south as Illinois.

7 – La Donna È Mobile

In my letter of 27 Apr 1955, I identified the avalanched town as Saint Jean de Mer, but I find no such community on Route 6. Saint Michel de Maurienne is the right distance from Modane and has the requisite railroad bridge.

Twenty years after we passed through, a road tunnel was built from Modane to Bardonnechia, so one can now hitchhike into Italy without going over the col. Bardonnechia meanwhile has become a considerable ski resort, with twenty-five hotels; it helped host the Winter Olympics in 2006.

As for the truck driver's: email 27 Mar 2011. *A woman is flighty*: my translation. Taught Shelley to swim: James Bieri, *Percy Bysshe Shelley: A Biography* (Univ. of Delaware 2005), p. 285. In 1975, I trekked to the Old Man of the Mountain and photographed a highway department crew that was patching and reinforcing his forehead. Alas, their work was in vain, and in 2003 the profile collapsed, the victim of erosion and the vibration of traffic. *This virtuous maid*: *Measure for Measure*, act 2, scene 2. *Oh yes, I do remember*: 27 Mar 2011. *I think you stayed*: 5 May 2011.

8 – Some Miracle from God

Glance only at a map: Lenin, quoted on The Red Comrades Documentation Project online (seen 9 Jun 2011). *The steppe rolls away* etc: Zajdlerowa, *Dark Side of the Moon* (cited ch. 4), pp. 174-75. *Privykniosh – pozhyviosh*: Ciesielski & Kuczynski,

Polacy w Kazachstanie (cited ch. 6), p. 310. Polish and Russian distinguish between the death of a human and that of an animal; in this sentence, the implication is of a degrading, animal-like death. *At first she had to milk* etc: emails 6 Feb, 24 Mar, and 4 Jul 2011. *The Russians brought us* and *Whenever I was in the market*: Maria Hadow, *Paying Guest in Siberia* (Harville Press 1959), pp. 55, 68.

All the most dangerous: Ciesielski & Kuczynski, p. 260. For foreign squadrons of the RAF, see Christopher Shores & Clive Wallace, *Aces High: A Tribute to the Most Notable Fighter Pilots of the British and Commonwealth Forces in WWII* (Grub Street 1994), pp. 58-63. *The War for me*: email 10 Dec 2010. *I remember the War* etc: 21 Feb, 4 Jul 2011. *Batko Stalin*: the "t" is soft, so the word comes out as "bash-ko." It may be Ukrainian in origin. *The Gulag Archipelago* regularly refers to "Daddy Stalin," perhaps a translation of the same expression. *It was just about the best*: 4 Jul 2011. *I probably could read*: 5 Mar 2011. *Now bear my sorrowing heart* and *What's our business*: Adam Mickiewicz, *Pan Tadeusz* (Hippocrene 1992; my translations), pp. 3, 437. Writing page numbers on the wall: interviews Jun 2011. Henryk Sienkiewicz won the Nobel Prize in 1905.

Georgievka hospital: Allen Paul, *Katyn* (cited ch. 6), p. 158. *One day Aunt Krysia* and *I think Kazakhstan*: email 4 July 2011. *The Poles were perceived* and *These huts would only last*: Kochanski, *Eagle Unbowed* (cited ch. 2), pp. 155, 141. *There was a tiny* and the following quotations about life in Georgievka: emails 16 Jan; 6 Feb, 13 Feb, and 15 Feb; 6 Mar, 14 Mar, and 16 Mar, and 4 Jul 2011; and Basia's comments on my draft manuscript. For the road to China, see Kochanski, p. 148. For *Szumia jodly*, see tinyurl.com/szumia (heard 14 Mar 2012).

Kochana Mamuiu: Mama put this birthday greeting in her treasure box, and it survived all her subsequent travels. The poem is as Basia wrote it, and the translation is hers. *In the space of two months*: Solzhenitsyn, *Gulag Archipelago* (cited ch. 4), vol. 3, p. 17. Russian casualties in the invasion came to a breathtaking 802,000 killed, 3 million wounded, and 3.2 million captured, June 22 to December 5, 1941.

9 – We Live in the Castle

If the name of my character seems preposterous, recall that James Joyce first called his protagonist . . . Stephen Hero! For the rank of marchese, see Wikipedia, "Nobility of Italy" (seen 16

Mar 2012). Prince Amadeo was eleven that summer. He now styles himself Duke of Savoy, and his claim to the throne is contested by his cousin Vittorio Emanuele, Prince of Naples, who at a royal wedding once punched the younger man in the nose. See Davies, *Vanished Kingdoms* (cited ch. 4), pp. 432-33.

I met him in Perugia: email 5 May 2011, and her comments on my draft manuscript. I find that the film was an appalling 1955 Japanese-Italian production with most singers dubbed. According to the Rick Steves website (seen 16 Mar 2012), one must now get reservations for the Uffizi "at least one month in advance." *He would come wheezing*: interviews Jun 2011. *In April, just before*: email 17 Feb 2011.

Our conversations are more or less exact. Basia insists that she never discussed our canoodling with her landlady, or that she was so naive as to confuse an erection with the prodding of a belt buckle. Yet the conversations are vivid in my memory. I am as sure of them as anything in my history, so I let them stand though I'm sorry they displease her.

Google Earth tells me that there's a Blue Grotto in the Gulf of Poets, though it's across the bay on the island of Palmaria. We couldn't have been so foolish as to let ourselves be rowed seven kilometers across the bay and the entrance to a major seaport and naval base. I puzzled this mystery for a time, until I struck up an email correspondence with a *Lericino* who told me that Enrico must have taken us to the *Tana del Brigantino*, well known to local boys.

An effective and hygienic: Luigi Faccini, email 21 Dec 2010. I am also indebted to an article published in *Il Lavoro*, 26 Jun 1974; to the Ostello di Lerici Facebook page; and to emails from Paolo Silvestri. Not only did the *Lericini* get rid of Madi, but in time they also voted to close the hostel. "The flow of young people ended," Sgr. Faccini recalled. "They did not carry money and they created disorder." No doubt that was also true of us in 1955.

10 – Last Boat to Pahlevi

This event, cataclysmic for millions: Kochanski, *Eagle Unbowed* (cited ch. 2), p. 161. Formation of the new Polish division: Anders, *Army in Exile* (cited ch. 4), p. 53. *The most rascally and dangerous*: from the series' origin script, tinyurl.com/ivanshark (heard 19 Jul 2011). When I was an undergraduate at the University of New Hampshire, I caught "Captain Midnight" on television in the East Hall lounge. Ivan Shark was brought back to life for the Cold War, and the Secret Squadron was battling him as before.

At 10 cents a week, 36 weeks to the school year, and $18.75 the cost of the bond, our savings book wouldn't have been entirely filled when the War ended. The question was moot, because Dad changed jobs again in the spring of 1942, and we exchanged our books for a conventional bank account. I still had the money when I set out for college in September 1950.

Chaotic, half-empty city: David Denby in *The New Yorker*, 13 Feb 2012. *Lebensborn* program: Kochanski, p. 271. *Most of them had no boots*: Anders (cited above), p. 64. *Vague, uncooperative, and worrisome*: Allen Paul, *Katyn* (cited ch. 6), p. 176. *To all Polish citizens*: Kochanski, p. 169. The author estimates (p. 137) that there were 196,000 PWs, 250,000 Gulag prisoners, and 210,000 Red Army conscripts. The figure 116,131 is from British Army records of those processed into Persia; it presumably omits the hundreds who died en route to Pahlevi. *This great avalanche*: Sword, *Deportation and Exile* (cited ch. 6), p. 43. *SS Atlantic*: Polish state archives at tinyurl.com/ssatlantic (seen 17 Mar 2012).

Had a third child, Were treated like goods, etc: Katherine Jolluck, *Exile and Identity: Polish Women in the Soviet Union during World War II* (Univ. of Pittsburgh 2002), pp. 174-177. *My life here is hell*: Jolluck in Nancy Wingfield et al, *Gender and War in Twentieth-Century Eastern Europe* (Indiana Univ. 2006), p. 211. Jolluck also makes a point (*Exile and Identity*, pp. 268-269) that would have been helpful to me in 1955, and again when I set out to write this book: "For these Poles, in accordance with Catholic doctrine and tradition, female sexuality is legitimate only within the bounds of marriage, and it constitutes an exceedingly private and taboo subject." Evidently so!

One hundred and eighty-six: Solzhenitsyn, *Gulag Archipelago* (cited ch. 4), vol. 2, p. 131n. *I saw arriving*: Anders (cited above), pp. 65-66. *Uncle Jan was in a labor camp* and *A Polish officer*: emails 4 Jul, 15 Feb, and 13 Aug 2011. *If the Poles do not want*: Sikorski Historical Institute, *Documents on Polish-Soviet Relations 1939-1945* (Heinemann 1961), vol. 1, pp. 231-44. *Sikorski displeased Stalin*: Solzhenitsyn, vol. 2, p. 134.

Exhausted by hard labor: Helena Woloch, quoted by Ryszard Antolak in the *Pars Times*, tinyurl.com/parstimes (seen 10 Dec 2010). *"Are we going to get nothing*: Sword, p. 67 (italics added).

To put matters brutally: "From Minister of State, Cairo to Foreign Office," 22 Jun 1942, januszandrzej.blogspot.com (seen 4 Nov 2013). Case was Australian. At the same website are detailed reports by Col. A. Ross on the spring and summer evacuations to Pahlevi.

Last transport to Pahlevi: email 15 Feb 2011. *Many of them remained*: tinyurl.com/ornatowski (seen 26 Mar 2012). *The empty tanker*: Aleksander Topolski, quoted on the Kresy-Siberia forum at tinyurl.com/topoloski (seen 22 Jul 2011). *I remember people* and *But then the joy*: email 3 Feb 2011. Anzali cemetery: tinyurl.com/anzali (seen 3 Aug 2011).

And then we were taken: emails 3 Jan, 3 Feb, and 13 Aug 2011. Mama's stipend equates to £80 today, about $120. *Mama's idea was to get*, *It was hard, being shut up* and *On Sundays we went*: interviews Jun 2011, phone interview 16 Feb 2011, email 15 May 2011.

11 – I Knew So Little of Love

They got a bit too amorous: email 30 Mar 2011. *As I remember it*: 22 May, 27 Nov 2011. The bistro is now a full service restaurant where lunch can be had at €35. *about what I spent for three weeks on the road in 1955*. *The tide is always high*: that much at least is true, for the tide range in the Mediterranean is measured in inches rather than in feet. *There was another beach* 27 Nov 2011.

Alas! I thought: Bernart de Ventardorn, *Can vei la lauzeta* (When I See the Lark, circa 1175); my translation. For Lieutenant Henry's escape to Switzerland, see Ernest Hemingway, *A Farewell to Arms* (Scribner Classics 1986), pp. 269-276. Hemingway gave the distance as 30 km; from hostel to hostel, I walked about 20 km. *Although I must have been*: 17 Aug 2011, 12 Sep 2011. *Germans by contrast*: there's a joke about the quandary faced by a Pole who meets a German and a Russian – which one should he shoot first? "Oh, the German, of course! Duty before pleasure!"

12 – Displaced Person

In launching this monstrous: U.S. Congress, *The Katyn Forest Massacre: Hearings before the Select Committee to Conduct an Investigation of the Facts, Evidence and Circumstances of the Katyn Forest Massacre* (GPO 1952), p. 1720. *The latest German attempt*: NYT, 16 Apr 1943, p. 4. *Hitler's Polish Collaborators*: U.S. Congress, p. 1725; Allen Paul, *Katyn* (cited ch. 6), ch. 16-17;

and *Amtliches Material zum Massenmord von Katyn* (Zentralverlag der NSDAP 1943), at www.katyn-books.ru (seen 12 Feb 2012). For Soviet sympathizers and agents in the Roosevelt administration, see John Haynes, "The Cold War Debate Continues" in *Journal of Cold War Studies*, Winter 2000. *Perhaps the greatest man* etc: *Life*, vol. 14, no. 13, pp. 29, 40.

Alas, the German revelations and *The less said*: Max Hastings, *Winston's War: Churchill, 1940-1945* (Knopf, 2010), p. 301. *If they are dead* and *We have got to beat Hitler*: Winston Churchill, *The Hinge of Fate* (Houghton Mifflin 1950), pp. 759, 761. *Until then, I hadn't*: email 21 Feb 2011. *Roosevelt winked*: Montefiore, *Stalin* (cited ch. 2), p. 467. *I just have a hunch*: Wilson Miscamble, *From Roosevelt to Truman: Potsdam, Hiroshima, and the Cold War* (Cambridge Univ. 2007), p. 52. *Stalin was the master*: Gellately, *Stalin's Curse* (cited ch. 6), loc. 3077. *I thought Poland might move* and *not prepared to make a great squawk*: Winston Churchill, *Closing the Ring* (Houghton Mifflin 1951), pp. 362, 397. *The bear belongs to me*: Montefiore, *Stalin*, p. 484.

The confusion of boundaries lay in the "Curzon Line" of 1920, meant to separate the Polish and Bolshevik armies. Lwow was first assigned to Poland but then, in the version presented to the Bolshevik government in Moscow, it was switched to present-day Ukraine. The matter became moot (and forgotten by everyone except Stalin) when the Poles drove the Russians far to the east in the spring of 1921. See Piotr Eberhardt, "The Curzon Line as the Eastern Boundary of Poland," in *Geographia Polonica*, vol. 85, issue 1 (2012).

Tom would take us: email 16 Jan 2011. Lincoln Continental: only 400 were built in 1941, and the cost at the factory was $2,865. *Passer-by, tell Poland*: Anders, *Army in Exile* (cited ch. 4), p. 285. *There is not a moment*: Allen Paul, *Katyn*, p. 293. *A ghoulish crew*: Montefiore, *Stalin*, p. 475. *The Poles were sickened*: Gellately, *Stalin's Curse*, loc. 4905. *I decided, however*: Dwight Eisenhower, *Crusade in Europe* (Doubleday 1948), p. 396. *So that's the end of the bastard*: Montefiore, p. 487. *A square deal for Poland* and *The prime minister was obliged*: Hastings, *Winston's War*, pp. 462, 466.

We lived in a ramshackle etc: email 3 Feb 2011, interviews Jun 2011. Zdzislaw in British Army: email from Janusz Deszberg, 19 Nov 2013. *The English did us proud*: 15 Feb 2011. *Franconia*'s manifest at tinyurl.com/ukcamps (seen 1 Aug 2011).

Holy Trinity was similar and *I had elocution*: interviews Jun 2011, and her revisions to the draft manuscript. *There was a military school*: email 28 Nov 2012. O levels, A levels: Ordinary and Advanced.

13 – We Meet Again

It gave my heart: my best recollection. *You wrote to me*: interviews Jun 2011. Under the guise of "Doncieres," M. Proust wrote about Orleans and Coligny Caserne in *The Guermantes Way* (tr. Mark Treharne, Viking Penguin 2004), pp. 64+. *Hallo Dan*: email 6 Dec 2010. *Ulysses* was translated by Maciej Slomczynski, son of the American adventurer (and later film producer) Merian Cooper, who had flown for Poland in 1919-1921.

Opinionated: Basia denies this, though with a wink: "I am not opinionated; I just have strong opinions!" (email 4 Dec 2011). *I think Katyn was always*: interviews Jun 2011. *Through Russia, Persia, Lebanon*: 23 Aug 2011. *Commander in chief*: 6 Feb 2011. *I paid very little attention* and *In the* end: 13 Feb 2011, interviews Jun 2011. *Wojtek's family*: 6 Mar 2011. *She was the strength* and *I was on a beach*: interviews Jun 2011. *Bloody British passport*: 5 Mar 2011. *Mama always felt*: 23 Aug and 11 Mar 2011; interviews Jun 2011. *Lwow is beautiful*: 19 Sep 2012. *Nor all your piety*: Edward Heron-Allen, *Edward FitzGerald's Rubaiyat of Omar Khayyam* (Bernard Quaritch 1899), p. 104.

Made in the USA
Monee, IL
07 July 2021